Data Structures

(Common to Computer Science and Information Technology)

R. Vinston Raja,
Assistant Professor,
Information Technology,
Panimalar Institute of Technology,
Chennai.

K. Hemapriya,
Assistant Professor,
Computer Science and Engineering,
Panimalar Institute of Technology,
Chennai.

R. Jeena,
Assistant Professor,
Information Technology,
Panimalar Institute of Technology,
Chennai.

Published by

Data Structures (Common to Computer Science and Information Technology)

9 789386 638939 >

ISBN 978-93-86638-93-9

Authors

R. Vinston Raja

K. Hemapriya

R. Jeena

Bonfring

309, 2nd Floor, 5th Street Extension, Gandhipuram,

Coimbatore-641 012.

Tamilnadu, India.

E-mail: info@bonfring.org

Website: www.bonfring.org

Phone: 0422 4213231

Preface

This book titled **"Data Structures"** is written to provide a significant amount of flexibility in the order in which the material is covered, as illustrated in the accompanying programs. Selected material from,

Chapters 1 and 6 cover detailed explanation about **Linear Data Structures(List, Stack, and Queue)**. Care has been taken throughout the chapters to include the set of exercises to have an in depth idea about the implementation of Linear Data Structures through C programming. Also included are suggested **sample programs** that incorporate the essential concepts in this chapter.

Chapters 7 to 11 cover the concepts of **Non-linear data structures**. Systematic care has been taken to support the topics with necessary routines and relevant diagrams about Non-Linear Data structure concepts like **Trees with types and Graphs with types**.

Chapters 12 to 14 cover the concepts of **Sorting, Searching and Hashing Techniques**. These topics are explained with necessary routines and relevant diagrams.

This book includes **University question papers** at the end. It also emphasizes the entire program development process. Readers will learn how to write well-designed programs and how to recognize them. At the same time, they will develop insight into program analysis and learn how to analyse programs in order to determine their correctness and efficiency.

R. Vinston Raja

K. Hemapriya

R. Jeena

Acknowledgement

We sincerely thank the almighty God, who is the source of life and strength of knowledge and wisdom.

Special acknowledgement to our **Honorable Chairman Dr. Jeppiaar, M.A., B.L., Ph.D.**, Chancellor, Sathyabama University, **Esteemed Secretary and Correspondent Dr. P. Chinnadurai, M.A., Ph.D.**, and respected Directors **Tmt. C. Vijayarajeswari, Thiru C. Sakthikumar, M.E., and Tmt. Saranya Sree Sakthikumar, B.E.**, of "Panimalar Group of Institutions" for their continuous support for the successful completion and publication of this book.

We thank our **Principal, Dr.T. Jayanthy M.E., Ph.D.**, Panimalar Institute of Technology.

We also thank our **HOD, Dr. A. Joshi, M.E., Ph.D.**, Department of Information Technology and **HOD, Dr. V. Subedha, M.E., Ph.D.**, Department of Computer Science and Engineering, Panimalar Institute of Technology.

We also thank all our **family, friends and colleagues** for their constant source of encouragement and help in various stages of writing this book.

Our sincere thanks to our publishers "**Bonfring Publication**", for their help and co-operation in publishing this book.

R. Vinston Raja

K. Hemapriya

R. Jeena

About the Authors

R. Vinston raja is currently working as Assistant Professor in the Department of Information Technology. He has Completed his M.Tech IT in Sathiyabama University in 2012 and Pursuing Ph.D in Sathyabama University. His area of interest is in IOT with Wireless Sensor Networks, Robotics and Artificial intelligence. He has published more than 20 papers in international journal and conference proceedings. He is also a recipient of Best Teacher Award in the academic year 2017-2018. He has experience in guiding student development projects.

K. Hema Priya is currently working as Assistant Professor in the Department of Computer Science and Engineering. She has Completed her M.Tech CSE in SRM University in 2013. Her area of interest includes Networks, Data Structure and programming Paradigm. She has published more than 12 papers in international journal and conference proceedings. She has experience in guiding student development projects.

R. Jeena is currently working as an Assistant Professor in the Department of Information Technology. She has 12 years of experience in teaching. She is currently doing her Ph.D in cloud computing at Veltech University, India. Her research interest are cloud computing and Data Mining. She has published more than 10 papers in international journal and she presented more than 20 papers in various International and National Conferences. She received Best Paper Presenter Award at International Conference from CSI TechNext India 2018.

Syllabus

CS8391 **DATA STRUCTURES**

Objectives

1. To understand the concepts of ADTs
2. To Learn linear data structures – lists, stacks, and queues.
3. To understand sorting, searching and hashing algorithms.
4. To apply Tree and Graph structures.

UNIT I **LINEAR DATA STRUCTURES – LIST** **9**

Abstract Data Types (ADTs) – List ADT – array-based implementation – linked list implementation –– singly linked lists - circularly linked lists- doubly-linked lists – applications of lists – Polynomial Manipulation – All operations (Insertion, Deletion, Merge, Traversal).

UNIT II **LINEAR DATA STRUCTURES – STACKS, QUEUES** **9**

Stack ADT – Operations - Applications - Evaluating arithmetic expressions- Conversion of Infix to postfix expression - Queue ADT – Operations - Circular Queue – Priority Queue- deQueue – applications of queues.

UNIT III **NON LINEAR DATA STRUCTURES – TREES** **9**

Tree ADT – tree traversals - Binary Tree ADT – expression trees – applications of trees – binary search tree ADT –Threaded Binary Trees- AVL Trees – B-Tree - B+ Tree - Heap – Applications of heap.

UNIT IV **NON LINEAR DATA STRUCTURES - GRAPHS** **9**

Definition – Representation of Graph – Types of graph - Breadth-first traversal - Depth- first traversal – Topological Sort – Bi-connectivity – Cut vertex – Euler circuits – Applications of graphs.

UNIT V **SEARCHING, SORTING AND HASHING TECHNIQUES** **9**

Searching- Linear Search - Binary Search. Sorting - Bubble sort - Selection sort - Insertion sort - Shell sort –Radix sort. Hashing- Hash Functions– Separate Chaining – Open Addressing – Rehashing – Extendible Hashing.

TOTAL: 45 PERIODS

Outcomes

At the end of the course, the student should be able to:

- Implement abstract data types for linear data structures.
- Apply the different linear and non-linear data structures to problem solutions.
- Critically analyze the various sorting algorithms.

Text Books

1. Mark Allen Weiss, "Data Structures and Algorithm Analysis in C", 2nd Edition, Pearson Education, 1997.
2. Reema Thareja, "Data Structures Using C", Second Edition, Oxford University Press, 2011.

References

1. Thomas H. Cormen, Charles E. Leiserson, Ronald L. Rivest, Clifford Stein, "Introduction to Algorithms", Second Edition, Mcgraw Hill, 2002.
2. Aho, Hopcroft and Ullman, "Data Structures and Algorithms", Pearson Education, 1983.
3. Stephen G. Kochan, "Programming in C", 3rd edition, Pearson Education.
4. Ellis Horowitz, Sartaj Sahni, Susan Anderson-Freed, "Fundamentals of Data Structures in C", Second Edition, University Press, 2008.

PART I

- Overview of Linear Data Structure
- List ADT
- Singly Linked list
- Doubly Linked List
- Circular linked List
- Polynomial ADT
- Review Questions

CHAPTER 1

Linear Datastructure–List

1.1. Introduction to Data Structures

A data structure is a specialized format for organizing and storing data.

General data structure types include the array, the file, the record, the table, the tree, and so on.

Any data structure is designed to organize data to suit a specific purpose so that it can be accessed and worked with in appropriate ways.

> *A data structure is a way of organizing, storing, retrieving data and their relationship with each other.*

Terms to be known

a) Data

A collection of facts, concepts, figures, observations, occurrences or instructions in a formalized manner.

b) Information

Processed data is called as information.

c) Record

Collection of related fields.

d) Data Type

Set of elements that share common set of properties used to solve a program.

1.2. Application of Data Structures

- Operating systems
- Compiler design
- Statistical and numerical analysis
- Database management systems
- Expert systems
- Network analysis

1.3. Classification of Data Structure

There are two main types of Data Structure classification.

1. Primitive Data Structure.
2. Non-primitive Data Structure

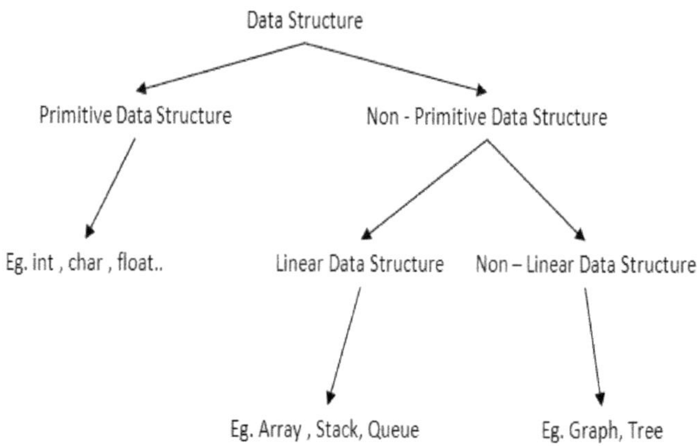

(i) **Primitive Data Structure**: It is a basic Data structure which can be directly operated by the machine instruction.

(ii) **Non-Primitive Data Structure**: It is a Data structure which emphasize on structuring of a group of homogeneous or heterogeneous data items. It is further classified into two types. They are:

- Linear Data Structures.
- Non- Linear Data Structures.

(iii) **Linear Data Structures**: It is a data structure which contains a linear arrangement of elements in the memory.

(iv) **Non-Linear Data Structure**: It is a data structure which represents a hierarchical arrangement of elements.

1.4. Abstract Data Type(ADT)

Abstract data types are mathematical models of a set of data values or information that share similar behavior or qualities and that can be specified and identified independent of specific implementations.

Abstract data types, or ADTs, are typically used in algorithms. An abstract data type is defined in term of its data items or its associated operations rather than by its implementation.

ADT is a set of operations that are written once in the program and can be used any time from any part of the program.

Benefits of Using ADTs

Modularity: Each data type can be considered independently.

Testing: Data type implementations can be tested separately to check that they meet the specifications.

Division of labour: Separate implementation of data types according to agreed specifications.

Reusability: Implemented data types can be reused.

Change of implementation: The implementation can be changed with no effect to users.

1.5. List ADT

A list is a linear data structure. It is a collection of elements.In general the List is in the form of elements A_1, A_2, ..., A_N, where N is the size of the list associated with a set of operations listed below.

- Insert( ): Add an element e.g. Insert(X,5)-Insert the element X after the position 5.
- Delete( ): Remove an element e.g. Delete(X)-The element X is deleted.
- Find( ): Find the position of an element (search) e.g. Find(X,L)-Returns the position of X in List L.
- PrintList( ): Display all the elements from the list.
- MakeEmpty( ): Make the list as empty list.

1.5.1. Methods to Implement a List

There are two ways to implement List.

1. Array implementation of list
2. Linked list implementation of list

1.5.2. Array Implementation of List

A set of data elements of same data type is called array. Array is a static data structure i.e., the memory should be allocated in advance and the size is fixed. This will waste the memory space when used space is less than the allocated space.

The basic operations performed on a list of elements are:

a. Creation of List.
b. Insertion of data element in the List.
c. Deletion of data element from the List.
d. Display all data elements in the List.
e. Searching for a data element in the list.

Global Declaration

```
#define maxsize 10
int list[maxsize], n ;
```

a) Create Operation

Initially the array is fixed with maximum size of 10 elements in our example. In the above global declaration section, list[maxsize] represents the array name as ' list ', and ' n ' denotes the number of elements present in the list.

Create( ) is used to initialize the list with ' n ' number of elements read from the user. The array elements are stored in the consecutive array locations (i.e.) list [0], list [1] and so on.

```
void Create()
  {
        int i;
        printf("\nEnter the number of elements to be added in the list:\t");
        scanf("%d",&n);
        printf("\nEnter the array elements:\t");
        for(i=0;i<n;i++)
         scanf("%d",&list[i]);
        Display();
  }
```

b) Insert Operation

Insert operation is used to insert an element at particular position in the list. Inserting the element in the last position of an array is easy. But inserting the element at a particular position in an array is quite difficult since it involves all the datas from the specified position to be moved one position right in the array.

Consider an array with 5 elements [max elements = 10]

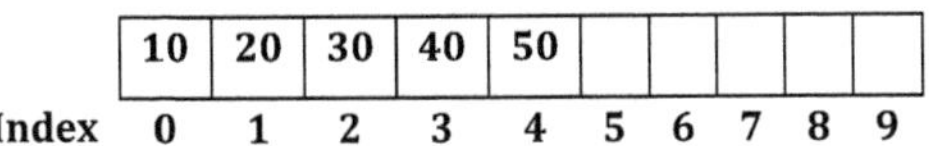

If data 15 is to be inserted in the 1st index then data 50 has to be moved to index 5, 40 has to be moved to index 4, 30 has to be moved to index 3 and 20 has to be moved to index 2.

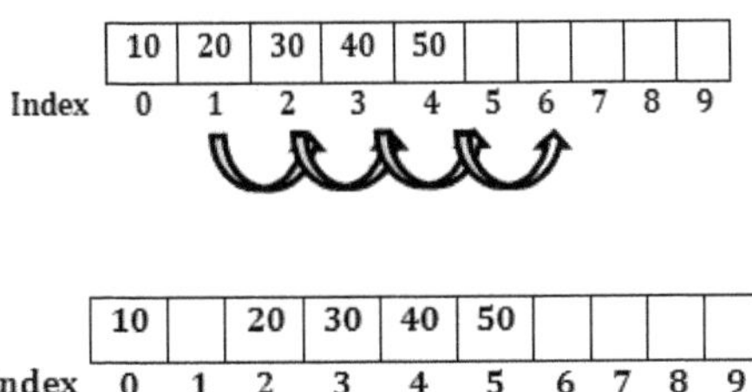

After four data movement, 15 is inserted in the index 1 of the array.

	10	15	20	30	40	50				
Index	0	1	2	3	4	5	6	7	8	9

```
void Insert( )
{
        int i,data,pos;
        printf("\nEnter the data to be inserted:\t");
        scanf("%d",&data);
        printf("\nEnter the position at which element to be inserted:\t");
        scanf("%d",&pos);
        for(i = n-1 ; i >= pos-1 ; i--)
          list[i+1] = list[i];
        list[pos-1] = data;
        n+=1;
        Display();
}
```

Here the elements are inserted one at a time. Once the element is inserted, the number of elements in the array 'n' is incremented by 1.Hence inserting an element at particular position in the array is costly and time consuming since it involves many data movements.

c) Deletion Operation

Delete operation is used to delete one element from the array. An element can be deleted from any position in the array. Deleting the element from the last position of an array is easy. But deleting the element at a particular position in an array is quite difficult since it involves all the datas from the specified position to be moved one position left in the array.Consider an array with 5 elements [max elements = 10]

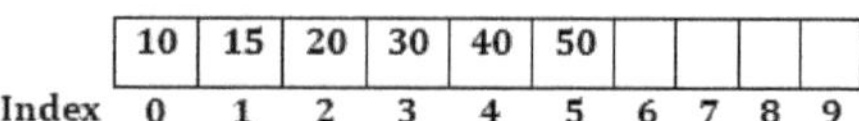

If data 15 is to be delete from the 1st index then data 20 has to be moved to index 1, 30 has to be moved to index 2, 40 has to be moved to index 3 and 50 has to be moved to index 4.

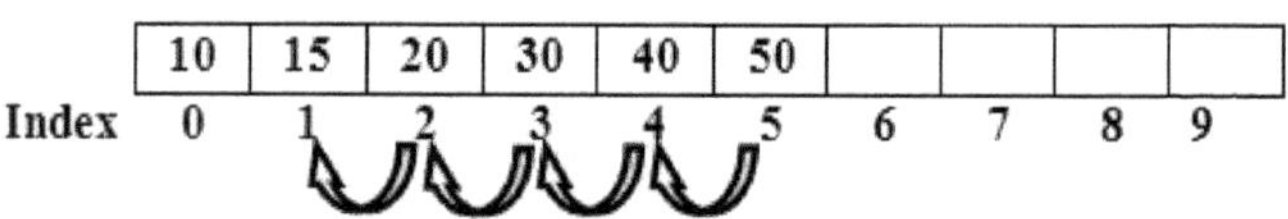

After four data movement, 15 is deleted from the index 1 of the array.

	10	20	30	40	50					
Index	0	1	3	4	5	6	7	8	9	

```
void Delete()
{
        int i,pos;
        printf("\nEnter the position of the data to be deleted:\t");
          scanf("%d",&pos);
        printf("\nThe data deleted is:\t %d", list[pos-1]);
        for(i=pos-1;i<n-1;i++)
          list[i]=list[i+1];
        n=n-1;
        Display();
}
```

d) Display Operation

Display( ) is used to display all the elements stored in the list. The elements are stored from the index 0 to n - 1. Using a for loop, the elements in the list are viewed.

```
void display()
{
        int i;
        printf("\n**********Elements in the array**********\n");
        for(i=0;i<n;i++)
          printf("%d\t",list[i]);
}
```

e) Search Operation

Search( ) is used to determine whether a particular element is present in the list or not. Input the search element to be checked in the list. There are two types of searching algorithm. They are Linear Search and Binary Search. Here Linear search technique is applied to search an element in the array.

```
void Search()
{
        int search,i,count = 0;
        printf("\nEnter the element to be searched:\t");
        scanf("%d",&search);
        for(i=0;i<n;i++)
        {
         if(search == list[i])
        count++;
         }
        if(count==0)
        printf("\nElement not present in the list");
        else
        printf("\nElement present in the list");
}
```

Program for Array Implementation of List

```
#include<stdio.h>
#include<conio.h>
#define maxsize 10
int list[maxsize],n;
void Create();
void Insert();
void Delete();
void Display();
void Search();
void main()
{
        int choice;
```

```
        clrscr();
        do
        {
        printf("\n Array Implementation of List\n");
        printf("\t1.create\n");
        printf("\t2.Insert\n");
        printf("\t3.Delete\n");
        printf("\t4.Display\n");
        printf("\t5.Search\n");
        printf("\t6.Exit\n");
        printf("\nEnter your choice:\t");
        scanf("%d",&choice);
        switch(choice)
        {
                case 1:  Create();
                         break;
                case 2:  Insert();
                         break;
                case 3:  Delete();
                         break;
                case 4:  Display();
                         break;
                case 5:  Search();
                         break;
                case 6:  exit(1);
                default: printf("\nEnter option between 1 -  6\n");
                         break;
        }
        }while(choice<7);
}
void Create()
{
        int i;
        printf("\nEnter the number of elements to be added in the list:\t");
```

```
        scanf("%d",&n);
        printf("\nEnter the array elements:\t");
        for(i=0;i<n;i++)
         scanf("%d",&list[i]);
        Display();
}
void Insert()
{
        int i,data,pos;
        printf("\nEnter the data to be inserted:\t");
        scanf("%d",&data);
        printf("\nEnter the position at which element to be inserted:\t");
        scanf("%d",&pos);
        for(i = n-1 ; i >= pos-1 ; i--)
          list[i+1] = list[i];
        list[pos-1] = data;
        n+=1;
        Display();
}
void Delete( )
{
        int i,pos;
        printf("\nEnter the position of the data to be deleted:\t");
        scanf("%d",&pos);
        printf("\nThe data deleted is:\t %d", list[pos-1]);
        for(i=pos-1;i<n-1;i++)
         list[i]=list[i+1];
        n=n-1;
        Display();
}
void Display()
{
        int i;
        printf("\n**********Elements in the array**********\n");
```

```
		for(i=0;i<n;i++)
		printf("%d\t",list[i]);
}
void Search()
{
		int search,i,count = 0;
		printf("\nEnter the element to be searched:\t");
		scanf("%d",&search);
		for(i=0;i<n;i++)
		{
		if(search == list[i])
		 {
		  count++;
		 }
		}
		if(count==0)
		printf("\nElement not present in the list");
		else
		printf("\nElement present in the list");
}
```

Output

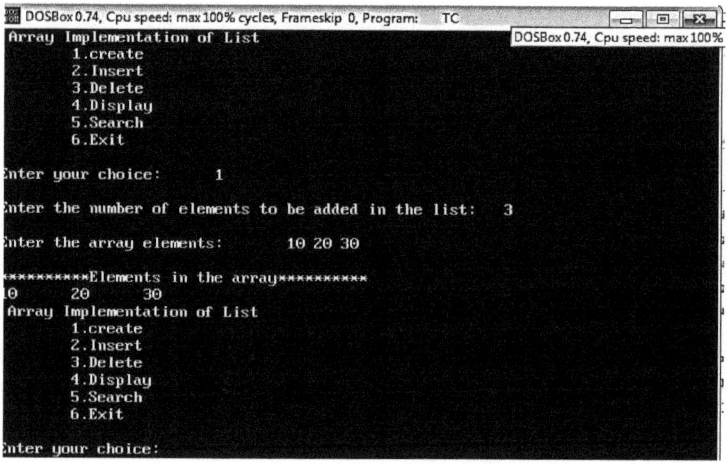

```
DOSBox 0.74, Cpu speed: max 100% cycles, Frameskip 0, Program:    TC
Array Implementation of List
        1.create
        2.Insert
        3.Delete
        4.Display
        5.Search
        6.Exit

Enter your choice:      1

Enter the number of elements to be added in the list:   3

Enter the array elements:       10 20 30

**********Elements in the array**********
10      20      30
Array Implementation of List
        1.create
        2.Insert
        3.Delete
        4.Display
        5.Search
        6.Exit

Enter your choice:
```

Limitation of Array Implementation

- An array size is fixed at the start of execution and can store only the limited number of elements.
- Insertion and deletion operation in array are expensive. Since insertion is performed by pushing the entire array one position down and deletion is performed by shifting the entire array one position up.

A better approach is to use a ***Linked List***implementation of List.

1.5.3. Linked List Implementation of List

Linked Lists

A linked list is a collection of nodes(Structure). Every node has a data field and an address field. The Address field contains the address of its successor.

Types of Linked List

1. Singly Linked List or One Way List
2. Doubly Linked List or Two-Way Linked List
3. Circular Linked List

1.5.4. Singly Linked List (SLL)

In this type of linked list two successive nodes are linked together in linear fashion. Each node contain address of the next node to be followed. In singly linked list only linear or forward sequential movement is possible. Elements are accessed sequentially, no direct access is allowed.

DATA	LINK (or)NEXT

SLL NODE

First node does not have predecessor while last node does not have any successor.last node have successor reference as "NULL".

Each SLL has a header node L to avoid confusion during Insertion and Deletion operation.

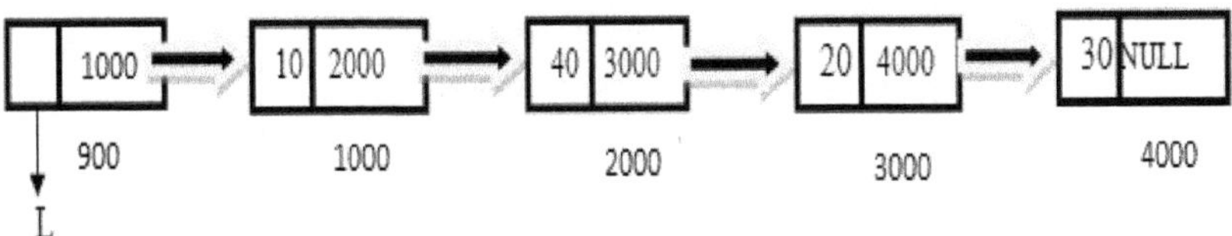

Basic operations on a singly-linked list are:

1. Insert( ) – Inserts a new node in the list.
2. Delete( ) – Deletes any node from the list.
3. Find( ) – Finds the position(address) of any node in the list.
4. FindPrevious( ) - Finds the position(address) of the previous node in the list.

Declaration of Linked List

```
void insert(int X,List L,position P);
void find(List L,int X);
void delete(int x , List L);
typedef struct node *position;
position L,p,newnode,temp;
```

Node Structure for Singly Linked List

```
struct node
{
        int data;
        position next;
};
```

Routine to Insert an Element in List

```
void Insert(int X,List L,position p)
{
        position newnode;
        newnode=malloc(sizeof(struct node));
        if(newnode==NULL)
                Fatal error("Out of Space");
        else
         {
                Newnode->data=x;
                Newnode->next=p->next;
                P ->next=newnode;
         }
}
```

Routine to Insert an Element in the List

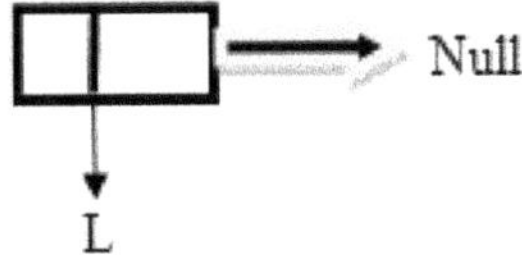

Insert(L,10) - A new node with data 10 is inserted and the next field is updated to NULL. The next field of previous node is updated to store the address of new node.

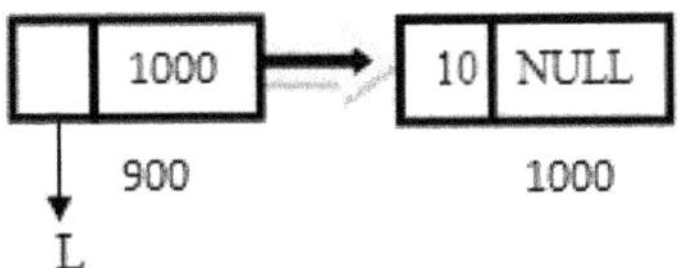

Insert(L,20) - A new node with data 20 is inserted and the next field is updated to NULL. The next field of previous node is updated to store the address of new node.

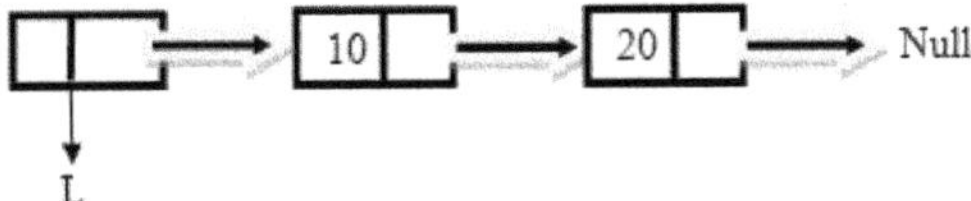

Insert(L,30) - A new node with data 30 is inserted and the next field is updated to NULL. Thenext field of previous node is updated to store the address of new node.

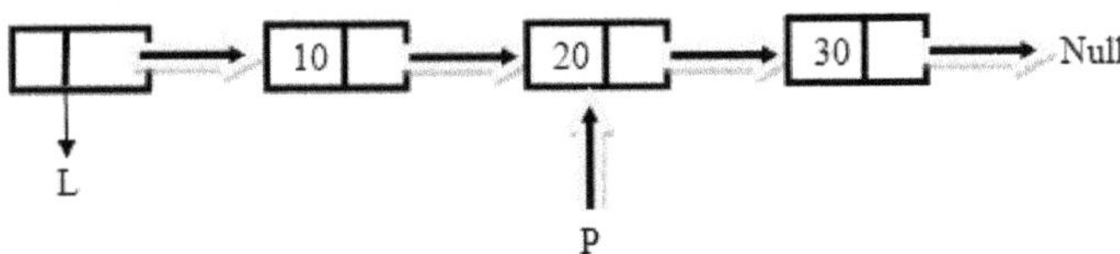

Routine to Check Whether a List is Empty

```
int IsEmpty(List L)
{
if (L->next==NULL)
                return(1);
}
```

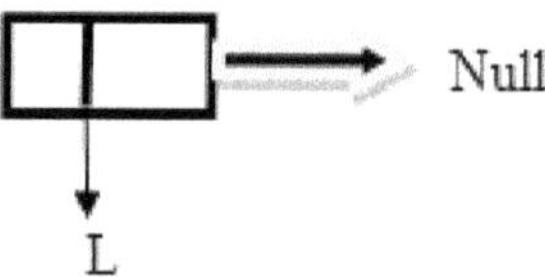

Routine to Check Whether the Current Position is Last in the List

```
int IsLast(List L , position p)
{
        if(p->next==NULL)
                return(1);
}
```

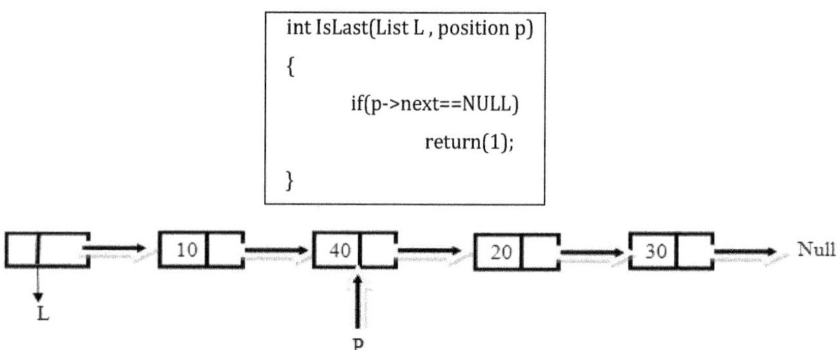

Routine to Find the Element in the List

```
position find(List  L,int  X)
{
    position p;
    p=L->next;
    while(p!=NULL && p->data!=X)
            p=p->next;
    return(p);
}
```

Find(L,20) - To find an element in the list, start from the first node of the list and traverse the list till the element is found.

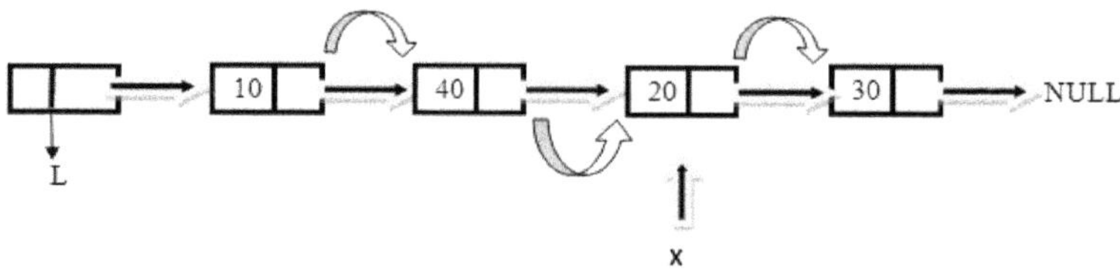

Routine to Find Previous Node

It returns the position of its predecessor.

```
position FindPrevious (int X, List L)
{
        position p;
        p=L;
        while(p->next!=NULL && p->next->data!=X)
                p=p->next;
        return P;
}
```

Routine to Count the Element in the List

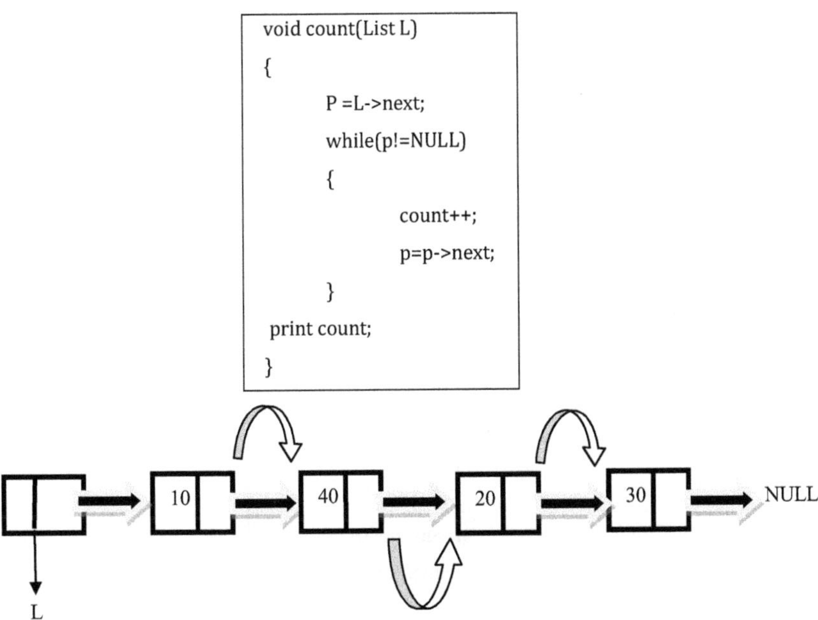

```
void count(List L)
{
        P =L->next;
        while(p!=NULL)
        {
                count++;
                p=p->next;
        }
 print count;
}
```


Routine to Delete an Element from the List

Delete(20,L) - A node with data 20 is found. Mark the node to be deleted as **temp**. Update the address part of the previous node from the temp node. Using free( ) release the memory of temp node.

```
void Delete(int x , List L)
{
    position p,Temp;
    p=FindPrevious(X,L);
    if(!IsLast(p,L))
    {
        temp=p->next;
        P ->next=temp->next;
        free(temp);
}
}
```

Before Deletion

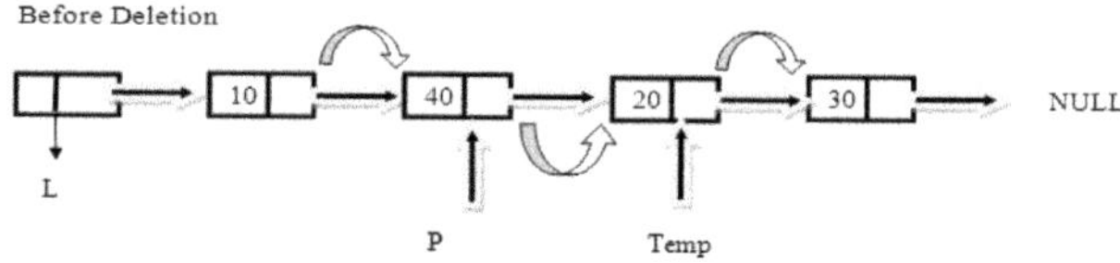

After Deletion

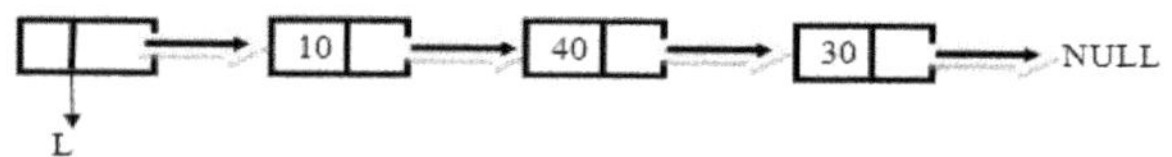

Routine to Delete the List

```
void Delete_list(List L)
{
    position P,temp;
    P=L->next;
    L->next=NULL;
    while(P!=NULL)
    {
        temp=P->next;
        free(P);
        P=temp;
    }
}
```

Routine to Find Next Element in the List

```
void FindNext(int X, List L)
{
    position P;
    P=L->next;
    while(P!=NULL && P->data!=X)
        P = P->next;
    return P->next;
}
```

1.5.5. Doubly Linked List (DLL)

It is a more sophisticated form of linked list. It is a collection of nodes where each node has three fields.

DLL NODE

PREV – Stores the address of the previous node.

DATA – Stores the actual data.

NEXT- Stores the address of the next node.

In comparison to singly-linked list, doubly-linked list requires handling of more pointers but less information is required as one can use the previous links to observe the preceding element. It has a dynamic size, which can be determined only at run time.

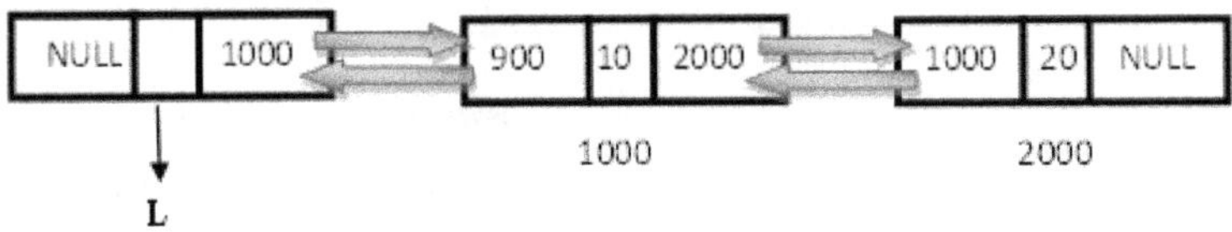

Doubly Linked List Operations

1. Insert( ) – Inserts a new element at the end of the list.
2. Delete( ) – Deletes any node from the list.
3. Find( ) – Finds any node in the list.
4. Print( ) – Prints the list.

Declaration of Doubly Linked List

```
typedef structnode *position;
struct node
{
        int data;
        position prev;
        position next;
};
```

Empty list

NULL L NULL

Routine to Insert an Element

```
void Insert (int x,List L,position p)
{
    position newnode;
    newnode = malloc(sizeof(struct node));
if(newnode==NULL)
Fatal error ("out of space");
      else
      {
newnode ->data = x;
newnode ->next =p->next;
 p->next ->prev = newnode;
 p->next= newnode;
newnode ->prev =p;
      }
}
```

i) Insert(L,10) - A newnode with data 10 is inserted, the next field is updated to NULL and the previous field is updated to store the address of the previous node. The next field of previous node is updated to store the address of new node.

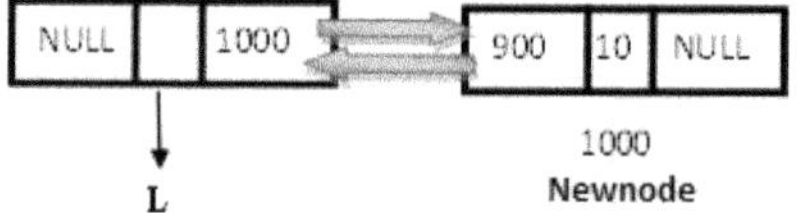

ii) Insert(L,20) - A newnode with data 20 is inserted, the next field is updated to NULL and the previous field is updated to store the address of the previous node. The next field of previous node is updated to store the address of new node.

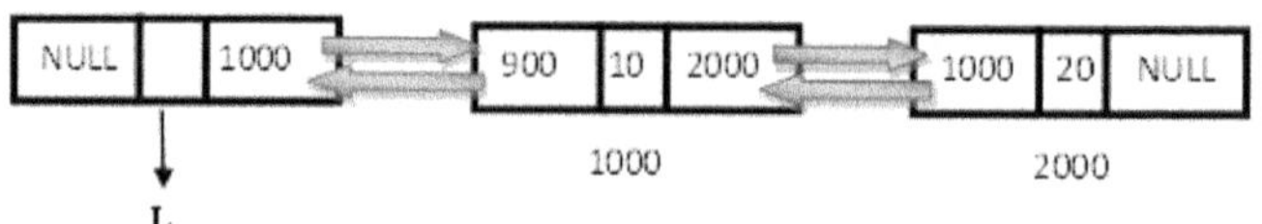

iii) Insert(L,30) - A new node with data 30 is inserted, the next field is updated to NULL and the previous field is updated to store the address of the previous node. The next field of previous node is updated to store the address of new node.

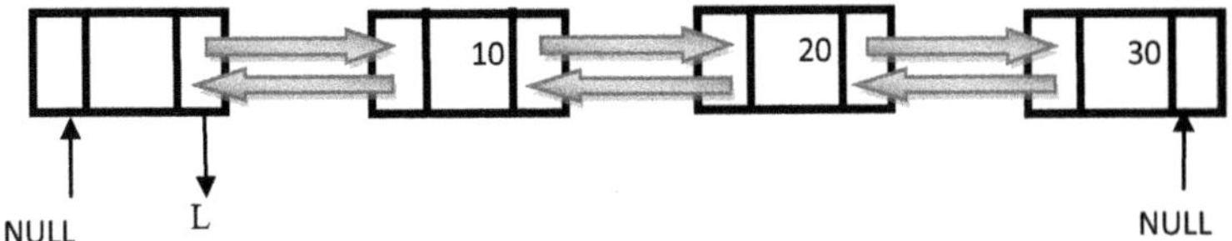

iv) Insert(L,40,P) - A new node with data 40 is inserted, the next field is updated to NULL and the previous field is updated to store the address of the previous node. The next field of previous node is updated to store the address of new node.

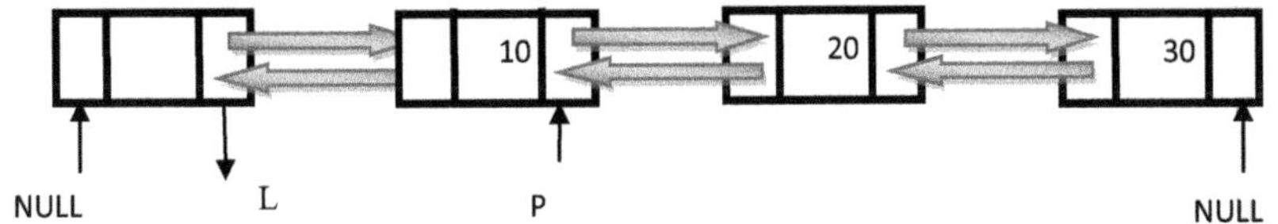

Inserting element 40 at the particular position in the list

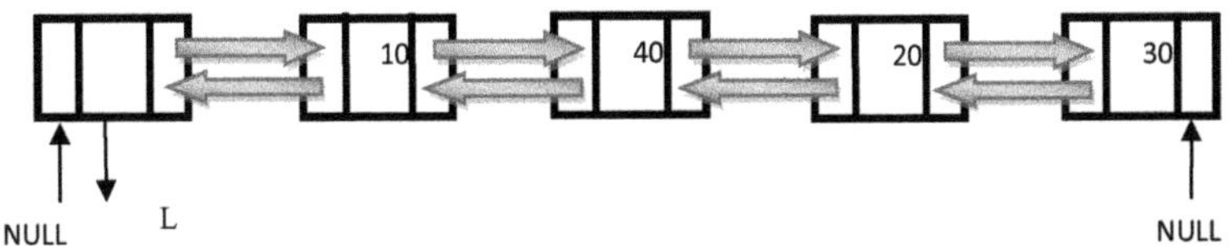

Routine to Display List Element

```
void Display(List L)
{
P =L->next;
while (p!=NULL)
{
    print p->data;
    p=p->next;
}
print NULL
}
```

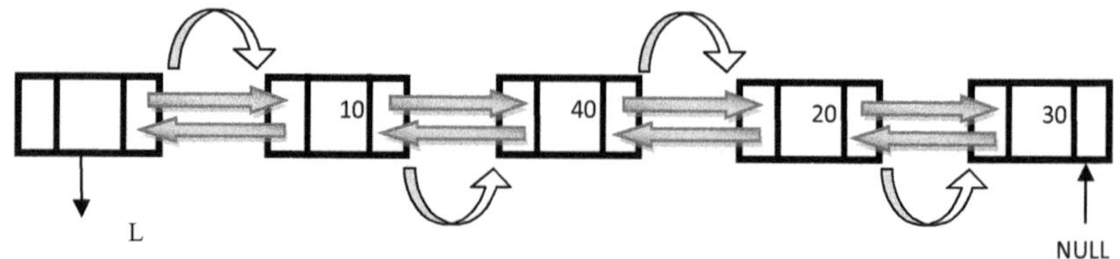

Routine to Delete an Element

```
void Delete (int x ,List L)
{
 Position p , temp;
P = Find(x,L);
 if(isLast(p,L))
  {
temp =p;
     p->prev->next=NULL;
     free(temp);
  }
 else
 {
  temp = p;
  p->prev->next=p->next;
  p->next->prev = p->prev;
 free(temp);
}
```

Delete(L,10) - A node with data 10 is found, the next and previous fields are updated to store the NULL value. The next field of previous node is updated to store the address of node next to the deleted node. The previous field of the node next to the deleted one is updated to store the address of the node that is before the deleted node.

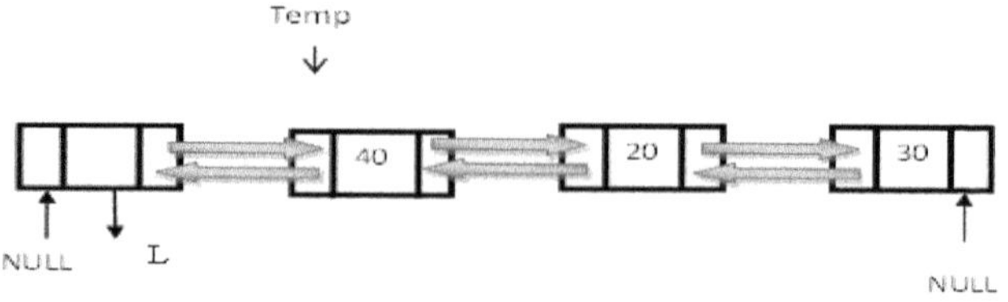

Find(start,10) 'Element Not Found'

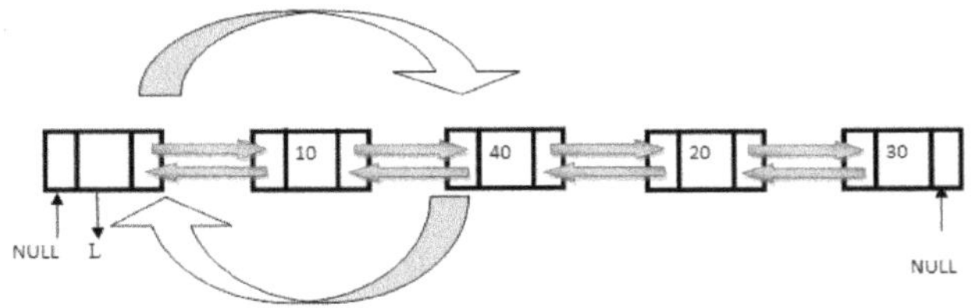

To print start from the first node of the list and move to the next with the help of the address stored in the next field.

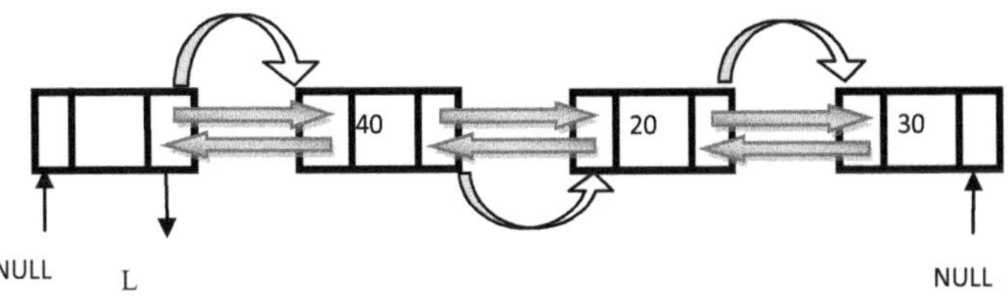

1.5.6. *Circular Linked List*

Circular linked list is a more complicated linked list. All nodes are linked in a continuous circle without using NULL.The next node after the last node is the first node.

Types of Circular Linked List

1. Singly circular linked list

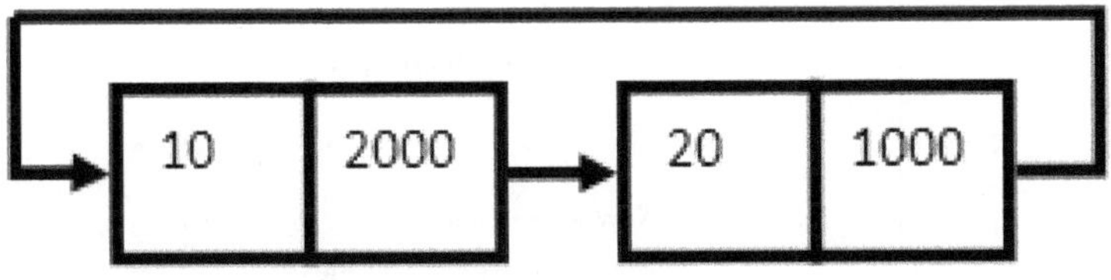

2. Doubly circular linked list

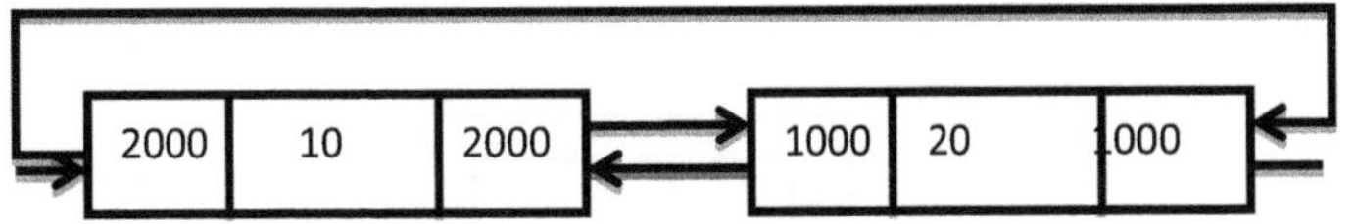

Basic operations of a singly circular linked list are same as SLL:

1. Insert ( )– Inserts a new element at the end of the list.
2. Delete( ) – Deletes any node from the list.
3. Find( ) – Finds any node in the list.
4. Print( ) – Prints the list.

Declaration of Linked List

```
void insert(int X,List L,position P);
void find(List L,int X);
void delete(int x , List L);
typedef struct node *position;
position L,p,newnode;
struct node
{
        int data;
        position next;
};
```

Routine to Insert an Element in List

```
void Insert(int X, List L, position p)
{
        position newnode;
        newnode = malloc( sizeof( struct node ));
        if( newnode = = NULL )
                Fatal error( " Out of Space " );
        else
         {
                Newnode -> data = x ;
                Newnode -> next = p ->next ;
                P -> next = newnode ;
}       }
```

singly circular with 1 node

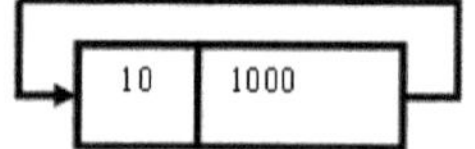

Insert(Start,20) - A new node with data 20 is inserted and the next field is updated to store the address of start node. The next field of previous node is updated to store the address of new node.

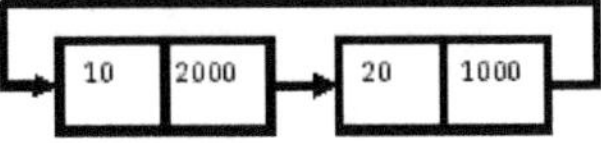

Insert(Start,30) - A new node with data 30 is inserted and the next field is updated to store the address of start node. The next field of previous node is updated to store the address of new node.

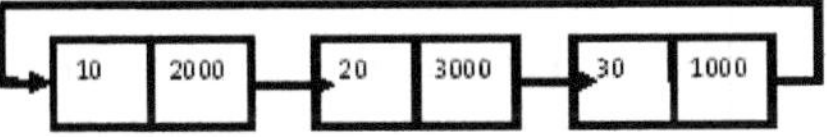

Find Previous

It returns the position of its predecessor.

```
position FindPrevious (int X, List L)
{
        position p;
        p = L;
        while( p -> next ! = NULL && p -> next -> data! = X )
                p = p -> next;
        return P;
}
```

Routine to Delete an Element from the List

```
void Delete( int x , List L)
{
        position p, Temp;
        p = FindPrevious( X, L);
        if( ! IsLast (p, L))
        {
                temp = p -> next;
                P -> next = temp -> next;
                free ( temp );
        }
}
```

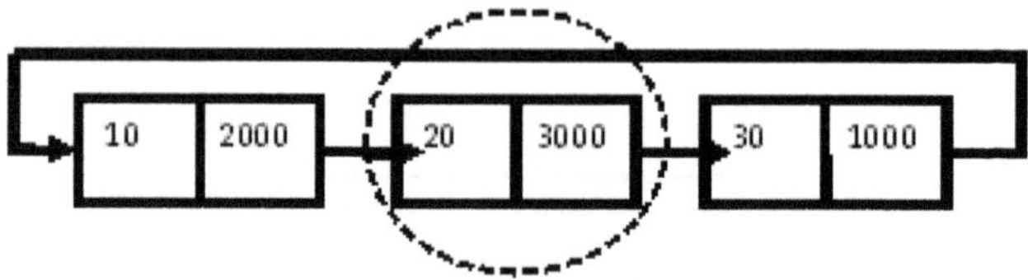

Routine to Delete the List

```
void Delete_list(List L)
    {
        position P,temp;
        P=L->next;
        L->next=NULL;
        while(P!=NULL)
        {
            temp=P->next;
            free(P);
            P=temp;
        }
    }
```

Routine to Find Next Element in the List

```
void FindNext(int X, List L)
{
    position P;
    P=L->next;
    while(P!=NULL && P->data!=X)
        P = P->next;
    return P->next;
}
```

Routine to Find the Element in the List

```
position find(List L, int X)
{
        position p;
        p=L->next;
        while(p!=NULL && p->data!=X)
                p=p->next;
        return(p);
}
```

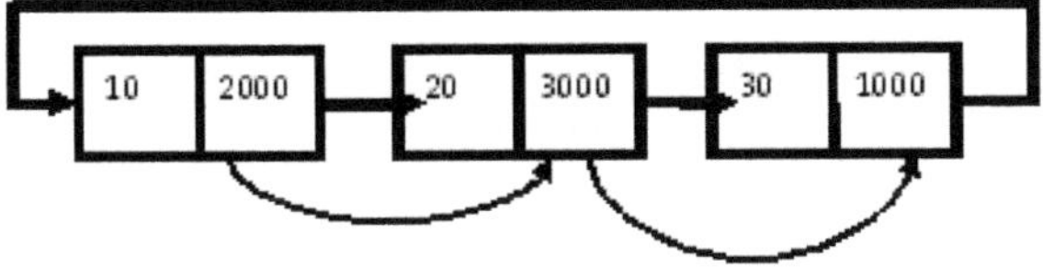

1.6. Applications of Linked List

Linked list is applicable in the following areas

1. Polynomial Manipulation
2. Multi list
3. Set operations
4. Radix sort
5. Dynamic memory management

Polynomial Manipulation

Polynomial manipulations such as addition, subtraction & differentiation etc.. can be performed using linked list

Declaration for Linked List Implementation of Polynomial ADT

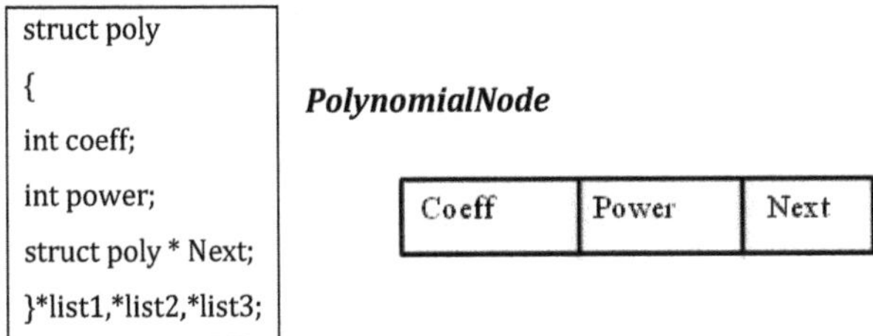

```
struct poly
{
int coeff;
int power;
struct poly * Next;
}*list1,*list2,*list3;
```

Creation of the Polynomial

```
poly create(poly*head1,poly*newnode1)
  {
        poly *ptr;
        if(head1==NULL)
        {
                head1=newnode1;
                return (head1);
        }
        else
        {
                ptr=head1;
                while(ptr->next!=NULL)
                ptr=ptr->next;
                ptr->next=newnode1;
        }
        return(head1);}
```

Addition of two Polynomials

```
void add()
{
      Poly*ptr1,*ptr2,*newnode;
      ptr1=list1;


      ptr2=list2;
      while(ptr1!=NULL&&ptr2!=NULL)
      {
            Newnode=malloc(sizeof(struct poly));
if(ptr1->power==ptr2->power)
            {
                  Newnode->coeff=ptr1->coeff+ptr2->coeff;
                  Newnode->power=ptr1->power;
```

```
                Newnode->next=NULL;
                list3=create(list3,newnode);
                ptr1=ptr1->next;
                ptr2=ptr2->next;
            }
            else if(ptr1->power>ptr2->power)
            {
                Newnode->coeff=ptr1->coeff;
                Newnode->power=ptr1->power;
                Newnode->next=NULL;
                list3=create(list3,newnode);
                ptr1=ptr1->next;
            }
            else
            {
                Newnode->coeff=ptr2->coeff;
                Newnode->power=ptr2->power;
                Newnode->next=NULL;
                list3=create(list3,newnode);
                ptr2=ptr2->next;
            }
    }}
```

Subtraction of two Polynomial

```
void sub()
{
    Poly *ptr1, *ptr2, *newnode;
    ptr1 = list1;
    ptr2 = list2;
    while( ptr1 != NULL && ptr2 != NULL )
    {
```

```
Newnode = malloc(sizeof(struct poly));
if(ptr1->power==ptr2->power)
{
        newnode->coeff=(ptr1-coeff)-(ptr2->coeff);
newnode->power=ptr1->power;
            newnode->next=NULL;
            list3=create(list3,newnode);
            ptr1=ptr1->next;
            ptr2=ptr2->next;
  }
  else
  {
            if(ptr1-power>ptr2-power)
            {
                    newnode->coeff=ptr1->coeff;
                    newnode->power=ptr1->power;
                    newnode->next=NULL;
                    list3=create(list3,newnode);
                    ptr1=ptr1->next;
            }
  else
  {
            newnode->coeff=-(ptr2->coeff);
            newnode->power=ptr2->power;
            newnode->next=NULL;
            list3=create(list3,newnode);
            ptr2=ptr2->next;
  }
        }
}
```

1.7. Sample Programs

Program 1: Implementation of Singly linked List	**Output**
#include<stdio.h>	1.create
#include<conio.h>	2.display
#include<stdlib.h>	3.insert
void create();	4.find
void display();	5.delete
void insert();	
void find();	
void delete();	Enter your choice
typedef struct node *position;	
position L,p,newnode;	1
struct node	
{	Enter the number of
int data;	nodes to be inserted
position next;	5
};	
void main()	Enter the data
{	1
int choice;	2
clrscr();	3
do	4
{	5
printf("1.create\n2.display\n3.insert\n4.find\n5.delete\n\n\n");	1.create
printf("Enter your choice\n\n");	2.display
scanf("%d",&choice);	3.insert
switch(choice)	4.find
{	5.delete
case 1:	
create();	
break;	Enter your choice
case 2:	
display();	2

break;	1 -> 2 -> 3 -> 4 -> 5 -> Null
case 3:	1.create
insert();	2.display
break;	3.insert
case 4:	4.find
find();	5.delete
break;	
case 5:	
delete();	Enter your choice
break;	
case 6:	3
exit(0);	
}	Enter ur choice
}	
while(choice<7);	1.first
getch();	2.middle
}	3.end
void create()	1
{	
int i,n;	Enter the data to be
L=NULL;	inserted
newnode=(struct node*)malloc(sizeof(struct node));	7
printf("\n Enter the number of nodes to be inserted\n");	7 -> 1 -> 2 -> 3 -> 4 -> 5 ->
scanf("%d",&n);	Null
printf("\n Enter the data\n");	1.create
scanf("%d",&newnode->data);	2.display
newnode->next=NULL;	3.insert
L=newnode;	4.find
p=L;	5.delete
for(i=2;i<=n;i++)	
{	
newnode=(struct node *)malloc(sizeof(struct node));	Enter your choice
scanf("%d",&newnode->data);	

newnode->next=NULL;
p->next=newnode;
p=newnode;
}
}
void display()
{
p=L;
while(p!=NULL)
{
printf("%d -> ",p->data);
p=p->next;
}
printf("Null\n");
}
void insert()
{
int ch;
printf("\nEnter ur choice\n");
printf("\n1.first\n2.middle\n3.end\n");
scanf("%d",&ch);
switch(ch)
{
case 2:
{
int pos,i=1;
p=L;
newnode=(struct node*)malloc(sizeof(struct node));
printf("\nEnter the data to be inserted\n");
scanf("%d",&newnode->data);
printf("\nEnter the position to be inserted\n");
scanf("%d",&pos);
newnode->next=NULL;	

while(i<pos-1)
{
p=p->next;
i++;
}
newnode->next=p->next;
p->next=newnode;
p=newnode;
display();
break;
}
case 1:
{
p=L;
newnode=(struct node*)malloc(sizeof(struct node));
printf("\nEnter the data to be inserted\n");
scanf("%d",&newnode->data);
newnode->next=L;
L=newnode;
display();
break;
}
case 3:
{
p=L;
newnode=(struct node*)malloc(sizeof(struct node));
printf("\nEnter the data to be inserted\n");
scanf("%d",&newnode->data);
while(p->next!=NULL)
p=p->next;	

```
        newnode->next=NULL;
        p->next=newnode;
        p=newnode;
        display();
        break;
        }
}
}
void find()
{
int search,count=0;
printf("\n Enter the element to be found:\n");
scanf("%d",&search);
p=L;
while(p!=NULL)
{
if(p->data==search)
 {
 count++;
 break;
 }
p=p->next;
}
if(count==0)
printf("\n Element Not present\n");
else
printf("\n Element present in the list \n\n");
}
void delete()
{
position p,temp;
int x;
p=L;
```

if(p==NULL)
{
printf("empty list\n");
}
else
{
printf("\nEnter the data to be deleted\n");
scanf("%d",&x);
if(x==p->data)
{
temp=p;
L=p->next;
free(temp);
display();
}
else
{
while(p->next!=NULL && p->next->data!=x)
{
p=p->next;
}
temp=p->next;
p->next=p->next->next;
free(temp);
display();
}
}
}	

Program 2 :Implementation of Doubly linked list	**Output**
#include<stdio.h>	
#include<conio.h>	1.INSERT
void insert();	2.DELETE
void delete();	3.DISPLAY
void display();	4.FIND
void find();	5.EXIT
struct list	Enter ur option
{	1
int info;	
struct list *next;	Enter the data to be inserted5
struct list *prev;	
}*node,*ptr,*head=NULL,*temp;	1.INSERT
void main()	2.DELETE
{	3.DISPLAY
int choice;	4.FIND
clrscr();	5.EXIT
do	Enter ur option1
{	
printf("\n1.INSERT");	Enter the data to be inserted7
printf("\n2.DELETE");	
printf("\n3.DISPLAY");	Enter the position where the data is to be inserted2
printf("\n4.FIND");	
printf("\n5.EXIT");	
printf("\nEnter ur option");	1.INSERT
scanf("%d",&choice);	2.DELETE
switch(choice)	3.DISPLAY
{	4.FIND
case 1:	5.EXIT
insert();	Enter ur option3
break;	
case 2:	The elements in the stack are
delete();	57
break;	1.INSERT
case 3:	2.DELETE
display();	3.DISPLAY
break;	4.FIND
	5.EXIT

case 4:
find();
break;
case 5:
exit(1);
}
}while(choice!=5);
getch();
}
void insert()
{
int pos,i;
temp=(struct list*)malloc(sizeof(struct list));
printf("\nEnter the data to be inserted");
scanf("%d",&temp->info);
if(head==NULL)
{
head=temp;
head->next=NULL;
head->prev=NULL;
}
else
{
printf("\nEnter the position where the data is to be inserted");
scanf("%d",&pos);
if(pos==1)
{
temp->next=head;
temp->prev=NULL;
head->prev=temp;
head=temp;
}
else
{
ptr=head;
for(i=1;i<pos-1&&ptr->next!=NULL;i++)
{
	Enter ur option1
	
	Enter the data to be inserted8
	
	Enter the position where the data is to be inserted1
	
	1.INSERT
	2.DELETE
	3.DISPLAY
	4.FIND
	5.EXIT
	Enter ur option3
	
	The elements in the stack are
	857
	1.INSERT
	2.DELETE
	3.DISPLAY
	4.FIND
	5.EXIT
	Enter ur option

```
ptr=ptr->next;
}
temp->next=ptr->next;
ptr->next=temp;
temp->prev=ptr;
ptr->next->prev=temp;
}
}
}
void delete()
{
int pos,i;
if(head==NULL)
printf("\nThe list is empty");
else
{
printf("\nEnter the position of the data to be
deleted");
scanf("%d",&pos);
temp=head;
if(pos==1)
{
printf("\nThe deleted element is %d",temp->info);
head=temp->next;
head->prev=NULL;
}
else
{
ptr=head;
for(i=1;i<pos-1;i++)
ptr=ptr->next;
node=ptr->next;
printf("\nThe deletedelement is %d",node->info);
ptr->next=node->next;
node->next->prev=ptr;
}
}
}
```

void display()
{
if(head==NULL)
printf("\nNo of elements in the list");
else
{
printf("\nThe elements in the stack are\n");
for(ptr=head;ptr!=NULL;ptr=ptr->next)
printf("%d",ptr->info);
}
}
void find()
{
int a,flag=0,count=0;
if(head==NULL)
printf("\nThe list is empty");
else
{
printf("\nEnter the elements to be searched");
scanf("%d",&a);
for(ptr=head;ptr!=NULL;ptr=ptr->next)
{
count++;
if(ptr->info==a)
{
flag=1;
printf("\nThe element is found");
printf("\nThe position is %d",count);
break;
}
}
if(flag==0)
printf("\nThe element is not found");
}
}	

Program 3: Implementation of Polynomial Addition

```
#include<stdio.h>
#include<malloc.h>
#include<conio.h>
struct link
{
int coeff;
int pow;
struct link *next;
};
struct link *poly1=NULL,*poly2=NULL,*poly=NULL;
void create(struct link *node)
{
char ch;
do
{
printf("\nEnter coeff:");
scanf("%d",&node->coeff);
printf("\nEnter power:");
scanf("%d",&node->pow);
node->next=(struct link*)malloc(sizeof(struct link));
node=node->next;
node->next=NULL;
printf("\ncontinue(y/n):");
ch=getch();
}
while(ch=='y'||ch=='Y');
}
void show(struct link *node)
{
while(node->next!=NULL)
{
```

Output

```
Enter the 1st number:
Enter coeff:4

Enter power:2

continue(y/n):
Enter coeff:
5

Enter power:2

continue(y/n):
Enter coeff:
6

Enter power:1

continue(y/n):
Enter the 2nd number:
Enter coeff:6

Enter power:4

continue(y/n):
1st number:4x^2+5x^2+6x^1
2nd number:6x^4Press any key to continue . . .
```

printf("%dx^%d",node->coeff,node->pow);
node=node->next;
if(node->next!=NULL)
printf("+");
}
}
void polyadd(struct link *poly1,struct link
*poly2,struct link *poly)
{
while(poly1->next&&poly2->next)
{
if(poly1->pow>poly2->pow)
{
poly->pow=poly1->pow;
poly->coeff=poly1->coeff;
poly1=poly1->next;
}
else if(poly1->pow<poly2->pow)
{
poly->pow=poly2->pow;
poly->coeff=poly2->coeff;
poly2=poly->next;
}
else
{
poly->pow=poly1->pow;
poly->coeff=poly1->coeff+poly2->coeff;
poly1=poly1->next;
poly2=poly2->next;
}
poly->next=(struct link *)malloc(sizeof(struct link));
poly=poly->next;
poly->next=NULL;	

```
}
while(poly1->next||poly2->next)
{
if(poly1->next)
{
poly->pow=poly1->pow;
poly->coeff=poly1->coeff;
poly1=poly1->next;
}
if(poly2->next)
{
poly->pow=poly2->pow;
poly->coeff=poly2->coeff;
poly2=poly2->next;
}
poly->next=(struct link *)malloc(sizeof(struct link));
poly=poly->next;
poly->next=NULL;
}
}
main()
{
char ch;
clrscr();
do{
poly1=(struct link *)malloc(sizeof(struct link));
poly2=(struct link *)malloc(sizeof(struct link));
poly=(struct link *)malloc(sizeof(struct link));
printf("\nEnter the 1st number:");
create(poly1);
printf("\nEnter the 2nd number:");
create(poly2);
printf("\n1st number:");
```

show(poly1);
printf("\n2nd number:");
show(poly2);
polyadd(poly1,poly2,poly);
printf("\nAdded Polynomial:");
show(poly);
printf("\nAdd two more numbers:");
ch=getch();
}
while(ch=='y'||ch=='Y');
}	

PART II

- Stack ADT
- Application of Stack
- Queue ADT
- Circular Queue
- Double Ended Queue
- Review Questions

CHAPTER 2

Linear Data Structures - Stacks

2.1. Introduction

Stack is a Linear Data Structure that follows Last In First Out(LIFO) principle.Insertion and deletion can be done at only one end of the stack called TOP of the stack.

Example: - Pile of coins.

TOP Pointer

It will always point to the last element inserted in the stack.

For empty stack, top will be pointing to -1. (TOP = -1)

2.2. Stack Model

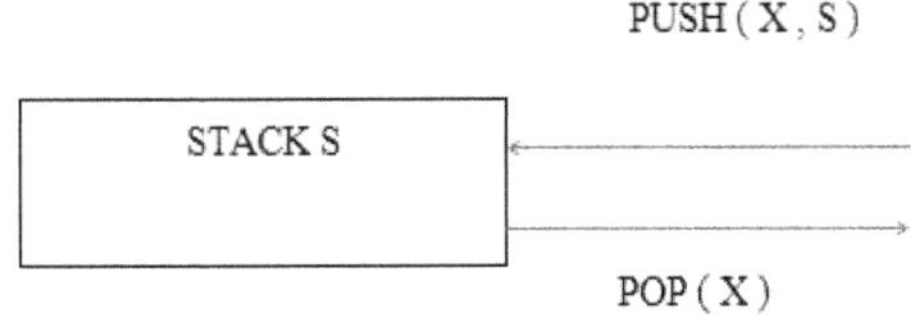

2.3. Operations on Stack(Stack ADT)

Two fundamental operations performed on the stack are PUSH and POP.

(a) PUSH:It is the process of inserting a new element at the Top of the stack.
For every push operation:

1. Check for Full stack (overflow).
2. Increment Top by 1. (Top = Top + 1)
3. Insert the element X in the Top of the stack.

(b) POP: It is the process of deleting the Top element of the stack.
For every pop operation:

1. Check for Empty stack (underflow).
2. Delete (pop) the Top element X from the stack
3. Decrement the Top by 1. (Top = Top - 1)

Exceptional Conditions of Stack

1. Stack Overflow

- An Attempt to insert an element X when the stack is Full, is said to be stack overflow.
- For every Push operation, check this condition.

2. Stack Underflow

- An Attempt to delete an element when the stack is empty, is said to be stack underflow.
- For every Pop operation, we need to check this condition.

2.4. Implementation of Stack

Stack can be implemented in 2 ways.

1. Static Implementation (Array implementation of Stack)
2. Dynamic Implementation (Linked List Implementation of Stack)

2.4.1. Array Implementation of Stack

- Each stackis associated with a Top pointer.
- For Empty stack, Top = -1.
- Stack is declared with its maximum size.

Array Declaration of Stack

```
#define ArraySize 5

int S [ Array Size];

  or

int S [ 5 ];
```

3. Stack Empty Operation

- Initially Stack is Empty.
- With Empty stack Top pointer points to – 1.
- It is necessary to check for Empty Stack before deleting(pop) an element from the stack.

Routine to Check Whether Stack is Empty

```
int IsEmpty ( Stack S )
{
  if( Top = = - 1 )
  return(1);
}
```

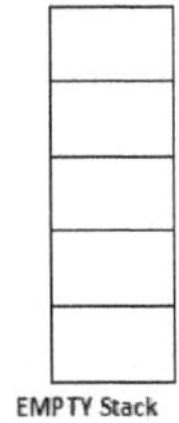

4. *Stack Full Operation*

- As we keep inserting the elements, the Stack gets filled with the elements.
- Hence it is necessary to check whether the stack is full or not before inserting a new element into the stack.

Routine to Check Whether a Stack is Full

```
int IsFull ( Stack  S )
    {  if( Top = = Arraysize – 1 )
       return(1);
    }
```

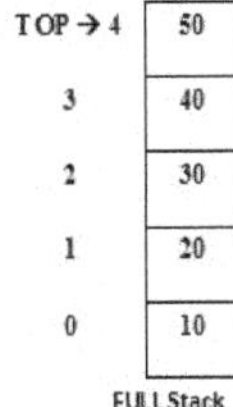

5. *Push Operation*

- It is the process of inserting a new element at the Top of the stack.
- It takes two parameters. Push(X, S) the element X to be inserted at the Top of the Stack S.
- Before inserting an Element into the stack, check for Full Stack.
- If the Stack is already Full, Insertion is not possible.
- Otherwise, Increment the Top pointer by 1 and then insert the element X at the Top of the Stack.

```
void Push ( int  X , Stack S )
{
 if ( Top = = Arraysize - 1)
      Error("Stack is full!!Insertion is not possible");
 else
      {      Top = Top + 1;
             S [ Top ] =X;
      }
}
```

Routine to Push an Element Into the Stack

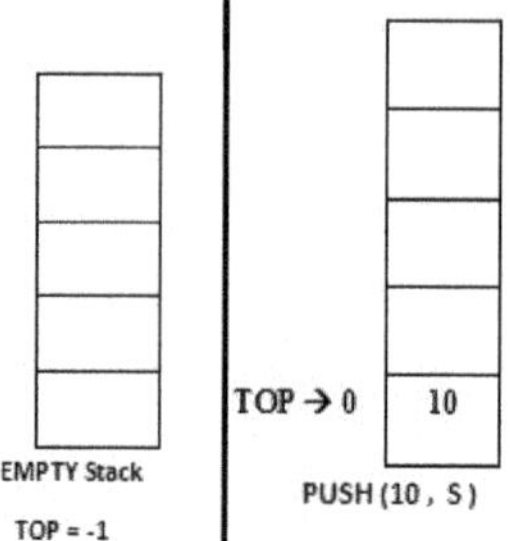

6. *Pop Operation*

- It is the process of deleting the Top element of the stack.
- It takes only one parameter. Pop(X).The element X to be deleted from the Top of the Stack.
- Before deleting the Top element of the stack, check for Empty Stack.
- If the Stack is Empty, deletion is not possible.
- Otherwise, delete the Top element from the Stack and then decrement the Top pointer by 1.

Routine to Pop the Top Element of the Stack

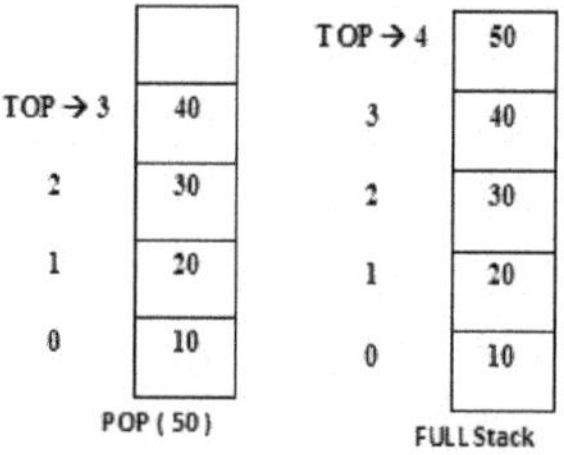


```
void Pop ( Stack  S )
{
 if ( Top = = - 1)
Error ( "Empty stack! Deletion not possible");
else
{     X = S [ Top ] ;
      Top = Top – 1 ;
 }
}
```

7. *Return Top Element*

- Pop routine deletes the Top element in the stack.
- If the user needs to know the last element inserted into the stack, then the user can return the Top element of the stack.
- To do this, first check for Empty Stack.
- If the stack is empty, then there is no element in the stack.
- Otherwise, return the element which is pointed by the Top pointer in the Stack.

Routine to Return Top Element of the Stack

```
int TopElement(Stack S)
{
  if(Top==-1)
  {
     Error("Empty stack!!No elements");
     return 0;
  }
 else
    return S[Top];
}
```

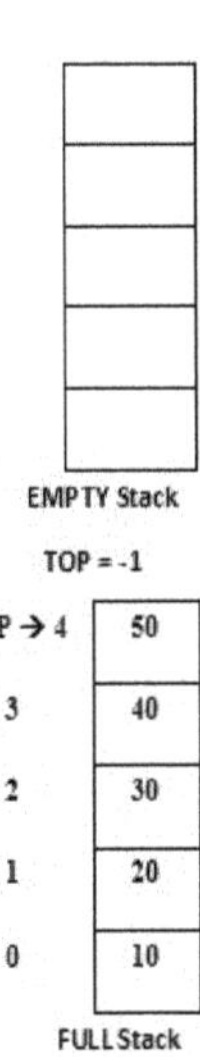

Implementation of Stack using Array

```
/* static implementation of stack*/
#include<stdio.h>
#include<conio.h>
#define size 5
int stack [ size ];
int top;
void push( )
{
      int n;
      printf( "\n Enter item in stack" );
      scanf( "%d", &n );
```

```
        if( top = =size - 1)
        {
                printf("\nStack is Full");
        }
        else
        {
                top=top+1;
                stack[top]=n;
        }
}
void pop()
{
        int item;
        if(top==-1)
        {
                printf("\n Stack is empty");
        }
        else
        {
                item=stack[top];
                printf("\n item popped is=%d", item);
                top--;
        }
}
void display()
{
        int i;
        printf("\n   item   in   stack
are");
        for(i =top; i >=0; i --)
        printf("\n %d", stack[ i] );
}
void main()
{
```

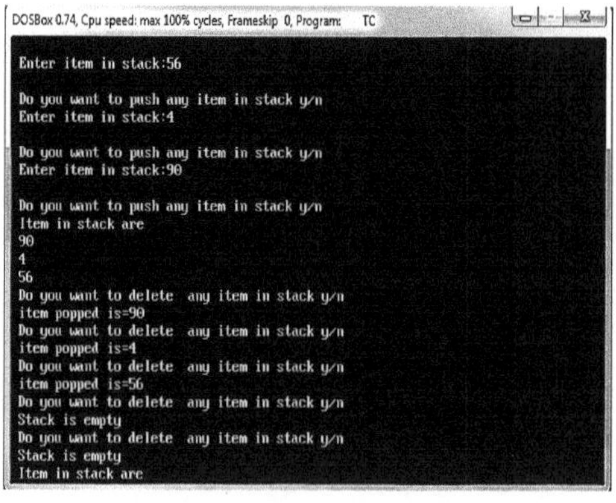

```
DOSBox 0.74, Cpu speed: max 100% cycles, Frameskip 0, Program:    TC
Enter item in stack:56

Do you want to push any item in stack y/n
Enter item in stack:4

Do you want to push any item in stack y/n
Enter item in stack:90

Do you want to push any item in stack y/n
Item in stack are
90
4
56
Do you want to delete  any item in stack y/n
item popped is=90
Do you want to delete  any item in stack y/n
item popped is=4
Do you want to delete  any item in stack y/n
item popped is=56
Do you want to delete  any item in stack y/n
Stack is empty
Do you want to delete  any item in stack y/n
Stack is empty
Item in stack are
```

```
        char ch,ch1;
        ch ='y';
        ch1='y';
        top=-1;
        clrscr();
        while(ch!='n')
        {
                push();
                printf("\n Do you want to push any item in stack y/n");
                ch=getch();
        }
        display();
        while(ch1!='n')
        {
                printf("\n Do you want to delete  any item in stack y/n");
                ch1=getch();
                pop();
        }
        display();
        getch();
}
```

2.4.2. Linked List Implementation of STACK

- Stack elements are implemented using SLL (Singly Linked List) concept.
- Dynamically, memory is allocated to each element of the stack as a node.

Type Declarations for Stack Using SLL

```
struct node;
typedef struct node *stack;
typedef struct node *position;
stack S;
struct node
{
int data;
position next;
};
int IsEmpty(Stack S);
void Push(int x, Stack S);
void Pop(Stack S);
int TopElement(Stack S);
```

1. *Stack Empty Operation*

- Initially Stack is Empty.
- With Linked List implementation, Empty stack is represented as S -> next = NULL.
- It is necessary to check for Empty Stack before deleting (pop) an element from the stack.

Routine to Check Whether the Stack is Empty

```
int IsEmpty( Stack S)
{
if ( S -> next = = NULL)
  return ( 1 );
}
```

S

Header	NULL

EMPTY STACK

2. *Push Operation*

- It is the process of inserting a new element at the Top of the stack.
- With Linked List implementation, a new element is always inserted at the Front of the List.(i.e.) S -> next.
- It takes two parameters. Push(X, S) the element X to be inserted at the Top of the Stack S.
- Allocate the memory for the newnode to be inserted.
- Insert the element in the data field of the newnode.
- Update the next field of the newnode with the address of the next node which is stored in the S -> next.

*Push Routine /*Inserts Element at Front of the List*

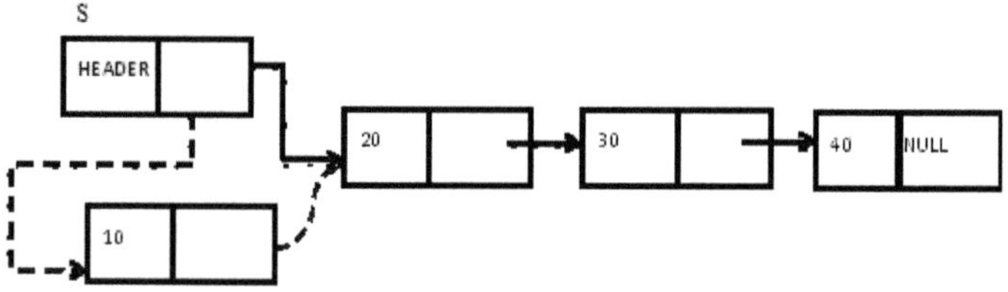

Before Insertion

Push Routine/*Inserts Element at Front of the List

```
void push(int X,  Stack S)
{
        Position newnode, Top;
             newnode = malloc (sizeof( struct
node ) );
             newnode -> data = X;
             newnode -> next = S -> next;
             S -> next = newnode;
             Top = newnode;
}
```

After Insertion

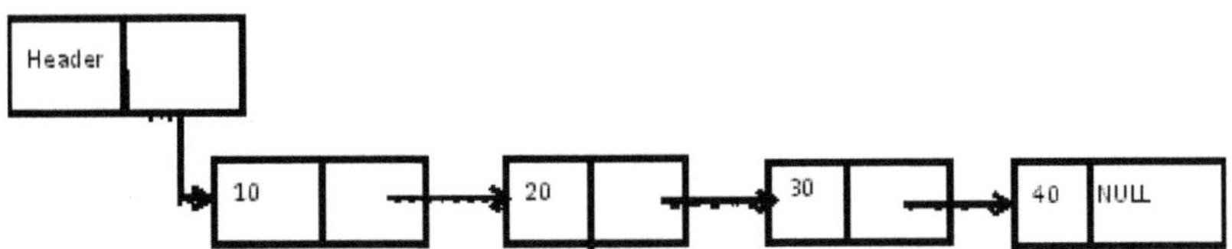

1. *Pop Operation*

- It is the process of deleting the Top element of the stack.
- With Linked List implementations, the element at the Front of the List (i.e.) S -> next is always deleted.
- It takes only one parameter. Pop(X).The element X to be deleted from the Front of the List.
- Before deleting the front element in the list, check for Empty Stack.
- If the Stack is Empty, deletion is not possible.
- Otherwise, make the front element in the list as "temp".
- Update the next field of header.
- Using free ( ) function, Deallocate the memory allocated for temp node.

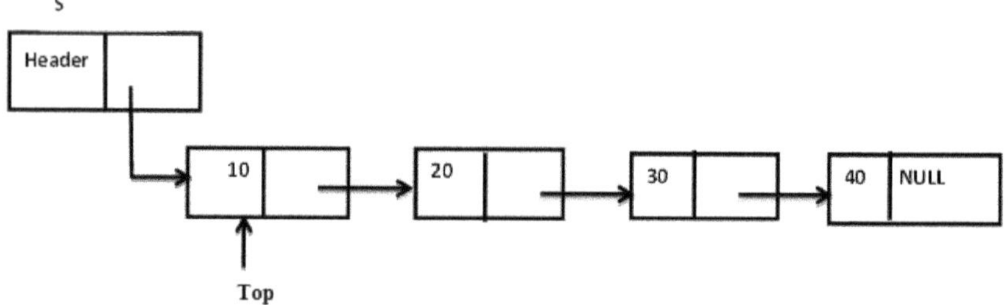

Pop Routine /*Deletes the Element at Front of List

```
void Pop(Stack S)
{
        Position temp,Top;
         Top=S->next;
         if(S->next==NULL)
                 Error("empty stack! Pop not possible");
         else
        {
                 Temp = S -> next;
                 S -> next = temp -> next;
                 free(temp);
                 Top = S -> next;
        }
}
```

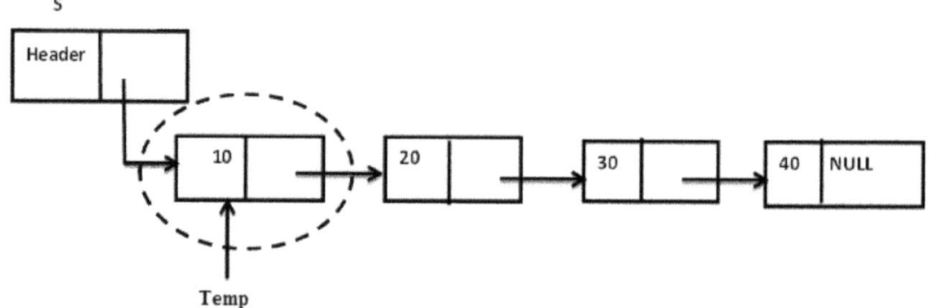

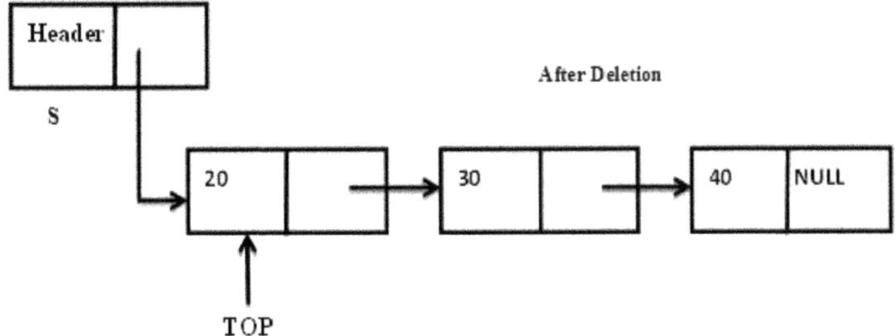

2. *Return Top Element*

- Pop routine deletes the Front element in the List.
- If the user needs to know the last element inserted into the stack, then the user can return the Top element of the stack.
- To do this, first check for Empty Stack.
- If the stack is empty, then there is no element in the stack.
- Otherwise, return the element present in the S -> next -> data in the List.

Routine to Return Top Element

```
int TopElement(Stack S)
{
  if(S->next==NULL)
   {
     error("Stack is empty");
     return 0;
  else
     return S->next->data;
}
```

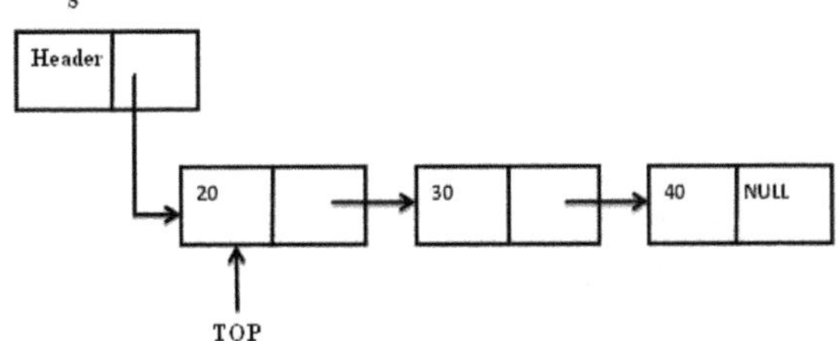

C Program for Linked List Implementation of Stack

```
#include<stdio.h>
#include<conio.h>
#include<stdlib.h>
typedef struct node *position;
struct node
{
        int data;
        position next;
};
 void create();
void push();
void pop();
void display();
position s,newnode,temp,top; /* Global Declarations */
void main()
{
        /* Main Program */
         int op;
        clrscr();
        do
        {
                printf("\n ### Linked List Implementation of STACK Operations ###
        \n\n");
                printf("\n Press 1-create\n 2-Push\n 3-Pop\n 4-Display\n5-Exit\n");
                printf("\n Your option ? ");
                scanf("%d", &op);
                switch (op)
                {
                case 1:
                        create();
                        break;
        case 2:
```

```
                push();
                break;
        case 3:
                pop();
                break;
        case 4:
                display();
                break;
        case 5:
                 exit(0);
        }
}while(op<5);
getch();
}
void create()
{
  int n,i;
 s=NULL;
 printf("Enter the no of nodes to be created\n");
 scanf("%d",&n);
 newnode=(struct node*)malloc(sizeof(struct node));
 printf("Enter the data\t");
 scanf("%d",&newnode->data);
 newnode->next=NULL;
 top=newnode;
 s=newnode;
 for(i=2;i<=n;i++)
 {
  newnode=(struct node*)malloc(sizeof(struct node));
 printf("Enter the data\t");
 scanf("%d",&newnode->data);
 newnode->next=top;
 s=newnode;
 top=newnode;
```

```
    }
}
void display()
{
        top=s;
        while(top!=NULL)
        {
                printf("%d->",top->data);
                top=top->next;
        }
        printf("NULL\n");
}
void push()
{
        top=s;
        newnode=(struct node*)malloc(sizeof(struct node));
        printf("Enter the data\t");
        scanf("%d",&newnode->data);
        newnode->next=top;
        top=newnode;
        s=newnode;
        display();
}
void pop()
{
        top=s;
        if(top==NULL)
        printf("Empty stack\n\n");
        else
        {
        temp=top;
        printf("Deleted element is \t %d\n\n",top->data);
        s=top->next;
        free(temp);
```

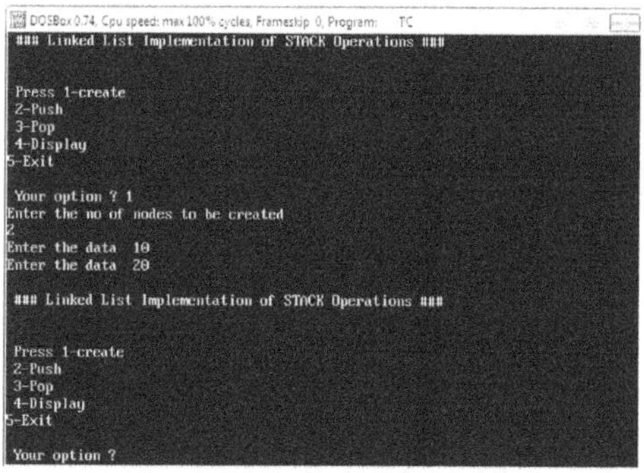

```
DOSBox 0.74, Cpu speed: max 100% cycles, Frameskip 0, Program:    TC
### Linked List Implementation of STACK Operations ###


 Press 1-create
 2-Push
 3-Pop
 4-Display
5-Exit

 Your option ? 1
Enter the no of nodes to be created
2
Enter the data  10
Enter the data  20

 ### Linked List Implementation of STACK Operations ###


 Press 1-create
 2-Push
 3-Pop
 4-Display
5-Exit

 Your option ?
```

```
        display();
        }
}
```

2.5. Applications of Stack

Application of Stack

1. Evaluating the arithmetic expressions.
    - Conversion of Infix to Postfix Expression
    - Evaluating the Postfix Expression
2. Balancing the Symbols
3. Function Call
4. Tower of Hanoi
5. 8 Queen Problem

2.5.1. Evaluating the Arithmetic Expression

There are 3 types of Expressions

- Infix Expression
- Postfix Expression
- Prefix Expression

Infix Expression

Operators appears between operands

Eg. A+B

A/B+C

Postfix Expression

Operators appears after the operands

E.g. AB+

AB/C+

Prefix Expression

Operators appears before the operands

E.g. +AB

+/ABC

Sr.No.	Infix Notation	Prefix Notation	Postfix Notation
1	a + b	+ a b	a b +
2	(a + b) * c	* + a b c	a b + c *
3	a * (b + c)	* a + b c	a b c + *
4	a / b + c / d	+ / a b / c d	a b / c d / +
5	(a + b) * (c + d)	* + a b + c d	a b + c d + *
6	((a + b) * c) - d	- * + a b c d	a b + c * d -

Evaluating Arithmetic Expressions

1. Convert the given infix expression to Postfix expression
2. Evaluate the postfix expression using stack.

Algorithm to Convert Infix Expression to Postfix Expression

1. Print operands as they arrive.
2. If the stack is empty or contains a left parenthesis on top, push the incoming operator onto the Stack.
3. If the character read is a left parenthesis, push it on the stack.
4. If the character read is a right parenthesis, pop the stack and print the operators until you see a left parenthesis. Discard the pair of parentheses.
5. If the character read has higher precedence than the top of the stack, push it on the stack.
6. If the character read has equal precedence with the top of the stack, use association. If the association is left to right, pop and print the top of the stack and then push the incoming operator. If the association is right to left, push the incoming operator.
7. If the character read has lower precedence than the symbol on the top of the stack, pop the stack and print the top operator. Then test the incoming operator against the new top of stack.
8. At the end of the expression, pop and print all operators on the stack. (No parentheses should remain.)

E.g. Consider the following Infix expression: - A*B+(C-D/E)#

Read char	Stack	Output
A		A
*	*	A
B	+ *	AB
+	+	AB*
(	(+	AB*
C	(+	AB*C

-	- (+	AB*C
D	- (+	AB*CD
/	/ - (+	
E	/ - (+	AB*CDE
)	/ - (+	AB*CDE/-
#		A B * C D E / - +

Output: Postfix expression:- AB*CDE/-+

Evaluating the Postfix Expression

Algorithm to evaluate the obtained Postfix Expression

1. Create a stack to store operands (or values).
2. Scan the given expression and do following for every scanned element.
   a. If the element is a operand, push its value into the stack.
   b. If the element is an operator, pop 2 values from the stack. Apply the operator and push the Result back to the stack
3. When the expression is ended, the number in the stack is the final answer.

E.g consider the obtained **Postfix expression:- AB*CDE/-+**

Operand	Value
A	2
B	3
C	4
D	4
E	2

Char Read	Stack
A	2
B	3, 2
*	6
C	4, 6
D	4, 4, 6
E	2, 4, 4, 6
/	2, 4, 6
-	2, 6
+	8

OUTPUT = 8

Example 2: Infix expression:- (a+b)*c/d+e/f#

Read char	Stack	Output
(	(	
a	(	a
+	+ (	a
b	+ (	ab
)		Ab+
*	*	ab
c	*	ab+c
/	/	ab+c*
d	/	ab+c*d
+	+	ab+c*d/
e	+	ab+c*d/e
/	/ +	ab+c*d/e
f	/ +	ab+c*d/ef
#		ab+c*d/ef/+

Postfix expression:- ab+c*d/ef/+

Evaluating the Postfix Expression

Operand	Value
a	1
b	2
c	4
d	2
e	6
f	3

Char Read	Stack
a	1
b	2 1
+	3
c	4 3
*	12
d	2 12
/	6
e	6 6
f	3 6 6
/	2 6
+	8

Output = 8

C program for Infix to Postfix Conversion	Output

#define SIZE 50 **/* Size of Stack */**
#include <ctype.h>
char s[SIZE];
int top=-1; ***/* Global declarations */***
 	
void push(char elem)
{
  s[++top]=elem;
}
 	
char pop()
{
  return(s[top--]);
}
 	
int pr(char elem)
{ ***/* Function for precedence */***
  switch(elem)
  {
  case '#': return 0;
  case '(': return 1;
  case '+':
  case '-': return 2;
  case '*':
  case '/': return 3;
  }
return 0;
}
 	
Void main()
{ ***/* Main Program */***
  char infx[50],pofx[50],ch,elem;
  int i=0,k=0;
  printf("\nRead the Infix Expression ? ");
  scanf("%s",infx);
  push('#');
	Read the Infix Expression ?
	(a+b)-(c-d)
	
	Given Infix Expn: (a+b)*(c-d)
	Postfix Expn: ab+cd-*

```
  while( (ch=infx[i++]) != '\0')
  {
    if( ch == '(') push(ch);
    else
      if(isalnum(ch)) pofx[k++]=ch;
      else
        if( ch == ')')
        {
          while( s[top] != '(')
            pofx[k++]=pop();
          elem=pop(); /* Remove */
        }
        else
        {    /* Operator */
          while( pr(s[top]) >= pr(ch) )
            pofx[k++]=pop();
          push(ch);
        }
  }
  while( s[top] != '#')   /* Pop from stack till empty
    pofx[k++]=pop();
  pofx[k]='\0';        /* Make pofx as valid string */
  printf("\n\nGiven Infix Expn: %s  Postfix Expn:
%s\n",infx,pofx);
}
```

2.5.2. *Towers of Hanoi*

Towers of Hanoi can be easily implemented using recursion. Objective of the problem is moving a collection of N disks of decreasing size from one pillar to another pillar. The movement of the disk is restricted by the following rules.

Rule 1 : Only one disk could be moved at a time.

Rule 2 : No larger disk could ever reside on a pillar on top of a smaller disk.

Rule 3 : A 3rd pillar could be used as an intermediate to store one or more disks, while moving the disk from source to destination.

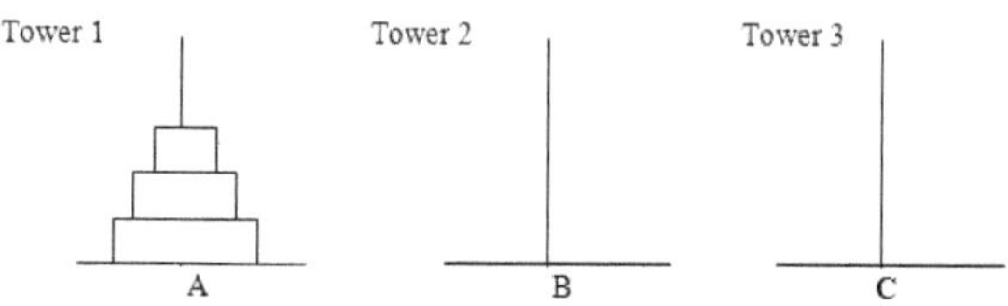

Initial Setup of Tower of Hanoi

Recursive Solution

N - Represents the Number of Disks

Step 1. If N = 1, move the disk from A to C.

Step 2. If N = 2, move the 1st disk from A to B. Then move the 2nd disk from A to C, The move the 1stdisk from B to C.

Step 3. If N = 3, Repeat the step (2) to more the first 2 disks from A to B using C as intermediate. Then the 3rd disk is moved from A to C. Then repeat the step (2) to move 2 disks from B to C using A as intermediate.

In general, to move N disks. Apply the recursive technique to move N - 1 disks from A to B using C as an intermediate. Then move the Nth disk from A to C. Then again apply the recursive technique to move N - 1 disks from B to C using A as an intermediate.

Recursive Routine for Towers of Hanoi

```
void hanoi (int n, char s, char d, char i)
{
/* n    no. of disks, s    source, d    destination i    intermediate */
if (n = = 1)
{
print (s, d);
return;
}
else
{
hanoi (n - 1, s, i, d);
print (s, d)
hanoi (n-1, i, d, s);
return;
}
}
```

Source Pillar Intermediate Pillar Destination Pillar

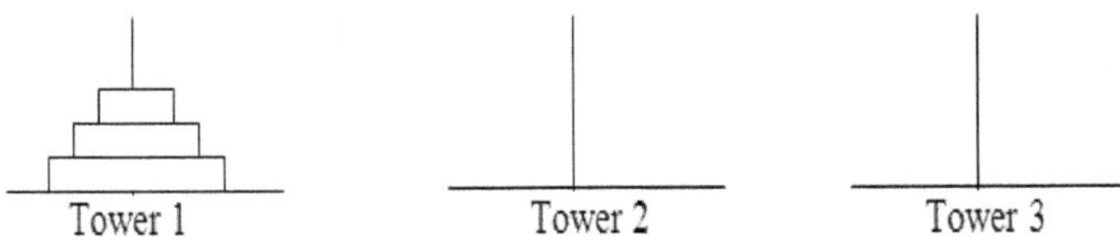

1. Move Tower1 to Tower3

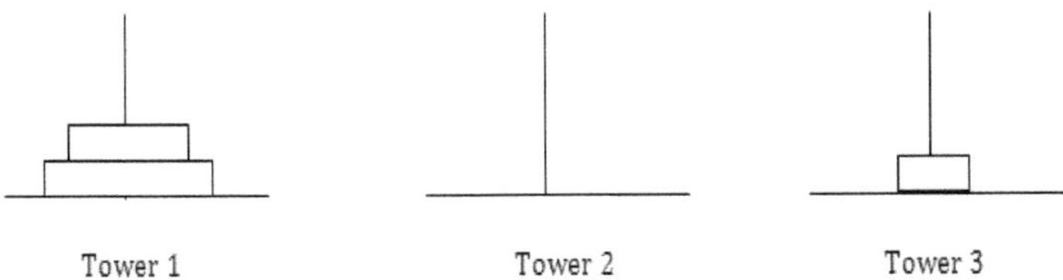

2. Move Tower1 to Tower2

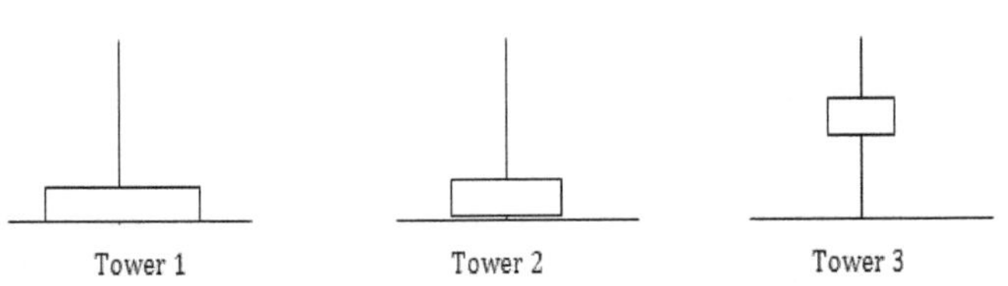

3. Move Tower 3 to Tower 2

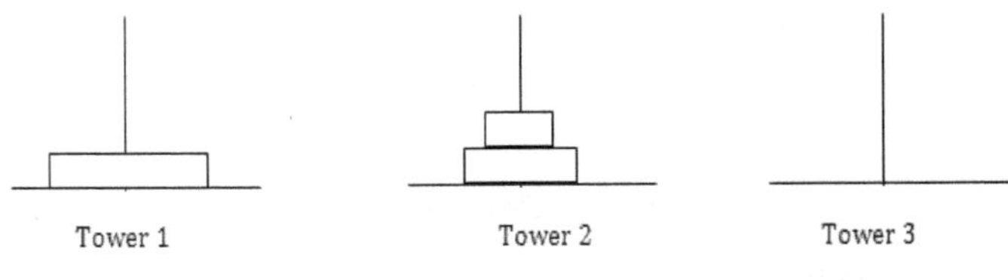

4. Move Tower 1 to Tower 3

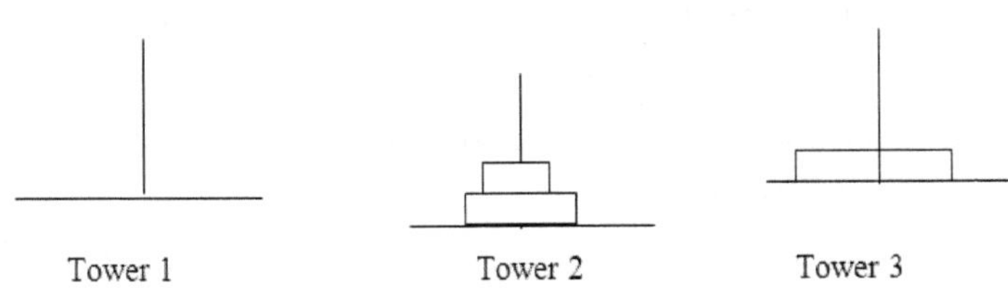

5. Move Tower 2 to Tower 1

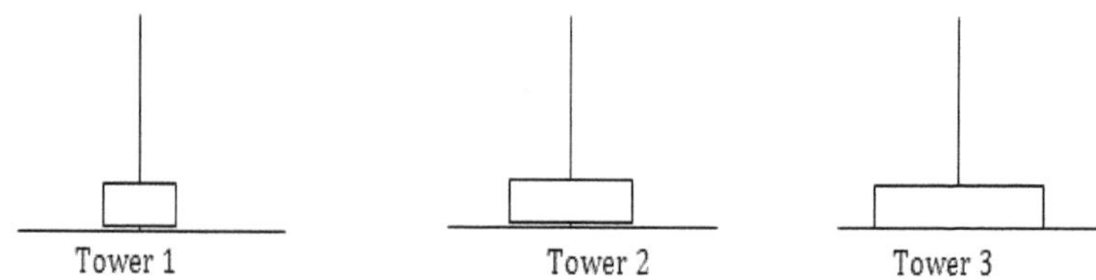

6. Move Tower 2 to Tower 3

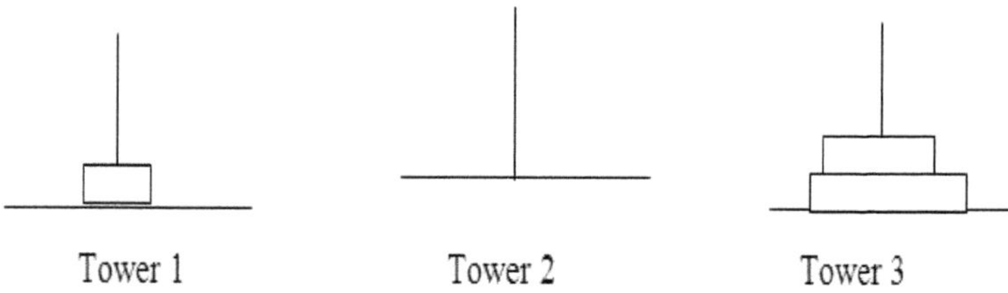

7. Move Tower 1 to Tower 3

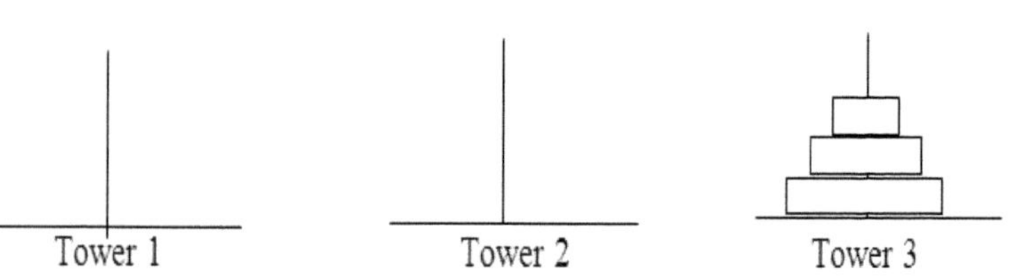

Since disks are moved from each tower in a LIFO manner, each tower may be considered as a Stack. Least Number of moves required solvingtheproblem according to our algorithm is given by,

$$O(N)=O(N-1)+1+O(N-1) =2^N-1$$

2.5.3. *Function Calls*

When a call is made to a new function all the variables local to the calling routine need to be saved, otherwise the new function will overwrite the calling routine variables.

Similarly the current location address inthe routine must be saved so that the new function knows where to go after it is completed.

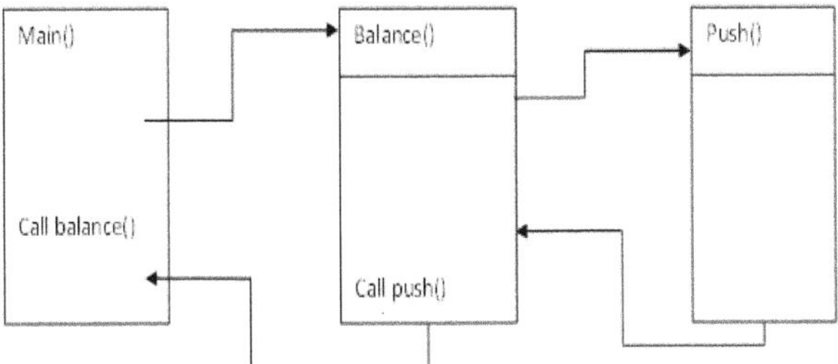

Recursive Function to Find Factorial

```
int fact(int n)
{
int S;
if(n==1)
    return(1);
else
            S=n*fact(n - 1);
            return(S)
}
```

2.5.4. Balancing the Symbols

- Compilers check the programs for errors, a lack of one symbol will cause an error.
- A Program that checks whether everything is balanced.
- Every right parenthesis should have its left parenthesis.
- Check for balancing the parenthesis brackets braces and ignore any other character.

Algorithm for Balancing the Symbols

Read one character at a time until it encounters the delimiter `#'.

Step 1 : - If the character is an opening symbol, push it onto the stack.

Step 2 : - If the character is a closing symbol, and if the stack is empty report an error as missing opening symbol.

Step 3 : - If it is a closing symbol and if it has corresponding opening symbol in the stack, POP it from the stack. Otherwise, report an error as mismatched symbols.

Step 4 : - At the end of file, if the stack is not empty, report an error as Missing closing symbol. Otherwise, report asbalanced symbols.

E.g. Let us consider the expression ((B*B)-{4*A*C}/[2*A]) #

((B*B)-{4*A*C}/[2*A]) #	
Read Character	**Stack**
(	(
(	((
)	(
{	{ (
}	(
[	[(
]	(
)	

Empty stack, hence the symbols are balanced in the given expression.

CHAPTER 3

Linear Data Structure-Queue

3.1. Introduction

- Itis a Linear Data Structure that follows First in First out(FIFO) principle.
- Insertion of element is done at one end of the Queue called "**Rear** "end of the Queue.
- Deletion of element is done at other end of the Queue called "**Front**"end of the Queue.
- Example: - Waiting line in the ticket counter.

Front Pointer

It always points to the first element inserted in the Queue.

Rear Pointer

It always points to the last element inserted in the Queue.

For Empty Queue

Front (F)= - 1

Rear(R) = - 1

3.2. Queue Model

3.3. Operations on Queue

Fundamental operations performed on the queue are:

1. EnQueue
2. DeQueue

1. EnQueue Operation

- It is the process of inserting a new element at the rear end of the Queue.
- For every EnQueue operation.

- Check for Full Queue
- If the Queue is full, Insertion is not possible.
- Otherwise, increment the rear end by 1 and then insert the element in the rear end of the Queue.

2. DeQueue Operation

- It is the process of deleting the element from the front end of the queue.
- For every DeQueue operation.
    - Check for Empty queue
    - If the Queue is Empty, Deletion is not possible.
    - Otherwise, delete the first element inserted into the queue and then increment the front by 1.

Exceptional Conditions of Queue

- Queue Overflow
- Queue Underflow

1. Queue Overflow

- An Attempt to insert an element X at the Rear end of the Queue when the Queue is full is said to be Queue overflow.
- For every Enqueue operation, we need to check this condition.

2. Queue Underflow

- An Attempt to delete an element from the Front end of the Queue when the Queue is empty is said to be Queue underflow.
- For every DeQueue operation, we need to check this condition.

3.4. Implementation of Queue

Queue can be implemented in two ways.

1. Implementation using Array (**Static Queue**)
2. Implementation using Linked List (**Dynamic Queue**)

3.4.1. Array Implementation of Queue

- Each Queue is associated with Front pointer and rear Pointer.
- For Empty Queue, Front = - 1 and Rear = -1.

- Queue is declared with its maximum size.

Array Declaration of Queue

```
#define ArraySize 5
int Q [ ArraySize];
  or
int Q [ 5 ];
```

Initial Configuration of Queue

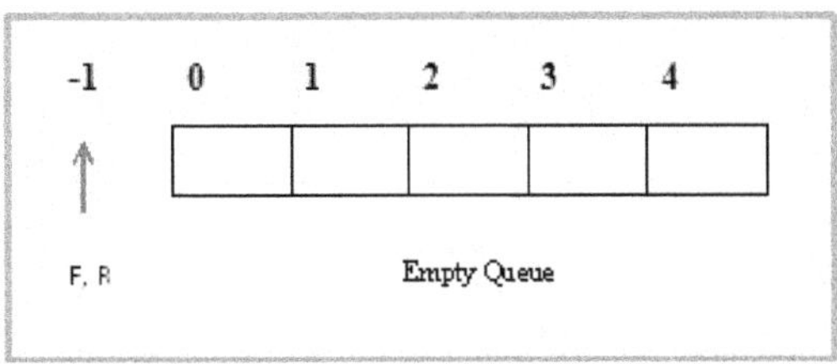

1. *Queue Empty Operation*

- Initially Queue is Empty.
- With Empty Queue, Front (F) and Rear (R) points to – 1.
- It is necessary to check for Empty Queue before deleting (DeQueue) an element from the Queue (Q).

Routine to Check for Empty Queue

```
int IsEmpty ( Queue Q )
{
if( ( Front = = - 1) && ( Rear = = - 1 ) )
        return ( 1 );
}
```

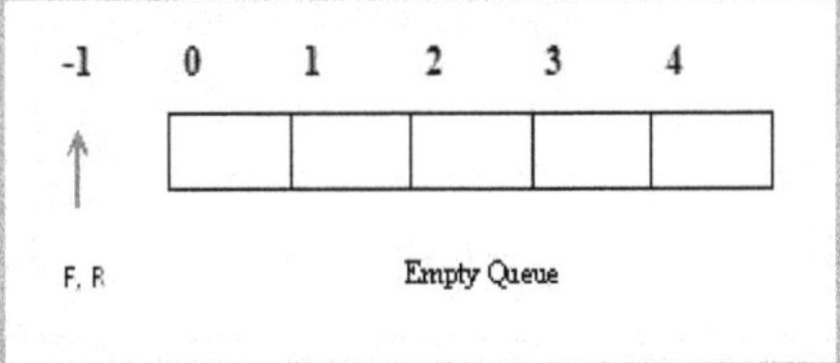

2. *Queue Full Operation*

- As we keep inserting the new elements at the Rear end of the Queue, the Queue becomes full.
- When the Queue is Full, Rear reaches its maximum Arraysize.
- For every Enqueue Operation, we need to check for full Queue condition.

Routine to Check for Full Queue

```
int IsFull( Queue Q )
{
if( Rear = = ArraySize - 1 )
    return ( 1 );
}
```

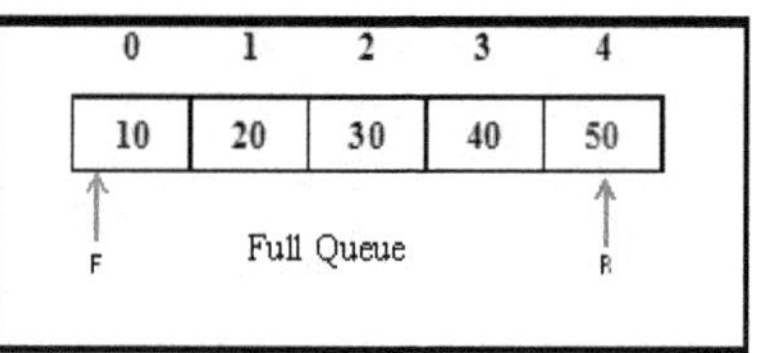

3. *Enqueue Operation*

- It is the process of inserting a new element at the Rear end of the Queue.
- It takes two parameters, Enqueue(X, Q). The elements X to be inserted at the Rear end of the Queue Q.
- Before inserting a new Element into the Queue, check for Full Queue.
- If the Queue is already Full, Insertion is not possible.
- Otherwise, Increment the Rear pointer by 1 and then insert the element X at the Rear end of the Queue.
- If the Queue is Empty, Increment both Front and Rear pointer by 1 and then insert the element X at the Rear end of the Queue.

Routine to Insert an Element in a Queue

```
void EnQueue (int X , Queue Q)
{
if ( Rear == Arraysize-1)
print (" Full Queue !!!!. Insertion not
possible");
else if (Rear = = - 1)
{
Front = Front + 1;
Rear = Rear + 1;
Q [Rear] = X;
}
else
{
Rear = Rear + 1;
Q [Rear] = X;
        }
}
```

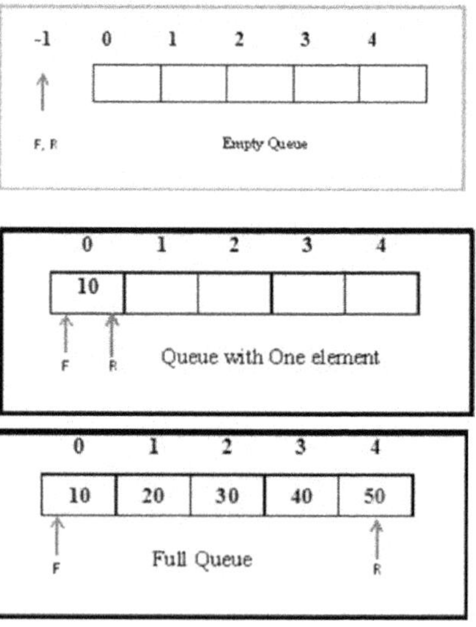

4. *DeQueue Operation*

- It is the process of deleting a element from the Front end of the Queue.
- It takes one parameter,DeQueue (Q). Always front element in the Queue will be deleted.
- Before deleting an Element from the Queue, check for Empty Queue.
- If the Queue is empty, deletion is not possible.
- If the Queue has only one element, then delete the element and represent the empty queue by updating Front = - 1 and Rear = - 1.
- If the Queue has many Elements, then delete the element in the Front and move the Front pointer to next element in the queue by incrementing Front pointer by 1.

Routine for Dequeue

```
void DeQueue ( Queue Q )
{
  if ( Front = = - 1)
print (" Empty Queue !. Deletion not possible ");
else if( Front = = Rear )
{
X = Q [Front];
        Front = - 1;
        Rear = - 1;
    }
          else
        {
          X = Q [ Front ];
          Front = Front + 1 ;
}
}
```

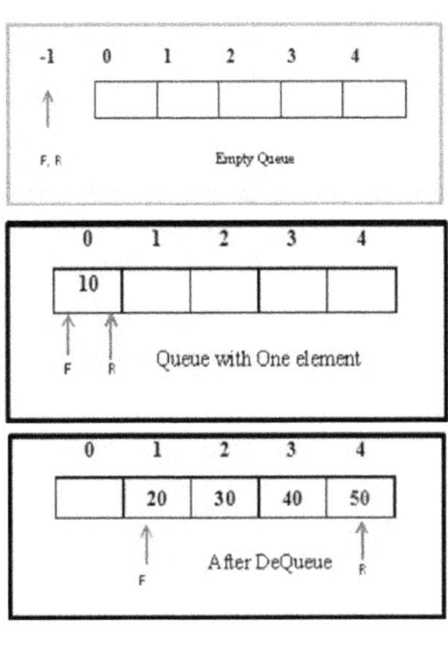

Array Implementation of Queue

```
#include<stdio.h>
#include<conio.h>
#define SIZE 5
int front=-1;
```

```
int rear=-1;
int q[SIZE];

void insert();
void del();
void display();
void main()
{
        int choice;
        clrscr();
        do
        {
                printf("\t Menu");
                printf("\n 1. Insert");
                printf("\n 2. Delete");
                printf("\n 3. Display ");
                printf("\n 4. Exit");
                printf("\n Enter Your Choice:");
                scanf("%d",&choice);
                switch(choice)
                {
                        case 1:
                                insert();
                                display();
                                break;
                        case 2:
                                del();
                                display();
                                break;
                        case 3:
                                display();
                                break;
                        case 4:
                                printf("End of Program....!!!!");
```

```
                                        exit(0);
                        }
        }while(choice!=4);
}
 void insert()
  {
        int no;
        printf("\n Enter No.:");
        scanf("%d",&no);

        if(rear < SIZE-1)
        {
                q[++rear]=no;
                if(front==-1)
                front=0;// front=front+1;
        }
        else
        {
                printf("\n Queue overflow");
        }
  }
void del()
  {
        if(front==-1)
        {
                printf("\nQueue Underflow");
                return;
        }
        else
        {
        printf("\nDeleted Item:-->%d\n",q[front]);
        }
        if(front==rear)
        {
```

```
                Front=-1;
                Rear=-1;
        }
        else
        {
                Front=front+1;
        }
}
void display()
{
        int i;
        if(front==-1)
        {
                printf("\nQueue is empty....");
                return;
        }
        for(i =front; i<=rear;i++)
                printf("\t%d",q[i]);
}
```

```
DOSBox 0.74, Cpu speed: max 100% cycles, Framesk
          Menu
1. Insert
2. Delete
3. Display
4. Exit
Enter Your Choice:1

Enter No.:40
        10      20      30      40_
```

3.4.2. *Linked List Implementation of Queue*

- Queue is implemented using SLL (Singly Linked List) node.
- Enqueue operation is performed at the end of the Linked list and DeQueue operation is performed at the front of the Linked list.
- With Linked List implementation, for Empty queue

Front = NULL & Rear = NULL

Linked List representation of Queue with 4 elements.

Q

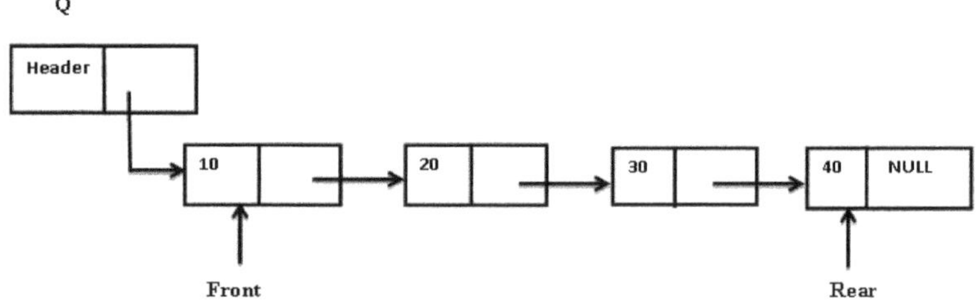

Declaration for Linked List Implementation of Queue ADT

```
struct node;
typedef  struct node * Queue;
typedef  struct node * position;
int IsEmpty (Queue Q);
Queue CreateQueue (void);
void MakeEmpty (Queue Q);
void Enqueue (int X, Queue Q);
void Dequeue (Queue Q);
struct node
{
int data ;
position next;
}* Front = NULL, *Rear = NULL;
```

1. *Queue Empty Operation*

- Initially Queue is Empty.
- With Linked List implementation, Empty Queue is represented as S -> next = NULL.
- It is necessary to check for Empty Queue before deleting the front element in the Queue.

Routine to Check Whether the Queue is Empty

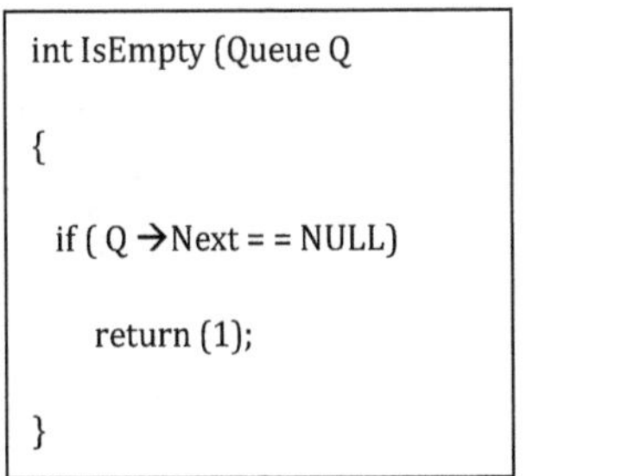

```
int IsEmpty (Queue Q
{
  if ( Q →Next = = NULL)
     return (1);
}
```

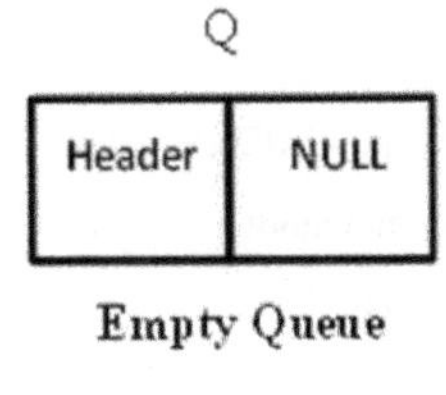

Empty Queue

2. *EnQueue Operation*

- It is the process of inserting a new element at the Rear end of the Queue.

- It takes two parameters, EnQueue (int X , Queue Q). The elements X to be inserted into the Queue Q.
- Using malloc ( ) function allocate memory for the newnode to be inserted into the Queue.
- If the Queue is Empty, the newnode tobe inserted will become first and last node in the list. Hence Front and Rear points to the newnode.
- Otherwise insert the newnode in the Rear -> next and update the Rear pointer.

Routine to EnQueue an Element in Queue

```
void EnQueue (int X, Queue Q )
{
struct node *newnode;
newnode = malloc (sizeof (struct node));
if (Rear = = NULL)
{
newnode →data = X;
newnode→next = NULL;
Q -> next = newnode;
Front = newnode;
Rear = newnode;
}
else
{
newnode →data = X;
newnode →next = NULL;
Rear →next = newnode;
Rear = newnode;
}
}
```

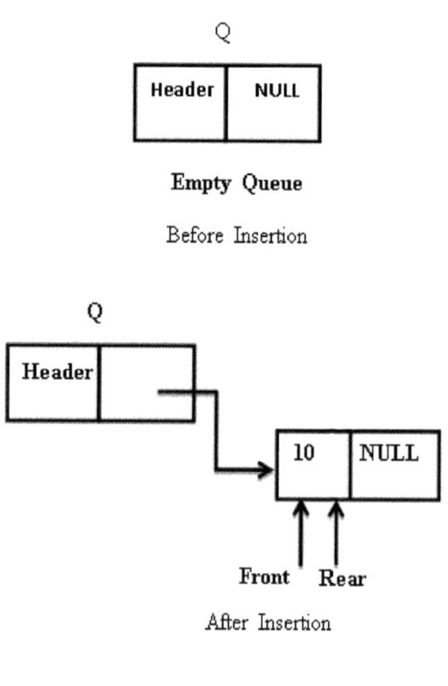

3. *DeQueue Operation*

- It is the process of deleting the front element from the Queue.
- It takes one parameter, Dequeue (Queue Q). Always element in the front (i.e) element pointed by Q -> next is deleted always.
- Element to be deleted is made "temp".
- If the Queue is Empty, then deletion is not possible.
- If the Queue has only one element, then the element is deleted and Front and Rear pointer is made NULL to represent Empty Queue.
- Otherwise, Front element is deleted and the Front pointer is made to point to next node in the list.
- The free ( ) function informs the compiler that the address that temp is pointing to, is unchanged but the data present in that address is now undefined.

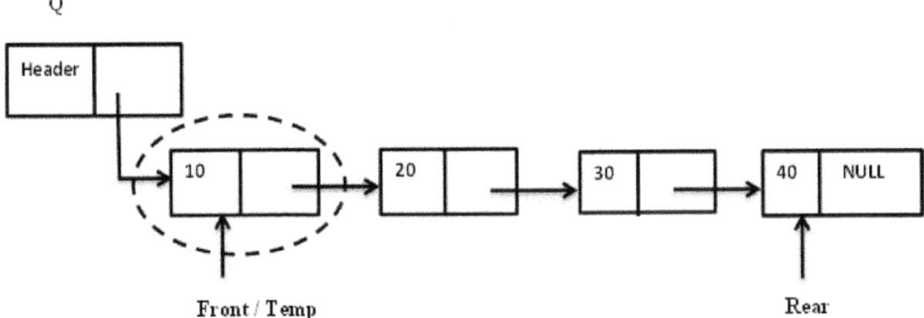

After DeQueue

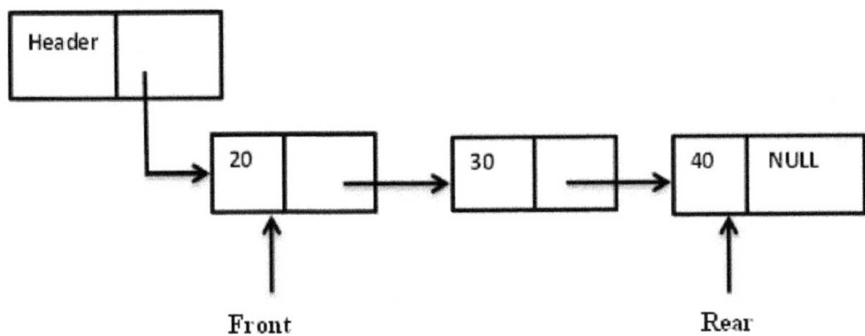

Routine to DeQueue an Element from the Queue

```
void DeQueue ( Queue Q )
{
struct node *temp;
if (Front = = NULL)
Error ("EmptyQueue!!! Deletion not possible." );
    else if (Front = = Rear)
{
         temp = Front;
         Q -> next = NULL;
Front = NULL;
Rear = NULL;
          free ( temp );
}
else
            {
               temp = Front;
               Q -> next = temp -> next;
               Front = Front →Next;
free (temp);
}
}
```

C Program for Linked List Implementation of Queue

```
#include<stdio.h>
#include<conio.h>
void enqueue();
void dequeue();
void display();
typedef struct node *position;
position front=NULL,rear=NULL,newnode,temp,p;
     struct node
     {
     int data;
```

```
  position next;
  };
void main()
{
int choice;
clrscr();
do
{
 printf("1.Enqueue\n2.Dequeue\n3.display\n4.exit\n");
 printf("Enter your choice\n\n");
 scanf("%d",&choice);
 switch(choice)
 {
 case 1:
        enqueue();
        break;
 case 2:
        dequeue();
        break;
 case 3:
        display();
        break;
 case 4:
        exit(0);
 }
 }
 while(choice<5);
 }
void enqueue()
{
        newnode=(struct node*)malloc(sizeof(struct node));
        printf("\n Enter the data to be enqueued\n");
        scanf("%d",&newnode->data);
        newnode->next=NULL;
```

```
        if(rear==NULL)
          front=rear=newnode;
        else
        {
          rear->next=newnode;
          rear=newnode;
        }
  display();
}
void dequeue()
{
        if(front==NULL)
          printf("\nEmpty queue!!!!! Deletion not possible\n");
        else if(front==rear)
         {
          printf("\nFront element %d is deleted from queue!!!! now queue is
                empty!!!! no more deletion possible!!!!\n",front->data);
          front=rear=NULL;
         }
        else
         {
          temp=front;
          front=front->next;
          printf("\nFront element %d is deleted from queue!!!!\n",temp->data);
          free(temp);
         }
  display();
}
void display()
{
 p=front;
 while(p!=NULL)
 {
 printf("%d -> ",p->data);
```

```
    p=p->next;
  }
  printf("Null\n");
}
```

Output

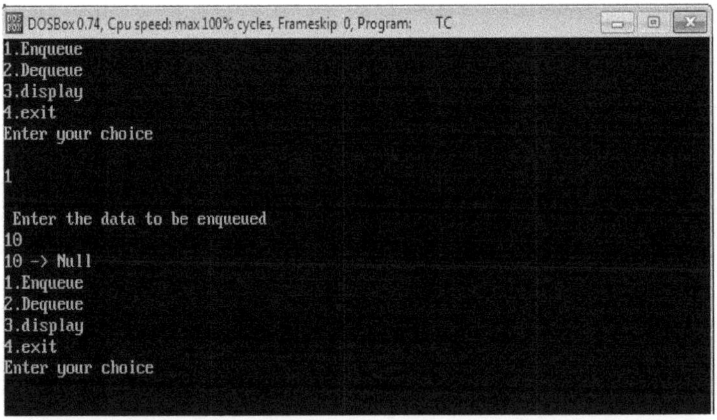

```
DOSBox 0.74, Cpu speed: max 100% cycles, Frameskip 0, Program: TC
1.Enqueue
2.Dequeue
3.display
4.exit
Enter your choice

1

 Enter the data to be enqueued
10
10 -> Null
1.Enqueue
2.Dequeue
3.display
4.exit
Enter your choice
```

3.5. Drawbacks of Queue (Linear Queue)

- With the array implementation of Queue, the element can be deleted logically only by moving Front = Front + 1.
- Here the Queue space is not utilized fully.

To overcome the drawback of this linear Queue, we use Circular Queue.

CHAPTER 4

Circular Queue

4.1. Introduction

- A circular queue is an abstract data type that contains a collection of data which allows addition of data at the end of the queue and removal of data at the beginning of thequeue.
- It has a fixed size.
- It follows FIFO principle.
- Data items are added at the rear end and deleted from the front end of the circular queue.
- Here the Queue space is utilized fully by inserting the element at the Front end if the rear end is full.

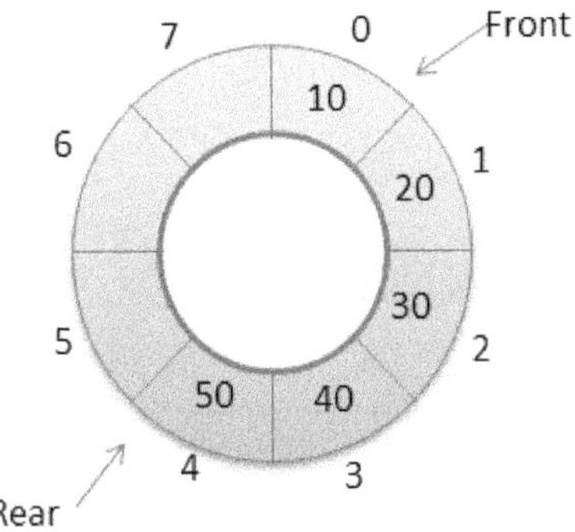

4.2. Operations on Circular Queue

Fundamental operations performed on the Circular Queue are

- Circular Queue Enqueue
- Circular Queue Dequeue

Formula to be used in Circular Queue

For Enqueue Rear = (Rear + 1) % ArraySize

For Dequeue Front = (Front + 1) % ArraySize

(i) Circular Queue Enqueue Operation

- It is same as Linear Queue EnQueue Operation (i.e) Inserting the element at the Rear end.
- First check for full Queue.
- If the circular queue is full, then insertion is not possible.
- Otherwise check for the rear end.
- If the Rear end is full, the elements start getting inserted from the Front end.

Routine to EnQueue an Element in Circular Queue

```
void Enqueue (int X,CircularQueue CQ)
{
   if(Front== ( Rear+1)% ArraySize)
          Error( "Queue is full!!Insertion not possible");
   else if( Rear == -1)
      {
                Front= Front+1;
                Rear= Rear+1;
                CQ[ Rear]= X;
      }
      else
     {
       Rear=( Rear+1)%Arraysize;
       CQ[ Rear]=X;
     }
}
```

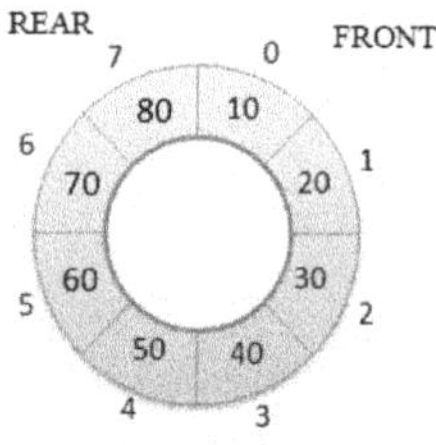

FULL QUEUE

(ii) Circular Queue DeQueue Operation

- It is same as Linear Queue DeQueue operation (i.e) deleting the front element.
- First check for Empty Queue.
- If the Circular Queue is empty, then deletion is not possible.

- If the Circular Queue has only one element, then the element is deleted and Front and Rear pointer is initialized to - 1 to represent Empty Queue.
- Otherwise, Front element is deleted and the Front pointer is made to point to next element in the Circular Queue.

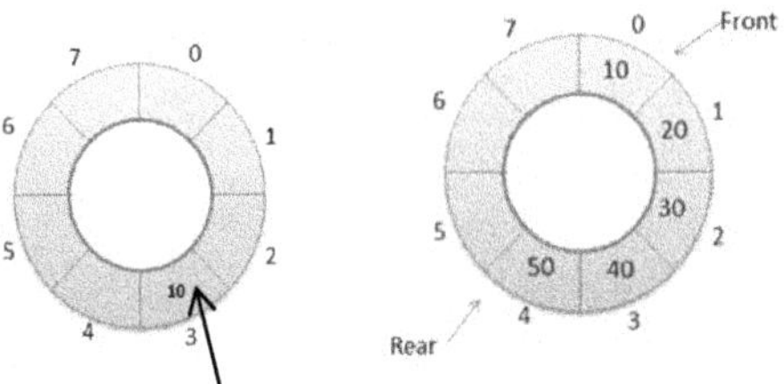

Routine To DeQueue An Element In Circular Queue

```
void DeQueue (CircularQueue CQ)
{
if(Front== - 1)
        Empty("Empty Queue!");
else if(Front==rear)
 {
X=CQ[Front];
 Front=-1;
  Rear=-1;
 }
else
{
 X=CQ[Front];
  Front=(Front+1)%Arraysize;
 }
}
```

C Program for Implementation of Circular Queue

```
#include<stdio.h>
#include<conio.h>
#define max 3
void insert();void delet();void display();
int q[10],front=0,rear=-1;
void main()
{
int ch;
 clrscr();
 printf("\nCircular Queue operations\n"); printf("1.insert\n2.delete\n3.display\n4.exit\n");
 while(1)
 {
 printf("Enter your choice:");
 scanf("%d",&ch);
 switch(ch)
 {
 case 1:
            insert();
            break;
 case 2:
            delet();
             break;
 case 3:
            display();
            break;
 case 4:
            exit();
 default:
            printf("Invalid option\n");
}}}

void insert()
{
```

```
int x;
if((front==0&&rear==max-1)||(front>0&&rear==front-1))
 printf("Queue is overflow\n");
else
 {
  printf("Enter element to be insert:");
  scanf("%d",&x);
  if(rear==max-1&&front>0)
   {
    rear=0;
    q[rear]=x;
   }
   else
   {
    if((front==0&&rear==-1)||(rear!=front-1))
    q[++rear]=x;
   }
 }
}
void delet()
{
 int a;
 if((front==0)&&(rear==-1))
    printf("Queue is underflow\n");
 if(front==rear)
  {
   a=q[front];
   rear=-1;
   front=0;
  }
  else if(front==max-1)
  {
   a=q[front];
```

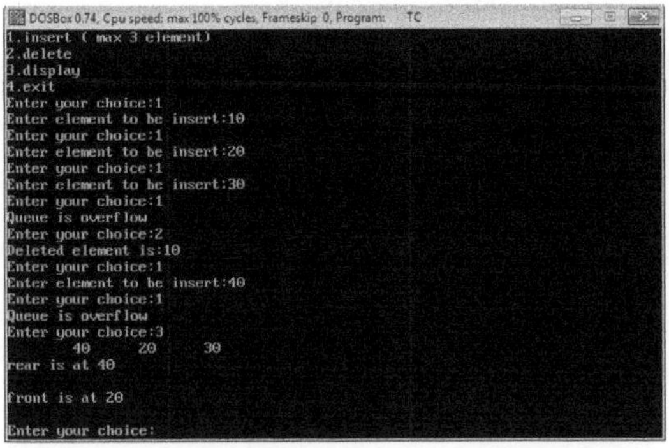

```
  front=0;
 }
 else
  a=q[front++];
  printf("Deleted element is:%d\n",a);
}
void display()
{
 int i,j;
 if(front==0&&rear==-1)
  printf("Queue is underflow\n");
 if(front>rear)
 {
  for(i=0;i<=rear;i++)
  printf("\t%d",q[i]);
  for(j=front;j<=max-1;j++)
  printf("\t%d",q[j]);
  printf("\nrear is at %d\n",q[rear]);
  printf("\nfront is at %d\n",q[front]);
 }
 else
 {
  for(i=front;i<=rear;i++)
    printf("\t%d",q[i]);
  printf("\nrear is at %d\n",q[rear]);
  printf("\nfront is at %d\n",q[front]);
 }
  printf("\n");
}
```

CHAPTER 5

Double-Ended Queue (Deque)

5.1. Introduction

- A double-ended queue is an abstract data type similar to an simple queue.
- In DEQUE, insertion and deletion operations are performed at both ends of the Queue.

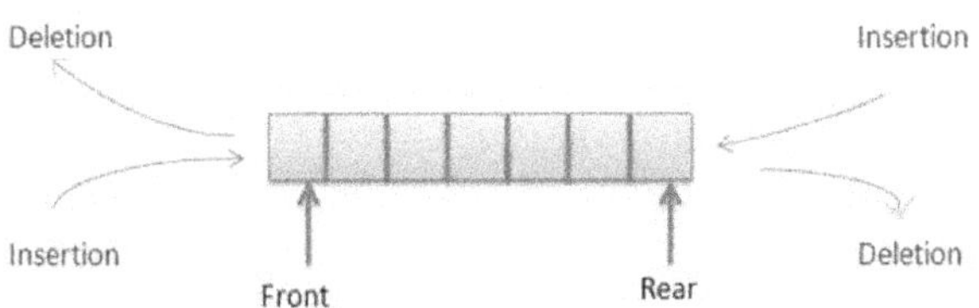

5.2. Exceptional Condition of DEQUE

(i) Input Restricted DEQUE

Here insertion is allowed at one end and deletion is allowed at both ends.

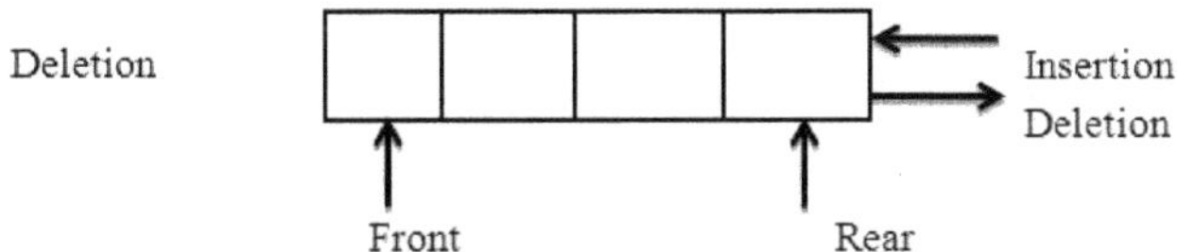

(ii) Output Restricted DEQUE

Here insertion is allowed at **both ends** and deletion is allowed at **one end.**

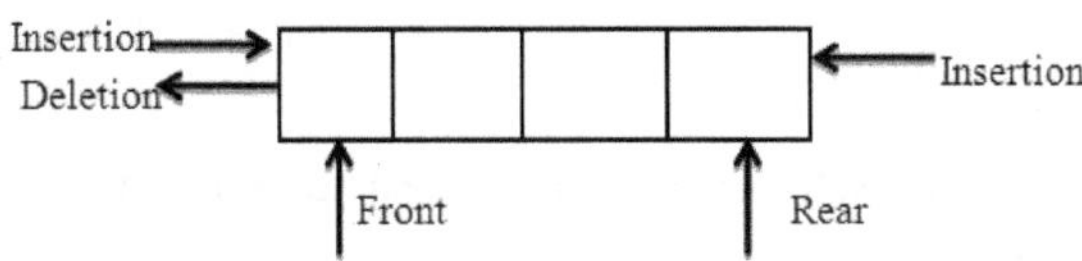

5.3. Operations on DEQUE

Four cases for inserting and deleting the elements in DEQUE are

- Insertion At Rear End [same as Linear Queue]
- Insertion At Front End

- Deletion At Front End [same as Linear Queue]
- Deletion At Rear End

```
void Insert_Rear(int X, DEQUE DQ)
{
  if( Rear ==Arraysize-1)
Error("Full Queue!!!! Insertion not possible");
else if(Rear == -1)
{
        Front =Front +1;
        Rear = Rear +1;
        DQ[Rear ] = X;
}
else
{
        Rear =Rear +1;
        DQ[ Rear ]=X;
}
 }
```

Case 1:Routine to insert an element at Rear end

- It is the process of inserting a new element at the Rear end of the Queue.
- It takes two parameters, Insert_Rear(X,DEQUE DQ) The elements X to be inserted at the Rear end of the Queue.
- Before inserting a new Element into the Queue, check for Full Queue.
- If the Queue is already Full, Insertion is not possible.
- Otherwise, Increment the Rear pointer by 1 and then insert the element X at the Rear end of the Queue.
- If the Queue is Empty, Increment both Front and Rear pointer by 1 and then insert the element X at the Rear end of the Queue.

Case 2: Routine to insert an element at Front end

- It is the process of inserting a new element at the Front end of the Queue.
- It takes two parameters, Insert_Front(X,DEQUE DQ) The elements X to be inserted at the Front end of the Queue.

- Before inserting a new Element into the Queue, check the Front end of the Queue.
- If an element is present in the Front end then Insertion is not possible.
- Otherwise, decrement the Front pointer by 1 and then insert the element X at the Front end of the Queue.
- If the Queue is Empty, Increment both Front and Rear pointer by 1 and then insert the element X at the Front end of the Queue.

```
void Insert_Front(int X, DEQUE DQ)
{
  if(Front ==0)
Error("Element present in Front!!!!! Insertion not possible");
else if(Front == -1)
{
Front =Front +1;
    Rear = Rear +1;
DQ[Front] = X;
}
else
{
Front =Front -1;
DQ[Front]=X;
  }
}
```

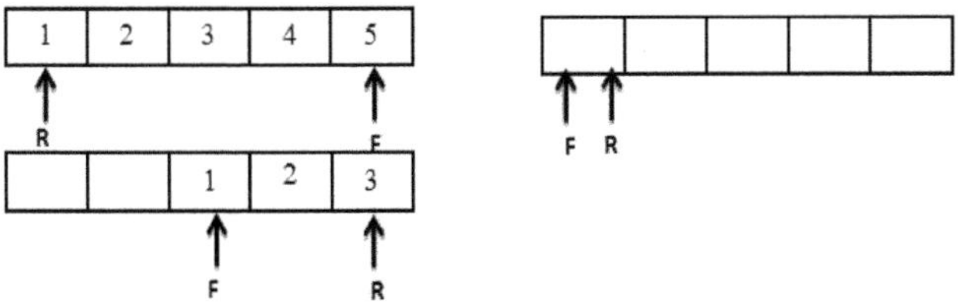

1	2	3	4	5

R (at 1), F (at 5)

		1	2	3

F (at 1), R (at 3)

F R

Case 3: Routine to delete an element from Front end

- It is the process of deleting a element from the Front end of the Queue.
- It takes one parameter, Delete_Front(DEQUE DQ). Always front element in the Queue will be deleted.
- Before deleting an Element from the Queue, check for Empty Queue.

- If the Queue is empty, deletion is not possible.
- If the Queue has only one element, then delete the element and represent the empty queue by updating Front = - 1 and Rear = - 1.
- If the Queue has many Elements, then delete the element in the Front and move the Front pointer to next element in the queue by incrementing Front pointer by 1.

```
void Delete_Front(DEQUE  DQ)
{
if(Front = = - 1)
Error("Empty queue!!!! Deletion not possible");
  else if( Front = = Rear )
  {
    X = DQ[ Front];
    Front = - 1;
    Rear = - 1;
 }
 else
 {
   X = DQ [ Front ];
   Front = Front + 1;
 }
}
```

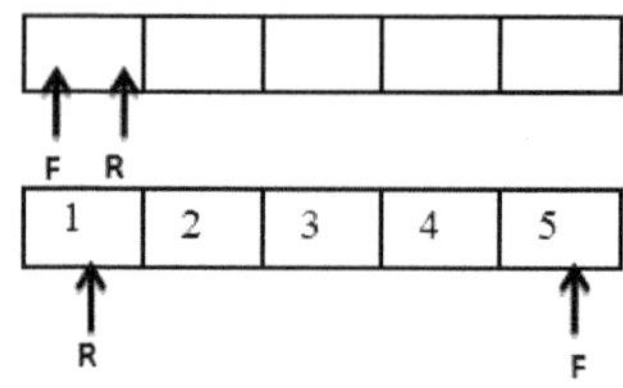

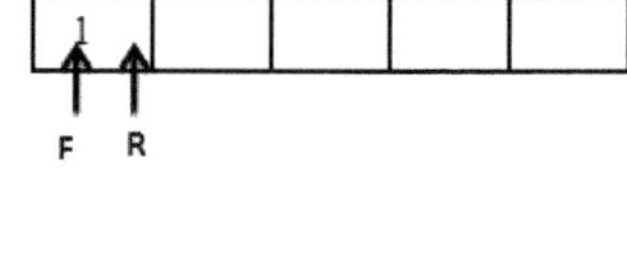

Case 4: Routine to delete an element from Rear End

- It is the process of deleting a element from the Rear end of the Queue.
- It takes one parameter, Delete_Rear(DEQUE DQ). Element in the Rear end of the Queue will be deleted.
- Before deleting an Element from the Queue, check for Empty Queue.
- If the Queue is empty, deletion is not possible.

- If the Queue has only one element, then delete the element and represent the empty queue by updating Front = - 1 and Rear = - 1.
- If the Queue has many Elements, then delete the element in the Rear endand move the Rear pointer to previous element in the queue by decrementing Rear pointer by 1.

```
void Delete_Rear(DEQUE DQ)
{
  if( Rear = = - 1)
Error("Empty queue!!!! Deletion not possible");
 else if( Front = = Rear )
  {
   X = DQ[ Rear ];
   Front = - 1;
   Rear = - 1;
}
 else
  {
   X = DQ[ Rear ];
   Rear = Rear - 1;
  }
}
```

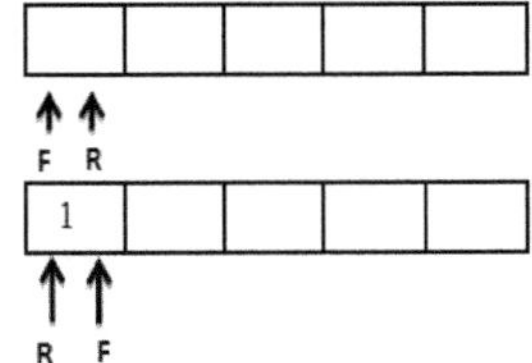

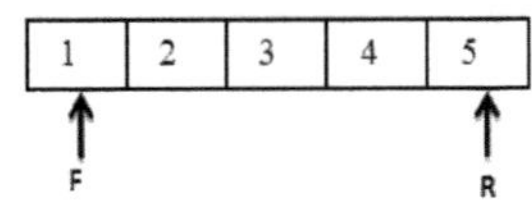

CHAPTER 6

Priority Queue

6.1. Priority Queue

In normal queue data structure, insertion is performed at the end of the queue and deletion is performed based on the FIFO principle. This queue implementation may not be suitable for all situations.

Consider a networking application where server has to respond for requests from multiple clients using queue data structure. Assume four requests arrived to the queue in the order of R1 requires 20 units of time, R2 requires 2 units of time, R3 requires 10 units of time and R4 requires 5 units of time. Queue is as follows...

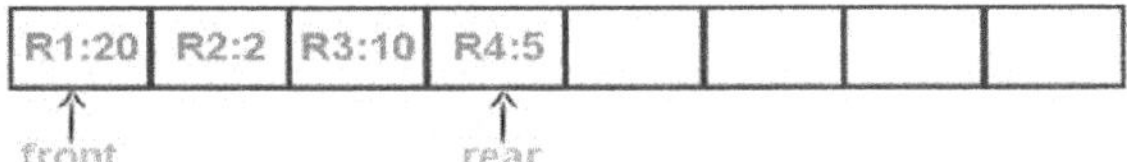

Now, check waiting time for each request to be complete.

- R1 : 20 units of time
- R2 : 22 units of time (R2 must wait till R1 complete - 20 units and R2 itself requeres 2 units. Total 22 units)
- R3 : 32 units of time (R3 must wait till R2 complete - 22 units and R3 itself requeres 10 units. Total 32 units)
- R4 : 37 units of time (R4 must wait till R3 complete - 35 units and R4 itself requeres 5 units. Total 37 units)

Here, average waiting time for all requests (R1, R2, R3 and R4) is (20+22+32+37)/4 ≈ 27 units of time.

That means, if we use a normal queue data structure to serve these requests the average waiting time for each request is 27 units of time. Now, consider another way of serving these requests. If we serve according to their required amount of time. That means, first we serve R2 which has minimum time required (2) then serve R4 which has second minimum time required (5) then serve R3 which has third minimum time required (10) and finally R1 which has maximum time required (20).

Now, check waiting time for each request to be complete.

1. **R2 : 2 units of time**
2. **R4 : 7 units of time (R4 must wait till R2 complete 2 units and R4 itself requires 5 units. Total 7 units)**
3. **R3 : 17 units of time (R3 must wait till R4 complete 7 units and R3 itself requeres 10 units. Total 17 units)**
4. **R1 : 37 units of time (R1 must wait till R3 complete 17 units and R1 itself requeres 20 units. Total 37 units)**

Here, average waiting time for all requests (R1, R2, R3 and R4) is (2+7+17+37)/4 ≈ 15 units of time.

From above two situations, it is very clear that, by using second method server can complete all four requests with very less time compared to the first method. This is what exactly done by the priority queue.

> **Priority queue is a variant of queue data structure in which insertion is performed in the order of arrival and deletion is performed based on the priority.**

6.2. Types of Priority Queue

There are two types of priority queues they are as follows...

1. **Max Priority Queue**
2. **Min Priority Queue**

6.2.1 In max priority queue, elements are inserted in the order in which they arrive the queue and always maximum value is removed first from the queue.

For example assume that we insert in order 8, 3, 2, 5 and they are removed in the order 8, 5, 3, 2. The following are the operations performed in a Max priority queue...

1. **isEmpty() - Check whether queue is Empty.**
2. **insert() - Inserts a new value into the queue.**
3. **findMax() - Find maximum value in the queue.**
4. **remove() - Delete maximum value from the queue.**

Max Priority Queue Representations

There are 6 representations of max priority queue.

1. **Using an Unordered Array (Dynamic Array)**
2. **Using an Unordered Array (Dynamic Array) with the index of the maximum value**
3. **Using an Array (Dynamic Array) in Decreasing Order**
4. **Using an Array (Dynamic Array) in Increasing Order**
5. **Using Linked List in Increasing Order**
6. **Using Unordered Linked List with reference to node with the maximum value**

#1. Using an Unordered Array (Dynamic Array)

In this representation elements are inserted according to their arrival order and maximum element is deleted first from max priority queue.

For example, assume that elements are inserted in the order of 8, 2, 3 and 5. And they are removed in the order 8, 5, 3 and 2.

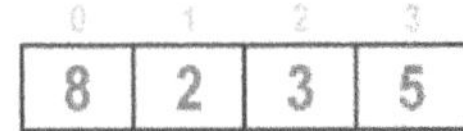

Now, let us analyse each operation according to this representation...

isEmpty() - If '**front == -1**' queue is Empty. This operation requires **O(1)** time complexity that means constant time.

insert() - New element is added at the end of the queue. This operation requires **O(1)** time complexity that means constant time.

findMax() - To find maximum element in the queue, we need to compare with all the elements in the queue. This operation requires **O(n)** time complexity.

remove() - To remove an element from the queue first we need to perform **findMax()** which requires **O(n)** and removal of particular element requires constant time **O(1)**. This operation requires **O(n)** time complexity.

#2. Using an Unordered Array (Dynamic Array) with the Index of the Maximum Value

In this representation elements are inserted according to their arrival order and maximum element is deleted first from max priority queue.

For example, assume that elements are inserted in the order of 8, 2, 3 and 5. And they are removed in the order 8, 5, 3 and 2.

0	1	2	3		maxIndex
8	2	3	5		0

Now, let us analyse each operation according to this representation...

isEmpty() - If **'front == -1'** queue is Empty. This operation requires **O(1)** time complexity that means constant time.

insert() - New element is added at the end of the queue with **O(1)** and for each insertion we need to update maxIndex with **O(1)**. This operation requires **O(1)**time complexity that means constant time.

findMax() - To find maximum element in the queue is very simple as maxIndex has maximum element index. This operation requires **O(1)** time complexity.

remove() - To remove an element from the queue first we need to perform **findMax()** which requires **O(1)**, removal of particular element requires constant time **O(1)** and update maxIndex value which requires **O(n)**. This operation requires **O(n)** time complexity.

#3. Using an Array (Dynamic Array) in Decreasing Order

In this representation elements are inserted according to their value in decreasing order and maximum element is deleted first from max priority queue.

For example, assume that elements are inserted in the order of 8, 5, 3 and 2. And they are removed in the order 8, 5, 3 and 2.

0	1	2	3
8	5	3	2

Now, let us analyse each operation according to this representation...

isEmpty() - If **'front == -1'** queue is Empty. This operation requires **O(1)** time complexity that means constant time.

insert() - New element is added at a particular position in the decreasing order into the queue with **O(n)**, because we need to shift existing elements inorder to insert new element in decreasing order. This operation requires **O(n)** time complexity.

findMax() - To find maximum element in the queue is very simple as maximum element is at the beginning of the queue. This operation requires **O(1)** time complexity.

remove() - To remove an element from the queue first we need to perform **findMax()** which requires **O(1)**, removal of particular element requires constant time **O(1)** and rearrange remaining elements which requires **O(n)**. This operation requires **O(n)** time complexity.

#4. Using an Array (Dynamic Array) in Increasing Order

In this representation elements are inserted according to their value in increasing order and maximum element is deleted first from max priority queue.

For example, assume that elements are inserted in the order of 2, 3, 5 and 8. And they are removed in the order 8, 5, 3 and 2.

0	1	2	3
2	3	5	8

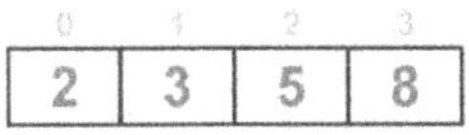

Now, let us analyse each operation according to this representation...

isEmpty() - If '**front == -1**' queue is Empty. This operation requires **O(1)** time complexity that means constant time.

insert() - New element is added at a particular position in the increasing order into the queue with **O(n)**, because we need to shift existing elements inorder to insert new element in increasing order. This operation requires **O(n)** time complexity.

findMax() - To find maximum element in the queue is very simple as maximum element is at the end of the queue. This operation requires **O(1)** time complexity.

remove() - To remove an element from the queue first we need to perform **findMax()** which requires **O(1)**, removal of particular element requires constant time **O(1)** and rearrange remaining elements which requires **O(n)**. This operation requires **O(n)** time complexity.

#5. Using Linked List in Increasing Order

In this representation, we use a single linked list to represent max priority queue. In this representation elements are inserted according to their value in increasing order and node with maximum value is deleted first from max priority queue.

For example, assume that elements are inserted in the order of 2, 3, 5 and 8. And they are removed in the order 8, 5, 3 and 2.

Now, let us analyse each operation according to this representation...

isEmpty() - If **'head == NULL'** queue is Empty. This operation requires **O(1)** time complexity that means constant time.

insert() - New element is added at a particular position in the increasing order into the queue with **O(n)**, because we need to the position where new element has to be inserted. This operation requires **O(n)** time complexity.

findMax() - To find maximum element in the queue is very simple as maximum element is at the end of the queue. This operation requires **O(1)** time complexity.

remove() - To remove an element from the queue is simply removing the last node in the queue which requires **O(1)**. This operation requires **O(1)** time complexity.

#6. Using Unordered Linked List with Reference to Node with the Maximum Value

In this representation, we use a single linked list to represent max priority queue. Always we maitain a reference (maxValue) to the node with maximum value. In this representation elements are inserted according to their arrival and node with maximum value is deleted first from max priority queue.

For example, assume that elements are inserted in the order of 2, 8, 3 and 5. And they are removed in the order 8, 5, 3 and 2.

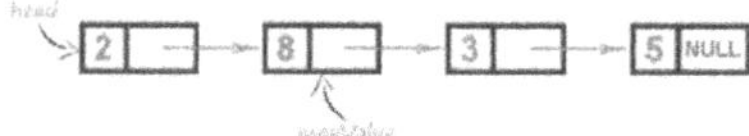

Now, let us analyse each operation according to this representation...

isEmpty() - If **'head == NULL'** queue is Empty. This operation requires **O(1)** time complexity that means constant time.

insert() - New element is added at end the queue with **O(1)** and update maxValue reference with **O(1)**. This operation requires **O(1)** time complexity.

findMax() - To find maximum element in the queue is very simple as maxValue is referenced to the node with maximum value in the queue. This operation requires **O(1)** time complexity.

remove() - To remove an element from the queue is deleting the node which referenced by maxValue which requires **O(1)** and update maxValue reference to new node with maximum value in the queue which requires **O(n) time complexity**. This operation requires **O(n)** time complexity.

6.2.2. Min Priority Queue

similar to max priority queue except removing maximum element first, we remove minimum element first in min priority queue.

The following operations are performed in Min Priority Queue...

1. **isEmpty()** - Check whether queue is Empty.
2. **insert()** - Inserts a new value into the queue.
3. **findMin()** - Find minimum value in the queue.
4. **remove()** - Delete minimum value from the queue.

Min priority queue is also has same representations as Max priority queue with minimum value removal.

Priority Queue in C

Here you will get implementation of priority queue in C and C++ with program example.

Priority Queue is an ordered list of homogeneous elements. In normal queue, service is provided on the basis of First-In-First-Out. In a priority queue service isn't provided on the basis of First-In-First-Out service, but rather then each element has a priority based on the urgency of the need.

An element with higher priority is processed before other elements with lower priority.

Elements with the same priority are processed on First-In-First-Out service basis.

An example of priority queue is a hospital waiting room. A patient having a more fatal problem would be admitted before other patients.

Other applications of priority queues are found in long term scheduling of jobs processed in a computer.

In practice, short processes are given a priority over long processes as it improves the average response of the system.Priority Queue can be implemented using a circular array.

As the service must be provided to an element having highest priority, there could be a choice between:

List is always maintained sorted on priority of elements with the highest priority element at the front. Here, deletion is trivial but insertion is complicated as the element must be inserted at the correct place depending on its priority.

List is maintained in the FIFO form but the service is provided by selecting the element with the highest priority. Deletion is difficult as the entire queue must be traversed to locate the element with the highest priority. Here, insertion is trivial (at the rear end).

Program for Priority Queue in C

```
#include <stdio.h>
#include <stdlib.h>
#define MAX 30
typedef struct pqueue
{
        int data[MAX];
        int rear,front;
}pqueue;
void initialize(pqueue *p);
int empty(pqueue *p);
int full(pqueue *p);
void enqueue(pqueue *p, int x);
int dequeue(pqueue *p);
void print(pqueue *p);
void main()
{
        int x,op,n,i;
        pqueue q;
        initialize(&q);
        do
        {
                printf("\n1)Create \n2)Insert \n3)Delete \n4)Print \n5)EXIT");
                printf("\nEnter Choice: ");
                scanf("%d",&op);
                switch (op)
                {
```

```
case 1: printf("\nEnter Number of Elements");
scanf("%d",&n );
initialize(&q);
printf("Enter the data");
for(i=0; i<n; i++)
{
        scanf("%d",&x);
        if(full(&q))
        {
                printf("\nQueue is Full..");
                exit(0);
        }
        enqueue(&q,x);
}
break;
case 2: printf("\nEnter the element to be inserted");
scanf("%d\n",&x);
if(full(&q))
{
printf("\nQueue is Full");
exit(0);
}
enqueue(&q,x);
break;
case 3: if(empty(&q))
{
        printf("\nQueue is empty..");
        exit(0);
}
x=dequeue(&q);
printf("\nDeleted Element=%d",x);
break;
case 4: print(&q);
break;
```

```
                    default: break;
                }
        }while (op!=5);
}
void initialize(pqueue *p)
{
        p->rear=-1;
        p->front=-1;
}
int empty(pqueue *p)
{
        if(p->rear==-1)
        return(1);
        return(0);
}
int full(pqueue *p)
{
        if((p->rear+1)%MAX==p->front)
        return(1);
        return(0);
}
void enqueue(pqueue *p, int x)
{
        int i;
        if(full(p))
        printf("\nOverflow");
        else
        {
                if(empty(p))
                {
                        p->rear=p->front=0;
                        p->data[0]=x;
                }
                else
```

```
		{
			i=p->rear;
			while(x>p->data[i])
			{
				p->data[(i+1)%MAX]=p->data[i];
				i=(i-1+MAX)%MAX; //anticlockwise movement inside the
				queue
				if((i+1)%MAX==p->front)
				break;
			}
			//insert x
			i=(i+1)%MAX;
			p->data[i]=x;
			//re-adjust rear
			p->rear=(p->rear+1)%MAX;
		}
	}
}
int dequeue(pqueue *p)
{
	int x;
	if(empty(p))
	{
		printf("\nUnderflow..");
	}
	else
	{
		x=p->data[p->front];
		if(p->rear==p->front)	//delete the last element
		initialize(p);
		else
		p->front=(p->front +1)%MAX;
	}
	return(x);
```

```
}
void print(pqueue *p)
{
	int i,x;

	if(empty(p))
	{
		printf("\nQueue is empty..");
	}
	else
	{
		i=p->front;
		while(i!=p->rear)
		{
			x=p->data[i];
			printf("\n%d",x);
			i=(i+1)%MAX;
		}
		//prints the last element
		x=p->data[i];
		printf("\n%d",x);
	}
}
```

Output

```
1)Create
2)Insert
3)Delete
4)Print
5)EXIT
Enter Choice: 1
Enter Number of Elements4
Enter the data9
12
```

```
4
6
1)Create
2)Insert
3)Delete
4)Print
5)EXIT
Enter Choice: 4
12
9
6
4
1)Create
2)Insert
3)Delete
4)Print
5)EXIT
Enter Choice: 3
Deleted Element=12
1)Create
2)Insert
3)Delete
4)Print
5)EXIT
Enter Choice: 5
```

6.3. Applications of Queue

1. Serving requests on a single shared resource, like a printer, CPU task scheduling etc.
2. In real life, Call Center phone systems will use Queues, to hold people calling them in an order, until a service representative is free.
3. Handling of interrupts in real-time systems. The interrupts are handled in the same order as they arrive, First come first served.
4. Batch processing in operating system.
5. Job scheduling Algorithms like Round Robin Algorithm uses Queue.

PART III

- Non Linear DataStructures–Trees
- Tree ADT
- Ttree traversals
- BinaryTreeADT
- ExpressionTrees
- Applications of Trees
- Binary search tree ADT
- Threaded BinaryTreesAVL Trees
- B-Tree
- B+Tree
- Heap
- Applications ofheap

CHAPTER 7

Non Linear Data Structures – Trees

7.1. Tree ADT

Definition: A tree is a collection of nodes. The collection can be empty; otherwise, a tree consists of a distinguished node r, called root, and zero or more nonempty (sub)trees T1, T2, ... Tk, each of whose roots are connected by a direct edge from r. A tree structure is shown in the figure below:

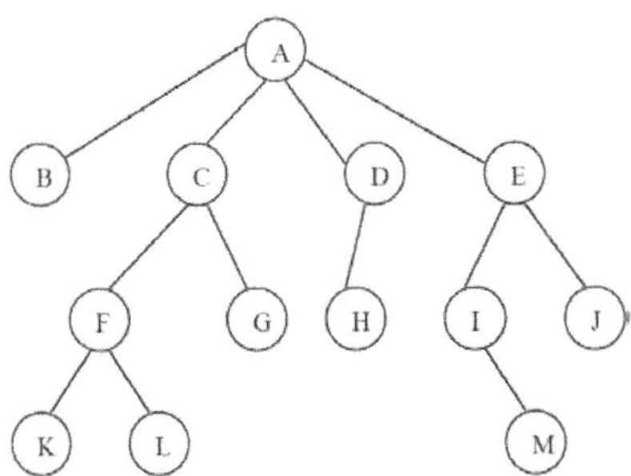

7.1.1. Tree Terminologies

Node

Item or information.

Root

The first and top node in a tree is called the root node. i.e. A node which doesn't have a parent is called a root.

Parent

A node that has a child is called the child's **parent node** (or ancestor node)

Edge

An edge is a connection between two nodes.

Child

A node of a tree referred to by a parent node. Every node, except the root, is the child of some parent. Here Node B is the child of node A, if A is the parent of B.

Sibling

Children of the same parent are said to be siblings. Here B, C, D, E are siblings of **A.** Similarly I, J, K, L are siblings.

Path

A **path** in a tree is a list of distinct nodes in which successive nodes are connected by edges in the tree. There is exactly only one path from each node to root.

Leaf

A node which doesn't have children is called leaf or terminal node. (Or) Nodes at the bottommost level of the tree are called leaf nodes . Here B,K,L,G,H,M,J are leaf nodes.

Ancestor

Node A is an ancestor of node B, if A is the parent of B.

Length

The length is defined as the number of edges on the path. The length for the path A to L is 3.

Degree

The number of subtrees of a node is called its degree.

Degree of A is 4

Degree of C is 2

Degree of D is 1

Degree of H is 0.

Level of a Node

Level of the root of a tree is 0, and the level of any other node in the tree is one more than the level of its parent.

Depth of a Tree

The depth of a tree is the maximum level of any leaf in the tree (also called the height of the tree).

For any node n, the depth of n is the length of the unique path from root to n.

The depth of the root is 0.

Depth of node L is 3.

Descendant

Node B is the descendant of node A, if A is an ancestor of node B

Subtree

Any node of a tree with all of its descendants is called its subtree.

Height

The **height** of a node is the length of the longest downward path to a leaf from that node. The height of the root is the height of the tree.

For any node n, the height of the node n is the length of the longest path from n to the leaf.

The height of the leaf is always 0.

Here - height of node F is 1.

- height of L is 0.

7.2. Tree Traversals

Traversing is the process of visiting every node in the tree exactly once. Therefore, a complete traversal of a binary tree implies visiting the nodes of the tree in some linear sequence.

In a linear list nodes are visited from first to last, but a tree being a non linear one we need definite rules. There are no. of ways to traverse a tree. All of them differ only in the order in which they visit the nodes.

The three main methods of traversing a tree are

- **Postorder** traversal strategy
- **Preorder** traversal strategy
- **Inorder** traversal strategy

Preorder Traversal (Depth-First Order)

1. Visit the root
2. Traverse the left subtree in preorder.
3. Traverse the right subtree in preorder.

Postorder Traversal

1. Traverse the left subtree in postorder
2. Traverse the right subtree in preorder

3. Visit the root

Inorder Traversal (Symmetric Order)

1. Traverse the left subtree in inorder
2. Visit the root
3. Traverse the right subtree in inorder

Example

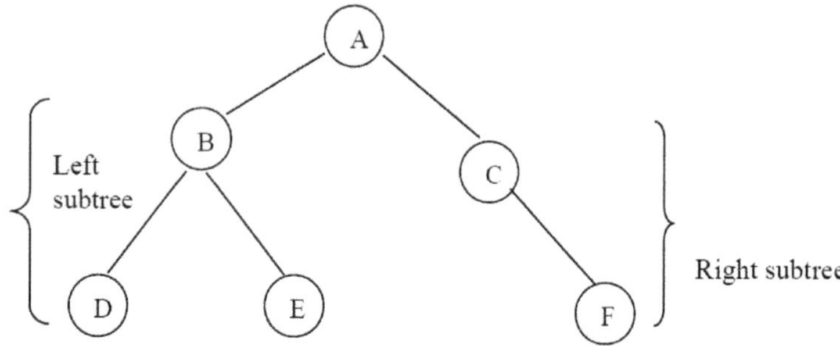

Preorder Traversal: ABDECF

- First, visit the Root **A**
- Now visit the left subtree in preorder .For left subtree, B is the root. So visit root B, then left of B and then visit right of B. It gives the traversing order **BDE.**
- Start visiting the right subtree of A in preorder. For right subtree, C is the root. So visit the root C, then left of C (In the given example there is no left of C), and then visit right of C. Now the order is **CF.**
- Finally, the preorder traversal of above tree is **ABDECF.**

Inorder Traversal: DBEACF

- First visit the left subtree in inorder .For left subtree, B is the root. So visit left of B, then root and then visit right of B. It gives the traversing order **DBE.**
- Now visit the Root **A.**
- Start visiting the right subtree of A in inorder. For right subtree, C is the root. So visit left of C (In the given example there is no left of C), then root C and then visit right of C. Now the order is **CF.**
- Finally, the inorder traversal of above tree is **DBEACF.**

Postorder Traversal: DEBFCA

- First visit the left subtree in postorder .For left subtree, B is the root. So visit the left of B,then visit right of B and then visit root B. It gives the traversing order **DEB.**
- Start visiting the right subtree of A in preorder. For right subtree, C is the root. So left of C (In the given example there is no left of C), then visit right of C and then visit root C. Now the order is **FC.**
- Now visit the Root **A**
- Finally, the postorder traversal of above tree is **DEBFCA.**

Example

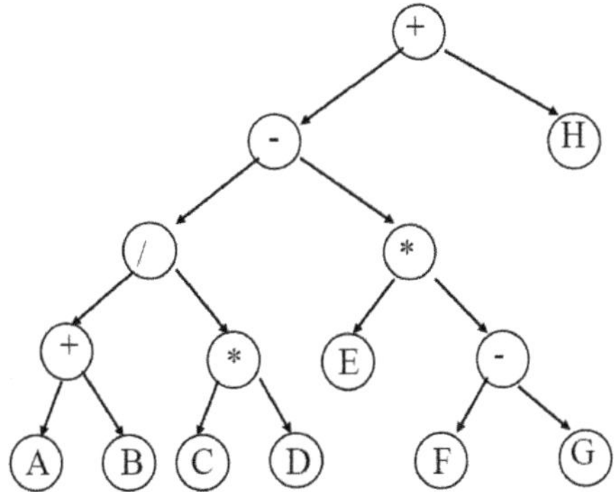

For the example given below, the traversals are given below:

Preorder

+-/+AB*CD*E-FGH

Inorder :

A+B/C*D-E*F-G+H

Postorder:

AB+CD*/EFG-*-H+

Left Child Right Sibling Data Structure:

Implementation of Tree

Tree can be implemented using linked list concept. A structure can be declared with 3 elements. One element contains the data. The second element points to the first child of the tree. The third element points to the next sibling of the first child. The syntax is given below:

Node Declaration for Trees

```
typedef struct TreeNode * PtrToNode;
          struct TreeNode
          {                   ElementType element;
                              PtrToNode FirstChild;
                              PtrToNode NextSibling;
          };
```

Example

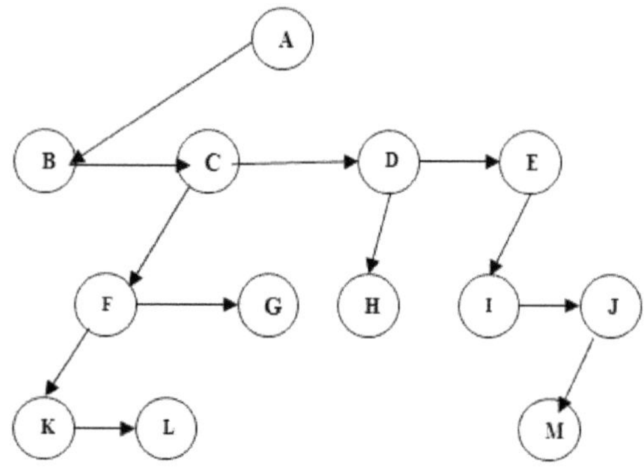

Explanation

- A is the root
- B is the first child of A
- C, D & E are the next siblings of B.

7.3. Binary Tree ADT

- A binary tree is a tree in which no node can have more than two children.
- A binary tree is called strictly binary tree if every nonleaf node in the tree has nonempty left and right subtrees i.e., every nonleaf node has two children.
- A complete binary tree of depth d is a strictly binary tree with all leaf nodes at level d.

A tree is a finite set of nodes having a distinct node called root. **Binary Tree** is a tree which is either empty or has at most two subtrees, each of the subtrees also being a binary tree. It means each node in a binary tree can have 0, 1 or 2 subtrees. A left or right subtree can be empty.

A binary tree is made of nodes, where each node contains a "left" pointer, a "right" pointer, and a data element. The "root" pointer points to the topmost node in the tree. The left and right pointers point to smaller "subtrees" on either side. A null pointer represents a binary tree with no elements -- the empty tree.

It has a distinct node called root i.e. 2. And every node has 0, 1 or 2 children. So it is a binary tree as every node has a maximum of 2 children.

If A is the root of a binary tree & B the root of its left or right subtree, then A is the parent or father of B and B is the left or right child of A. Those nodes having no children are leaf nodes. Any node say, A is the ancestor of node B and B is the descendant of A if A is either the father of B or the father of some ancestor of B. Two nodes having same father are called brothers or Siblings.

Going from leaves to root is called climbing the tree & going from root to leaves is called descending the tree.

A binary tree in which every non leaf node has non empty left & right subtrees is called a strictly binary tree. The tree shown below is a strictly binary tree.

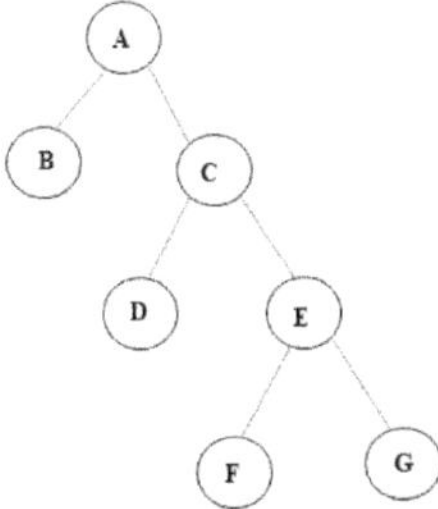

The no. of children a node has is called its degree. The level of root is 0 & the level of any node is one more than its father. In the strictly binary tree shown above A is at level 0, B & C at level 1, D & E at level 2 & F & g at level. The depth of a binary tree is the length of the longest path from the root to any leaf. In the above tree, depth is 3.

7.4. Linked List Representation of Binary Tree

The structure of each node of a binary tree contains one data field and two pointers, each for the right & left child. Each child being a node has also the same structure.The structure of a node is shown below.

Value	
Left	**Right**

Binary trees can be represented by links where each node contains the address of the left child and the right child. If any node has its left or right child empty then it will have in its respective link field, a null value. A leaf node has null value in both of its links.

7.4.1. Pictorial Represention of a Binary Tree

Address of the Left Child	Data Element	Address of the Right Child

Representation of a Leaf

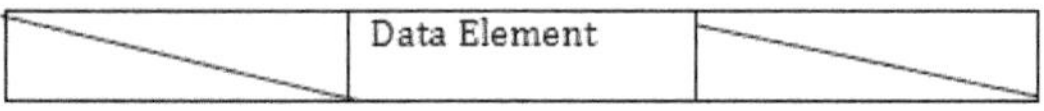

Note: Addresses of the Left Child and Right child are NULL.

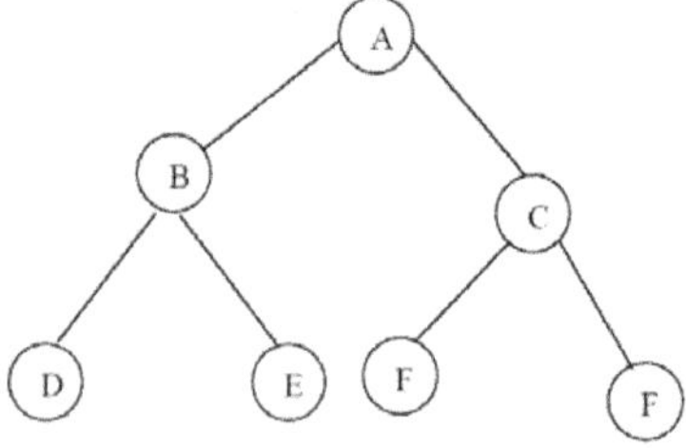

Left and Right Skewed Trees

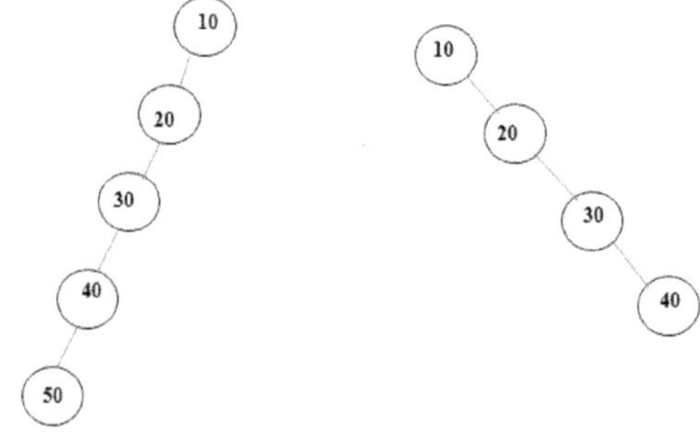

The tree in which each node is attached as a left child of pal left skewed tree. The tree in which each node is attached as a i node then it is called right skewed tree.

7.4.2. Representation of Trees

There are two ways of representing the binary tree.

1. Sequential representation
2. Linked representation.

Let us see these representations one by one.

1. Sequential Representation of Binary Trees or Array Representation

Each node is sequentially arranged from top to bottom and understand this matter by numbering each node. The numbering of root node and then remaining nodes will give ever increasing number direction. The nodes on the same level will be numbered from left to right. The numbering will be as shown below.

7.4.3. Linked List Implementation

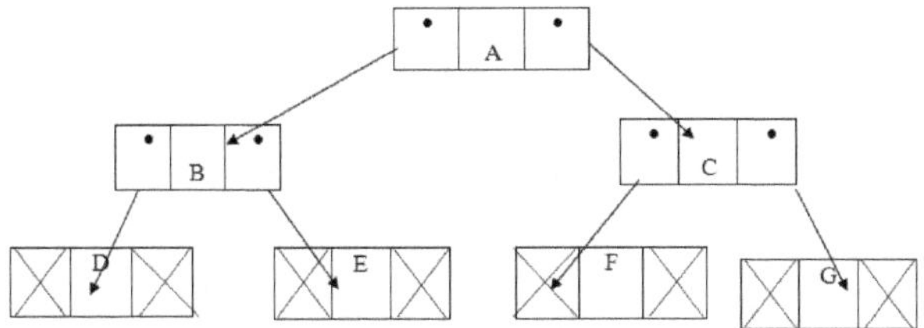

Binary Tree: Array Implementation

Binary tree can be implemented using array. The structure is given below.

```
typedef struct TreeNode *PtrToNode;
typedef struct TreeNode *Tree;
struct TreeNode
{
 ElementType Element;
 Tree Left;
 Tree Right;
};
```

7.5. Expression Tree

Expression tree is also a binary tree in which the leaf or terminal nodes are operands and non-terminal or intermediate nodes are operators used for traversal.

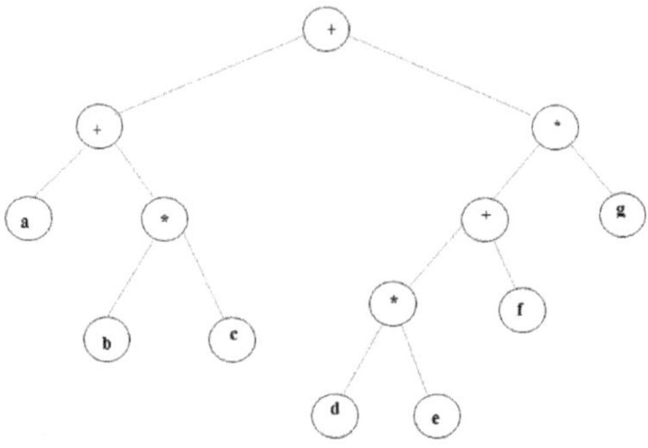

To Construct an Expression Tree the Following Steps are to be Followed

- Read out the given expression one symbol at a time.
- If the symbol is an operand, create a one-node tree and push a pointer to it onto a stack.
- If the symbol is an operator, pop pointers to two trees T1 and T2 from the stack and form a new whose root is the operator and whose left and right children point to T2 and T1, respectively.
- A pointer to this new tree is then pushed onto the stack.

Example

Input: **ab+cde+****

1. The two symbols are operands, so create one-node trees and push pointers to them onto a stack.

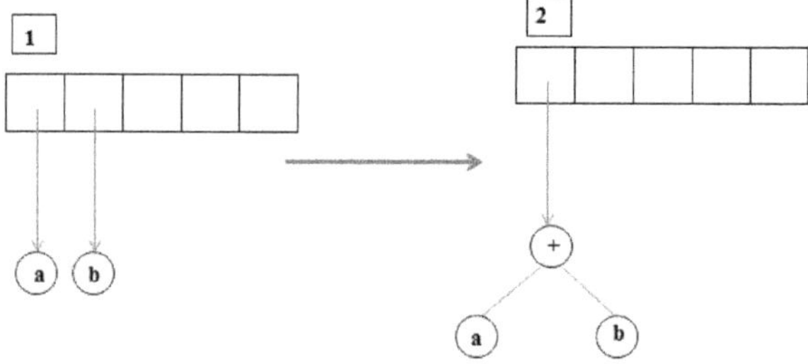

2. Next + is read , so two pointers to trees are popped, a new tree is formed, a new tree is formed, and a pointer to it is pushed onto the stack.
3. Now, c, d and e are read, and for each a one-node tree is created and a pointer to the corresponding tree is pushed onto the stack.

4. Now '+' is read, so two trees are merged.
5. Continuing, '*' is read, so we pop two tree pointers and form a new tree with a '*' as root.
6. Finally, the last symbol '*' is read, two trees are merged, and a pointer to the final tree is left on the stack.

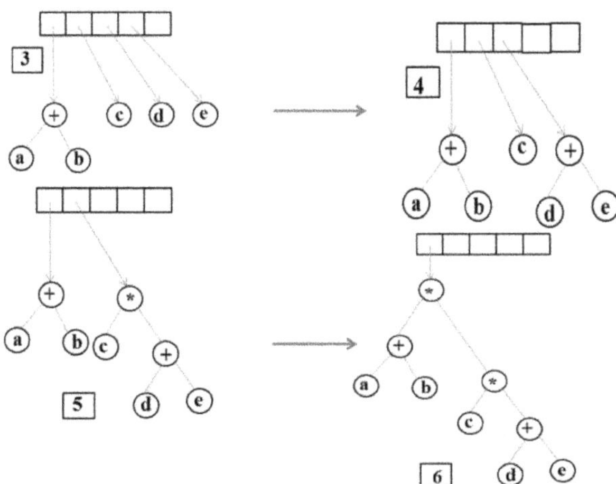

7.6. Applications of Trees

There are many applications for trees. One of the popular uses is the directory structure in many common operating systems, including UNIX and DOS.

- The root of this directory is /usr.
- /usr has 3 children namely mark, alex and bill, which are directories.
- ./usr contains 3 directories and no regular files.
- The filename /usr/mark/book/ch1.r is obtained by following the leftmost child 3 times.
- Each / after the first name indicates an edge; the result is the full pathname.

Advantages of Hierarchical File System

1. It allows users to organize the data logically.
2. Two files in different directories can share the same name, because their path is different from the root.

Routine to List a Directory in a Hierarchical File System

```
Static void listdir(directoryorfile D, int depth)
{
    if(D is a legitimate entry)
   {
     printname(D, depth);
      if(D is a directory)
         for each child, c, of D
              listdir(C, depth+1);
    }
}
```

Explanation

- This is executed by a recursive function call listdir.
- This procedure starts with the directory name and the depth 0. (Note: The depth of the root is 0).
- D can be either a directory or a file.
- It prints entry of D.
- If D is a Directory, it prints the children C recursively.
- This procedure terminates when the parameter for listdir is a not a valid parameter.

Routine which Call the Listdir Routine

```
void listdirectory(directoryorfile D)
{
listdir(D,0);
}
```

Explanation

- This routine call listdir with two parameters D and 0, where 0 denotes the depth of the root.

7.7. Binary Search Tree ADT

For every node, X, in the tree, the values of all the keys in its left subtree are smaller than the key value of X, and the values of all the keys in its right subtree are larger than the key value of X.

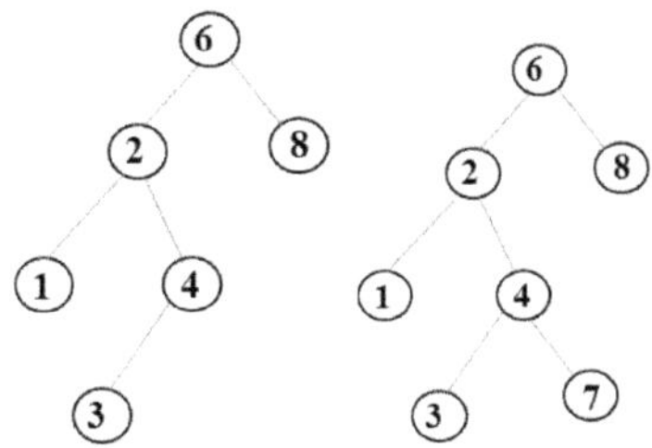

BST: Implementation

```
Struct TreeNode;
typedef struct TreeNode *Position;
typedef struct TreeNode *SearchTree;
SearchTree MakeEmpty( SearchTree T );
Position Find (ElementType X, SearchTree T);
Position FindMin( SearchTree T );
Position FindMax( SearchTree T );
SearchTree Insert (ElementType X, SearchTree T );
SearchTree Delete (ElementType X, SearchTree T );
ElementType Retrieve (Position P);
```

Binary Search Tree Declaration

```
struct TreeNode
{
        ElementType Element;
        SearchTree Left;
        SearchTree Right;
};
```

BST Implementation: MakeEmpty

This operation is mainly for initialization. The implementation follows recursive function call technique.

Procedure

```
SearchTree MakeEmpty( SearchTree T )
{       if( T != NULL )
        {
```

```
            MakeEmpty( T→Left );
            MakeEmpty( T→ Right );
            free( T );
        }
        return NULL;
    }
```

- This function uses recursive function call.
- This function initially makes the left subtrees empty.
- Then the function makes the right subtrees empty.

BST Implementation: Find

This operation generally requires returning a pointer to the node in tree T that has key X, or NULL if there is no such node.

- If T is NULL, then we can just return NULL.
- Otherwise, if the key stored at T is X, return T.
- Otherwise make a recursive call on a subtree of T, either left or right.
- If X is less than the key stored at T, then search Left subtree, otherwise search the right tree recursively.

Procedure

```
Position Find( ElementType X, SearchTree T )
{       if( T == NULL )
          return NULL;
        if ( X < T → Element )
          return Find( X, T → Left );
        else if ( X > T → Element )
          return Find( X, T → Right );
        else
          return T;
}
```

Note: Here, key denotes the data element.

- The function compares the searching element with the element in the root.
- If the element is less than the root, it searches the left subtree recursively.

- Otherwise it searches the right subtree recursively.
- This function returns the element if it is found in the tree.
- Otherwise it returns NULL

BST Implementation: FindMin

This routine will return the position of the smallest elements in the tree. To perform the **FindMin** start at the root and go left as long as there is a left child. The stopping point is the smallest element, which will be always the left most child of the tree.

Procedure

```
Position FindMin( SearchTree T )
{      if ( T == NULL )
 return NULL;
       else if( T → Left == NULL )
         return T;
       else
         return FindMin( T → Left );
}
```

- In a Binary Search Tree, The minimum element is availabe in the left subtree.
- Hence, this function searches the left subtree of the tree.
- Searching takes place recursively.
- The last node in the left subtree contains the minimum element. If T->left is NULL, then it returns the element in that node.
- If no tree is available, i.e T=NULL, then it returns NULL.

BST Implementation: FindMax

This routine will return the position of the largest elements in the tree. To perform the **FindMax** start at the root and go right as long as there is a right child. The stopping point is the largest element.

```
Position FindMax( SearchTree T )
{
                    if ( T != NULL )
          while ( T → Right != NULL )
T = T → Right;
      return T;
}
```

- In a Binary Search Tree, The maximum element is availabe in the right subtree.
- Hence, this function searches the right subtree of the tree.
- If T->right is not equal to NULL, T moves to T->right. This is done till T->right is equal to NULL.
- The last node in the right subtree contains the maximum element. If T->right is NULL, then it returns the element in that node.
- If no tree is available, i.e T=NULL, then it returns NULL.

BST Implementation: Insert

- To insert X in to tree T, proceed down the tree with a **Find.** If X is found do nothing because BST will not have duplicate values. Otherwise, insert X at the appropriate spot on the path traversed.

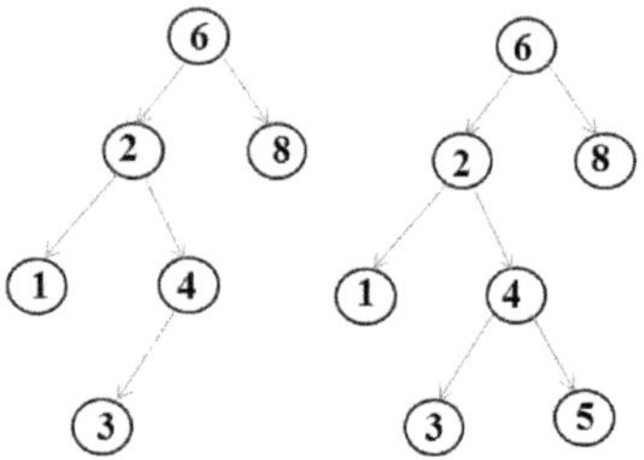

BST Implementation: Insert

In this routine T points to the root of the tree, and the root changes on the first insertion. **Insert** is written as a function that returns a pointer to the root of the new tree.

```
SearchTree Insert( ElementType X, SearchTree T )
{                    if ( T == NULL )
   {
T = malloc( sizeof( struct TreeNode ) );
          if ( T == NULL )
                              FatalError( "Out of space!!!" );
          else
          {
               T → Element = X;
               T → Left = T → Right = NULL;
          }
```

```
            }
        else if ( X < T → Element )
                T → Left = Insert( X, T → Left );
          else if( X > T → Element )
                T → Right = Insert( X, T → Right );
          /* Else X is in the tree already; we'll do nothing */
                          return T;  /* Do not forget this line!! */
        }
```

Explanation

1. This function has two parameters namely, the element X to be inserted and T, the address of the root of the tree.
2. If T is NULL, a new node is created and the address is stored in T, else go to 5
3. If T is NULL, it implies that memory allocation is not done and terminates.
4. Otherwise the new element X is inserted into the node T. The left and right pointer is made NULL.
5. The element X is compared with the element present in T. If X < T->element, then the element is to be inserted in the left. A recursive function call is made with two parameters X and T->left.
6. Otherwise if X > T->element, then the element is to be inserted in the right. A recursive function call is made with two parameters X and T->right.
7. Otherwise, it implies that X is already present in the BST. Hence the element cannot be inserted.
8. After the element is inserted in the appropriate position, the address of the new tree is returned to the main function.

BST Implementation: Delete

If the node is a leaf it can be deleted immediately.

If the node has one child, the node can be deleted after its **parents** adjust a pointer to bypass the node.

The following figure shows an initial tree and the result of a deletion; the key value is 2. It is replaced smallest data in its right subtree(3), and then that node is deleted as before.

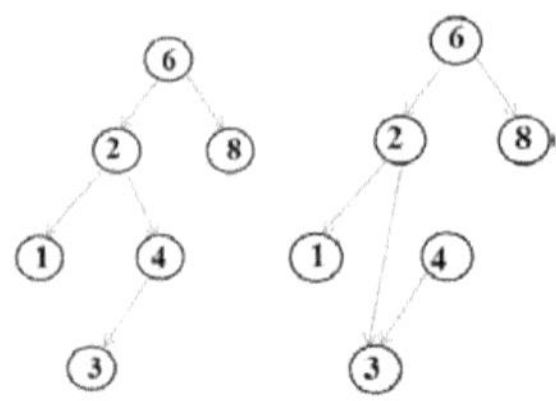

BST Implementation: Delete

```
SearchTree Delete( ElementType X, SearchTree T )
{                    Position TmpCell;
   if ( T == NULL )
     Error( "Element not found" );
  else  if ( X < T → Element )  /* Go left */
     T → Left = Delete( X, T → Left );
  else  if ( X > T → Element )  /* Go right */
     T → Right = Delete( X, T → Right );
  else  /* Found element to be deleted */

if ( T → Left && T → Right )  /* Two children */
  {
        TmpCell = FindMin( T → Right );
        T → Element = TmpCell → Element;
        T → Right = Delete( T → Element, T → Right );
  }
  else  /* One or zero children */
  {     TmpCell = T;
        if ( T → Left == NULL ) /* Also handles 0 children */
            T = T → Right;
        else if ( T → Right == NULL )
            T = T → Left;
        free( TmpCell );
  }
  return T;
}
```

Explanation

1. This function has two parameters namely, the element X to be deleted and T, the address of the root of the tree.
2. If T is NULL, it implies that the tree is not present and the function terminates.
3. Otherwise, the element X is compared with the element present in T. If X < T->element, then the element to be deleted is present in in the left. A recursive function call is made with two parameters X and T->left.
4. Otherwise if X > T->element, then the element to be deleted is present in the right. A recursive function call is made with two parameters X and T->right.
5. If the element is found, it checks where the node contains two children. If yes, It finds the minimum element from the two children and the minimum element is inserted into the node where the element is deleted.
6. If the node contains one or zero children, the left or children node value is inserted into the node where the element is deleted.
7. The function returns the address of the root of the newly formed tree after deletion to the main function.

Program

```
// C program to demonstrate insert operation in binary search tree
#include<stdio.h>
#include<stdlib.h>
struct node
{
        int key;
        struct node *left, *right;
};

// A utility function to create a new BST node
struct node *newNode(int item)
{
        struct node *temp = (struct node *)malloc(sizeof(struct node));
        temp->key = item;
        temp->left = temp->right = NULL;
        return temp;
```

```
}

// A utility function to do inorder traversal of BST
void inorder(struct node *root)
{
	if (root != NULL)
	{
		inorder(root->left);
		printf("%d \n", root->key);
		inorder(root->right);
	}
}

/* A utility function to insert a new node with given key in BST */
struct node* insert(struct node* node, int key)
{
	/* If the tree is empty, return a new node */
	if (node == NULL) return newNode(key);

	/* Otherwise, recur down the tree */
	if (key < node->key)
		node->left = insert(node->left, key);
	else if (key > node->key)
		node->right = insert(node->right, key);

	/* return the (unchanged) node pointer */
	return node;
}

// Driver Program to test above functions
int main()
{
	/* Let us create following BST
```

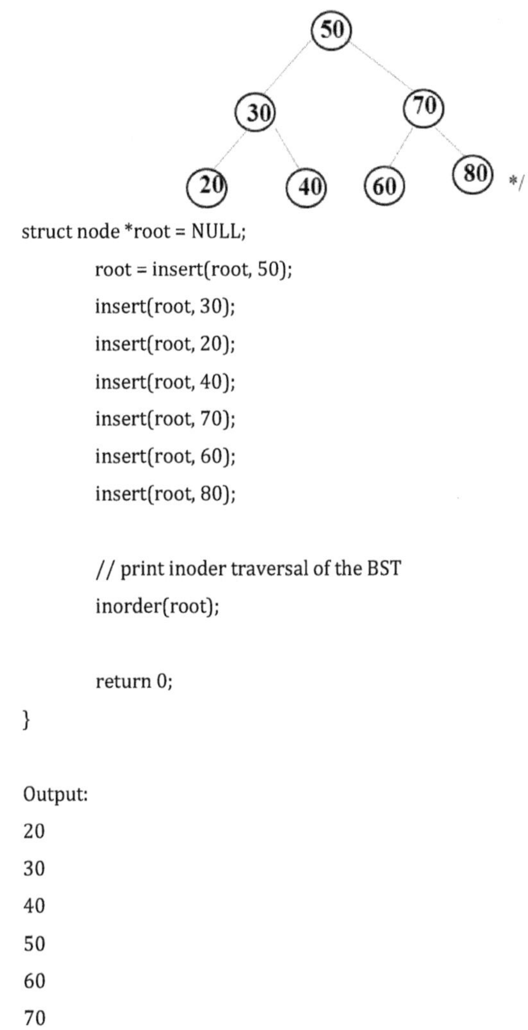


```
struct node *root = NULL;
        root = insert(root, 50);
        insert(root, 30);
        insert(root, 20);
        insert(root, 40);
        insert(root, 70);
        insert(root, 60);
        insert(root, 80);

        // print inoder traversal of the BST
        inorder(root);

        return 0;
}
```

Output:

20

30

40

50

60

70

80

7.8. Threaded Binary Tree

A binary search tree in which each node uses an otherwise-empty left child link to refer to the node's in-order predecessor and an empty right child link to refer to its in-Order Successor.

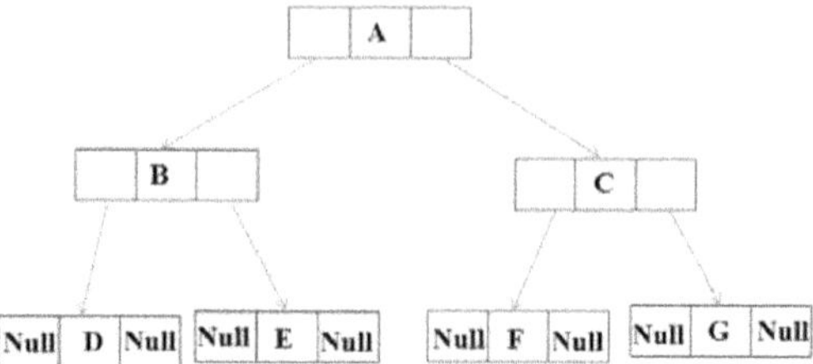

In above binary tree, there are 8 null pointers & actual 6 pointers.

In all there are 14 pointers.

We can generalize it that for any binary tree with n nodes there will be (n+1) null pointers and 2n total pointers.

The objective here to make effective use of these null pointers. J. perils & C. Thornton jointly proposed idea to make effective use of these null pointers.

According to this idea we are going to replace all the null pointers by the appropriate pointer values called threads.

And binary tree with such pointers are called threaded tree. In the memory representation of a threaded binary tree, it is necessary to distinguish between a normal pointer and a thread.

Threaded Binary Tree: One-Way

We will use the right thread only in this case. To implement threads we need to use in-order successor of the tree.

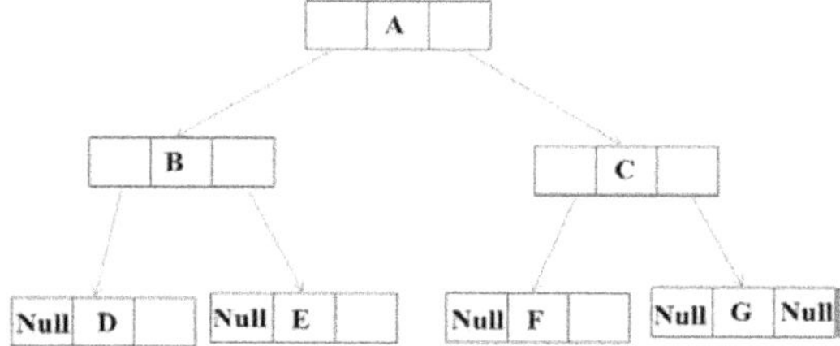

Inorder Traversal of The tree: D, B, E, A, F, C, G

Two Way Threaded Tree/Double Threads

Again two-way threading has left pointer of the first node and right pointer of the last node will contain the null value. The header nodes is called two-way threading with header node threaded binary tree.

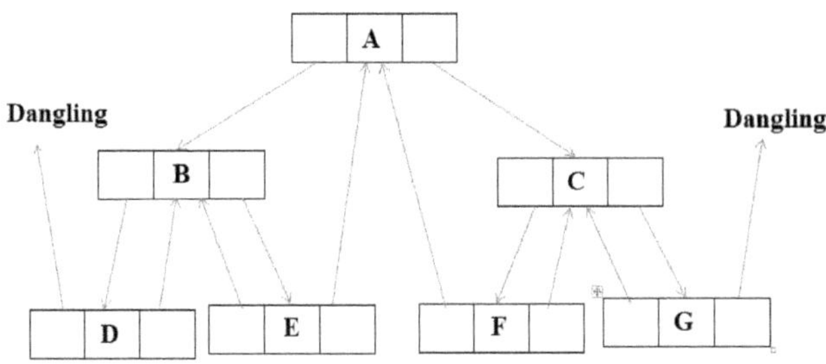

Inorder Traversal of The tree: D, B, E, A, F, C, G E C F G

Dangling can be Solved as Follows

Introduce a header node. The left and right pointer of the header node are treated as normal links and are initialized to point to header node itself.

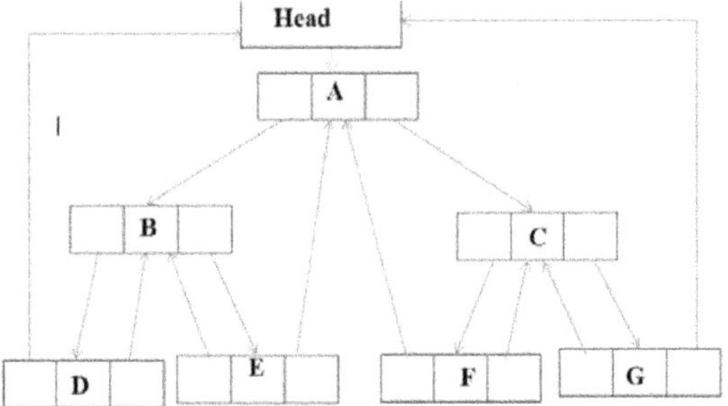

Inorder Traversal of The tree: D, B, E, A, F, C, G E C F G

Node Structure

For the purpose of our evaluation algorithm, we assume each node has five fields:

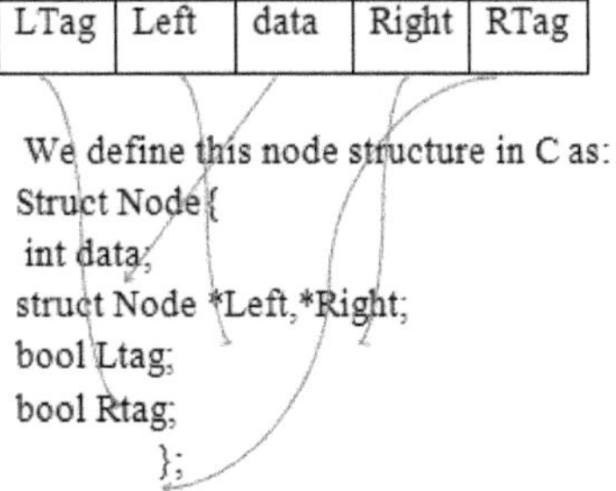

LTag	Left	data	Right	RTag

We define this node structure in C as:

```
Struct Node{
 int data;
struct Node *Left,*Right;
bool Ltag;
bool Rtag;
        };
```

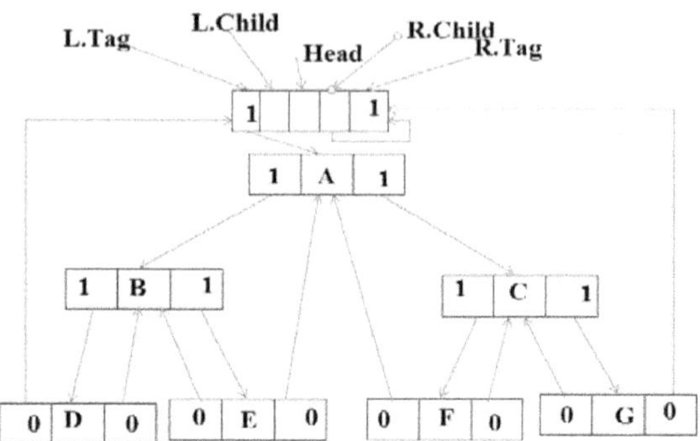

Inorder Traversal of The tree: D B E A F C G

Threaded Tree Traversal

- We start at the leftmost node in the tree, print it, and follow its right thread
- If we follow a thread to the right, we output the node and continue to its right.
- If we follow a link to the right, we go to the leftmost node, print it, and continue.

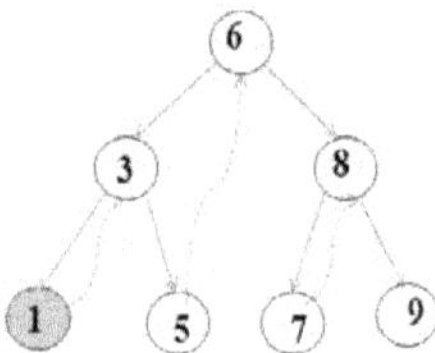

Start at leftmost node, print it.

O**utput**

1

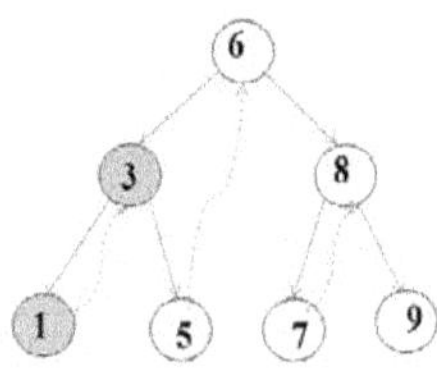

Follow thread to right, print it.

Output

13

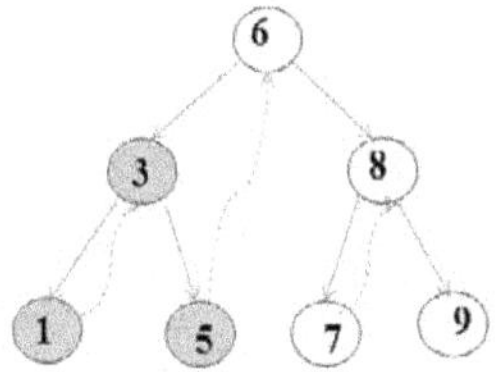

Follow link to right, go to leftmost node and print

Output 1 3 5

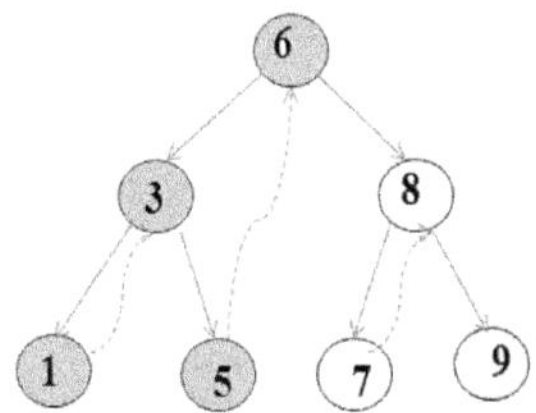

Follow thread to right, print node

Output 1 3 5 6

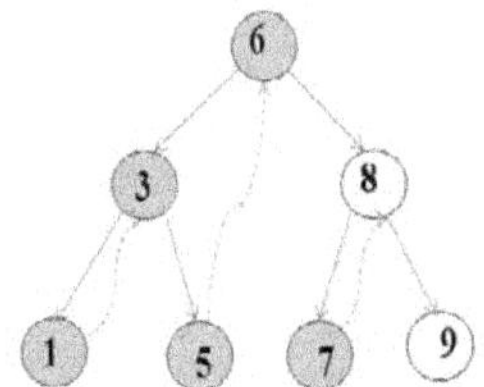

Follow link to right, go to leftmost node and print

Output 1 3 5 6 7

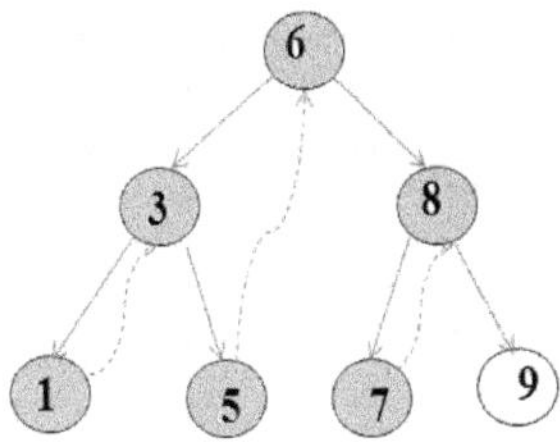

Follow thread to right, print node

Output 1 3 5 6 7 8

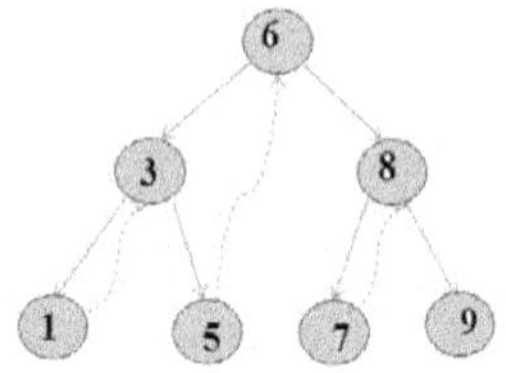

Follow link to right, go to leftmost node and print

Output 1 3 5 6 7 8 9

```
void inOrder(struct Node *root)
{
struct Node *cur = leftmost(root);
while (cur != NULL)
{
printf("%d ", cur->data);
// If this node is a thread node, then go to
// inorder successor
if (cur->rightThread)
 cur = cur->right;
 else
// Else go to the leftmost child in right subtree
cur = leftmost(cur->right);
}
}
```

Comparison of Threaded Binary Tree with Normal Binary Tree

Threaded Binary Tree	Normal Binary Tree
• In threaded binary trees, The null pointers are used as thread. • We can use the null pointers which is a efficient way to use computers memory. • Traversal is easy. • Completed without using stack or reccursive function. • Structure is complex. • Insertion and deletion takes more time.	• In a normal binary trees, the null pointers remains null. • We can't use null pointers so it is a wastage of memory. • Traverse is not easy and not memory efficient. • Less complex than Threaded binary tree. • Less Time consuming than Threaded Binary tree.

Inserting a node to Threaded Binary Tree

Inserting a node X as the right child of a nodes.

1st Case

If G has an empty right subtree, then the insertion is simple

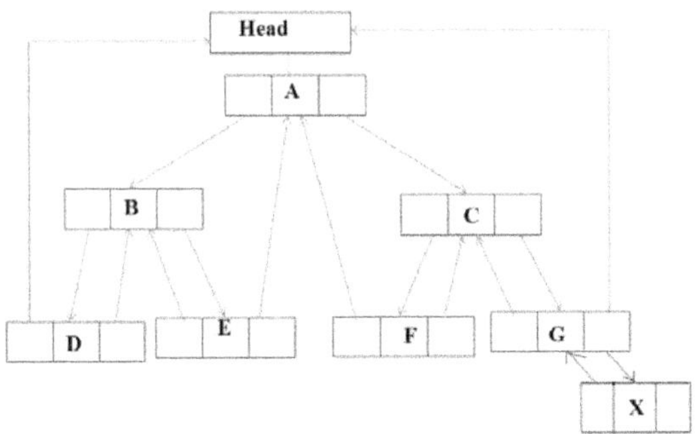

Inserting X as a right child of G.New inorder traversal is: D,B,E,A,F,C,G,X

2nd Case: If the right subtree of C is not empty, then this right child is made the right child of X after insertion.

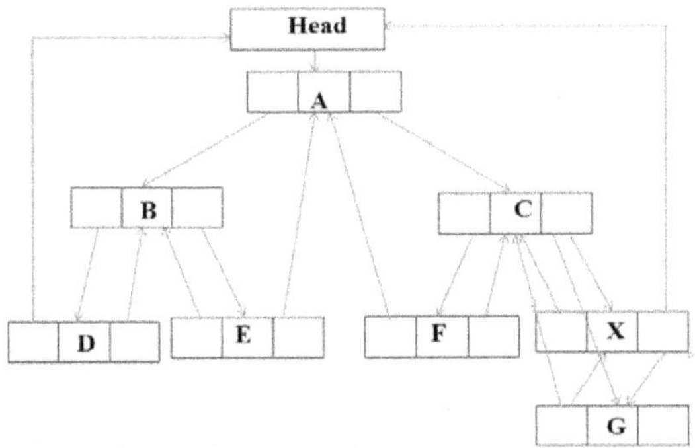

New Inorder Traversal of The tree: D, B, E, A, F, C, X,G

Advantages	Disadvantages
1. By doing threading we avoid the recursive method of traversing a Tree , which doesn't use of stack and consumes a lot of memory and time . 2. The node can keep record of its root . 3. Backward Traverse is possible. 4. Applicable in most types of the binary tree.	1. This makes the Tree more complex . 2. More prone to errors when both the child are not present & both values of nodes pointer to their ancestors. 3. Lot of time consumes when deletion or insertion is performed.

Applications

- Same as any kind of Binary Tree.
- Used in search and Traverse based work.

7.9. AVL Tree

- An AVL (Adelson-Velskii and Landis) tree is a binary search tree with a balance condition.

  For every node in the AVL tree, the height of left subtree and the height of the right subtree can differ by at most one.

  Height of left subtree- Height of right subtree < = 1

- The height of the left subtree minus the height of the right subtree of a node is called the balance factor of the node. For an AVL tree, the balances of the nodes are always -1, 0 or 1.
  - The height of an empty tree is defined to be -1.
- Given an AVL tree, if insertions or deletions are performed, the AVL tree may not remain height balanced.

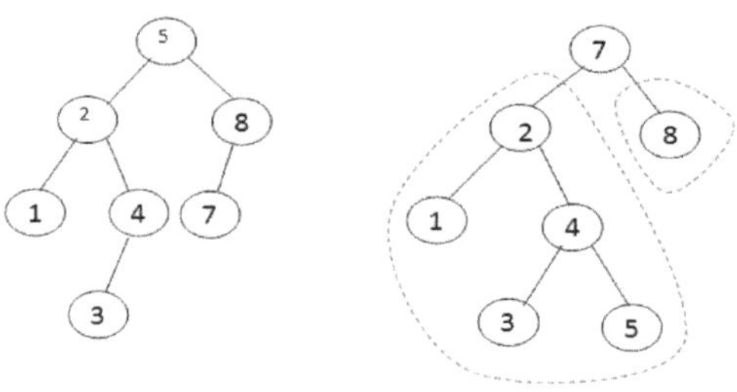

An AVL Tree

Not an AVL Tree

Balancing Trees

The tree becomes unbalanced whenever a node is inserted or deleted. The unbalanced tree is balanced by rotating the tree to the left or right.

There are four cases that require rebalancing. All unbalanced trees fall into one of these four cases:

1. **Left of Left** - A sub tree of a tree that is left high has become left high after the insertion of an element.

Diagram

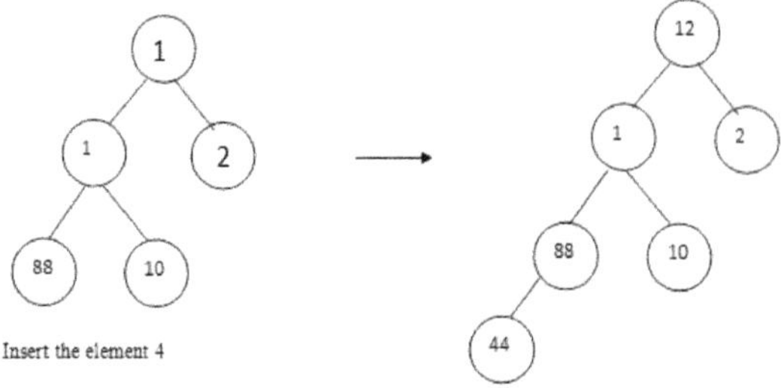

2. **Right of right** - A sub tree of a tree that is right high has become right high after insertingan element.

Diagram

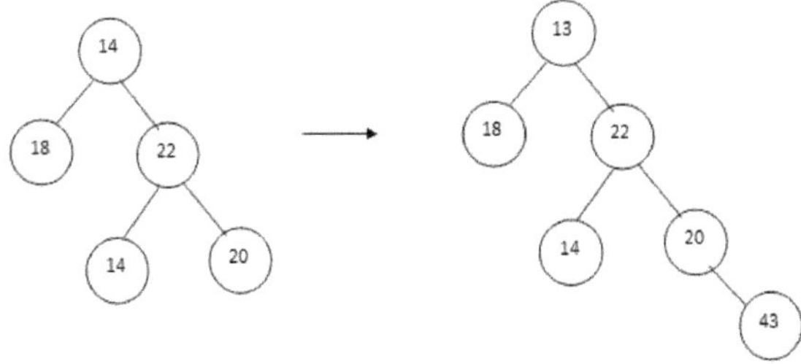

3. **Right of Left** - A sub tree of a tree that is left high has become right high after inserting an element.

Diagram

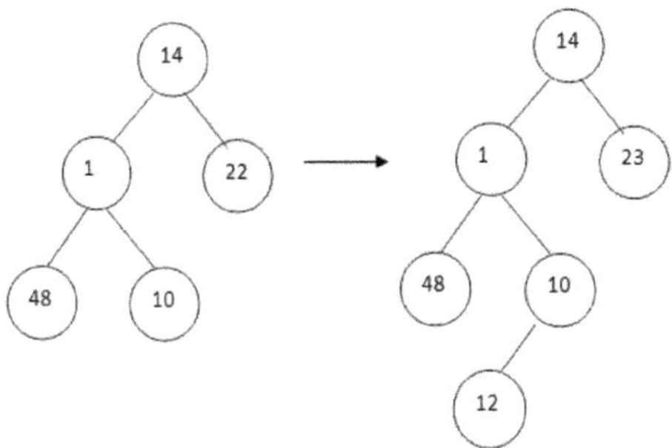

4. **Left of Right** - A sub tree of a tree that is right high has become left high after inserting an element.

Diagram

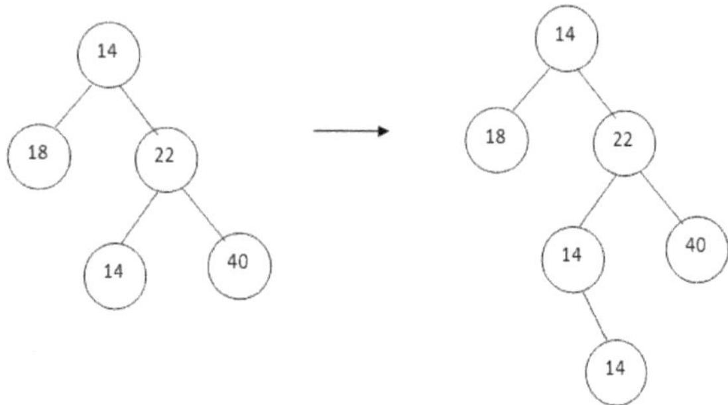

Rotation

An A VL tree becomes unbalanced when there is an insertion or deletion of a node from an existing A VL tree.

To balance the tree, transformation of the tree is performed. This transformation is called Rotation.

Rotation is a technique in which an unbalanced A VL tree is rotated either left or right side, so that the tree becomes balanced again. i.e

$$|H_L - H_R| <= 1$$

There are two types of Rotation. They are:

- Single Rotation
- Double Rotation

Single Rotation: Rotation of the tree is performed only once either left or right side of the unbalanced tree. Single Rotation is performed for the two cases namely left of left and right of right

Double Rotation: Rotation of the tree is performed twice, one on the left side and the other one on the right side and vice versa of the unbalanced tree. Double Rotation is performed for the two cases namely left of right and right of left.

Single Rotation

Case 1: Left of Left: When the out-of-balance condition has been created by a left high subtree of a left high tree, the tree is balanced by rotating the out-of-balance node to the right.

Diagram

Simple Right Rotation

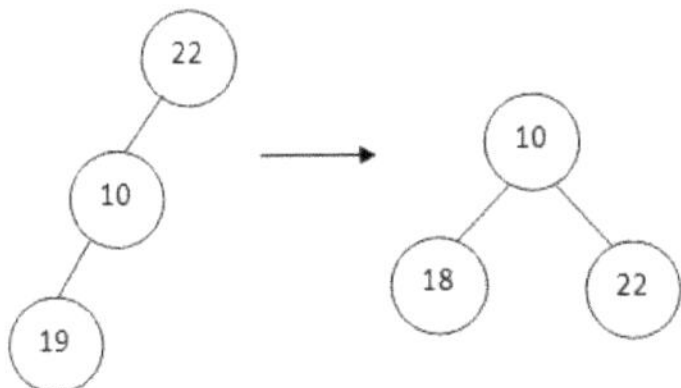

Case 2: Right of Right: When the out-of-balance condition has been created by a right high subtree of a right high tree, the tree is balanced by rotating the out-of-balance node to the left.

DoubleRotation

Case 3: Right of Left: Double rotation is needed for balancing the A VL tree in this case. The tree is out of balance in which the root is left high and the left subtree is right high.

- The left subtree which is right high is rotated first in the left side.
- The root of the subtree which is left high is rotated second in the right side.

Basic Operations performed in an A VL Tree:

The basic operations performed in an A VL tree are as follows:

- Inserting an element.
- Deleting an element

Whenever these two operations are done, the balance condition has to be checked after the operation. If the balance condition is not satisfied then rotation is performed. Single or double rotation is performed depending upon the violation in the balance factor.

AVL Trees: Implementation

A VL tree is implemented using linked list concept. The node declaration for A VL trees is given below:

```
struct AvlNode;
typedef struct AvlNode *Position;
typedefstruct AvlNode * AvlTree;
AvlTree MakeEmpty( AvlTree T);
Position Find(ElementType X, AvlTree T);
```

```
Position FindMin( AvlTree T );
Position FindMax( AvlTree T);
AvlTree Insert( ElementType X, AvlTree T);
AvlTree Delete( ElementType X, AvlTree T);
ElementType Retrieve( Position P );
struct AvlNode
{
ElementType Elemcnt; A vlTree Left; AvlTree Right;
int Height;
};
```

A structure AvlNode is created which contains four data elements. They are:

- The data to be stored in the node.
- Address of the left child
- Address of the right child
- Height of the node

Procedure to Compute the Height of a Node

```
static int Height( Position P )
{
if( P == NULL)
   return -1 ; else
return P->Height;
}
```

Explanation

- This function has a parameter P, which contains the address of the node.
- If P is NULL, it implies that there is no node, hence the height is returned as -1.
- Otherwise it returns the height of the node stored in the structure.

Procedure to Insert an Element Into the Tree

```
AvlTree lnsert( ElementType X, AvlTree T)
{
if ( T = NULL)
{
```

```
/* Create and return a one-node tree * /
T = malloc( sizeof( struct A vi Node ) ); if( T == NULL)
   FatalError( "Out ofspace!!!" );
   else
{ T->Element = X; T->Height- 0;
T->Left = T->Right = NULL;
}
}
else
if ( X < T ->Element )
          { T->Left = Insert( X, T->Left)
          if ( Height( T ->Left ) - Height( T -> Right) = 2 )
if ( X < T ->Left->Element )
  T = SingleRotateWithLeft( T)
          else
         T = DoubleRotate WithLeft( T );
}
else
if (X> T->Element)
          { T->Right = Insert( X, T->Right);
          if( Height( T->Right ) - Height( T->Left ) == 2 )
          if( X > T->Right->Element)
  T = SingleRotateWithRight( T);
          else
        T = DoubleRotatcWithRight( T);
}
/* Else X is in the tree already; we'll do nothing * /
T->Height = Max( Height( T->Left), Height{ T>Right» + 1;
return T;
}
```

Explanation

1. This function has two parameters namely, the clement X to be inserted and T, the addressof the root of the tree.

2. if T is NULL, a new node is create p and the address is stored in T, else go to 5.
3. if T is NULL, it implies that memory allocation is not done and terminates.
4. Otherwise the new element X is inserted into the node T. The left and right pointer are made NULL. The height of the node is initialized to O. Go to step 8.
5. The element X is compared with the element present in T. If X < T->element, then the element is to be inserted in the left. A recursive function call is made with two parameters X and T->left.
6. Otherwise if X > T->element, then the element is to be inserted in the right. A recursive function call is made with two parameters X and T ->right.
7. Otherwise, itimplies that X is already present in the A VL. Hence the element cannot be inserted.
8. After the element is inserted in the appropriate position, the balance factor is checked. If the Balance factor is equal to 2, then it implies that the tree is not balanced. Hence, rotation is to be performed.
9. The element is compared with T->left->elcment or T->right->element. If X is less, then single rotation is performed. Otherwise, double rotation is performed.
10. After the rotation is performed, the height of each node is calculated again and the address of the new tree is returned back to the main function.

Procedure for Single Rotation with Left

```
static Position SingleRotateWithLeft( Position K2 )
Position KI;
KI = K2->Left;
K2->Left = KI->Right;
Kl->Right = K2;
K2->Height = Max( Height(K2->LeH), Height(K2->Right) )+1;
 Kl->Height = Max( Height(KI->Lell), K2->Height) + 1;
return Kl; /* New root */
}
```

Explanation

1. This function takes a parameter K2, which is the address of the node where rotation is tobe done.
2. The rotation takes place on the right side.
3. K1 becomes the root node and K2 becomes the right child ofKl.

4. The height of KI and K2 are calculated and the address of Kl is returned to the calling function.

Procedure for Sine:le Rotation with Rie:ht:

```
static Position SingleRotateWithRight( Position K2 )
{
Position K 1 ;
KI = K2->right;
K2->right = K I->Ieft;
KI->left = K2:
K2->Height = Max( Height(K2->Left), Hcight(K2->Right) ) + 1;
KI->Height = Max( Height(KI->Left), K2->Hcight).oj. I;
return KI; 1* New root */
```

Explanation

1. This function takes a parameter K2, which is the address of the node where rotation is to be done.
2. The rotation takes place on the left side.
3. KI becomes the root node and K2 becomes the left child of KI.
4. The height of K I and K2 are calculated and the address of K 1 is returned to the calling function.

Proeedure for Double Rotation with Left

```
static Position DoubleRotateWithLcft( Position K3 )
{
/* Rotate between K I and K2 * /
K3->Left = SingleRotateWithRight( K3->Left );
/* Rotate between K3 and K2 * /
return SingleRotateWithLeft( K3 );
}
```

Explanation

1. This function takes a parameter K3, which is the address of the node
2. The first rotation takes place on thc len side with KJ->Ieft (K I)as Ihl.: parameter.
3. The rotation takes place between K I and K2.

4. K2 becomes the root node and Kl becomes the left child of K2.
5. The height of Kl and K2 are calculated and the address of K2 is returned to the calling function.
6. The address of K2 is assigned to K3->left.
7. The second rotation takes between K3 and K2. The rotation takes place on the right side.
8. K2 becomes the root node and K3 becomes the right child of K2.
9. The height of K3 and K2 are calculated and the address of K2 is returned to the calling function.

Procedure for Double Rotation with Rieht

```
static Position DoubleRotate WithRight( Position K 3)
{
/* Rotate between K I and K2 * /
K3->Right = SingleRotateWithRight( K3->Right );
 /* Rotate between K3 and K2 >I< /
return SingleRotatcWithRight( K3 );
}
```

Explanation

1. This function takes a parameter K3, which is the address of the node.
2. The first rotation takes place on the right side with K3->right (Kl) as the parameter.
3. The rotation takes place between Kl and K2.
4. K2 becomes the root node and Kl becomes the right child ofK2.
5. The height of KI and K2 are calculated and the address of K2 is returned to the calling function.
6. The address ofK2 is assigned to K3->right.
7. The second rotation takes between K3 and K2. The rotation takes place on the left side.
8. K2 becomes the root node and K3 becomes the left child of K2.
9. The height of K3 and K2 at'e calculated and the address of K2 is returned to the callingfunction.

7.10. B-Tree

B-Tree is a self-balancing search tree. B Trees are multi-way trees. That is each node contains a set of keys and pointers. A B Tree with four keys and five pointers represents the minimum size of a B Tree node. B Trees are dynamic. That is, the height of the tree grows and contracts as records are added and deleted.

In most of the other self-balancing search trees (like AVL and Red Black Trees), it is assumed that everything is in main memory. To understand use of B-Trees, we must think of huge amount of data that cannot fit in main memory. When the number of keys is high, the data is read from disk in the form of blocks. Disk access time is very high compared to main memory access time. The main idea of using B-Trees is to reduce the number of disk accesses. Most of the tree operations (search, insert, delete, max, min, ..etc) require O(h) disk accesses where h is height of the tree. B-tree is a fat tree. Height of B-Trees is kept low by putting maximum possible keys in a B-Tree node. Generally, a B-Tree node size is kept equal to the disk block size. Since h is low for B-Tree, total disk accesses for most of the operations are reduced significantly compared to balanced Binary Search Trees like AVL Tree, Red Black Tree, ..etc.

Properties of B-Tree

1. All leaves are at same level.
2. A B-Tree is defined by the term minimum degree 't'. The value of t depends upon disk block size.
3. Every node except root must contain at least t-1 keys. Root may contain minimum 1 key.
4. All nodes (including root) may contain at most 2t – 1 keys.
5. Number of children of a node is equal to the number of keys in it plus 1.
6. All keys of a node are sorted in increasing order. The child between two keys k1 and k2 contains all keys in range from k1 and k2.
7. B-Tree grows and shrinks from root which is unlike Binary Search Tree. Binary Search Trees grow downward and also shrink from downward.
8. Like other balanced Binary Search Trees, time complexity to search, insert and delete is O(Logn).

Following is an example B-Tree of minimum degree 3. Note that in practical B-Trees, the value of minimum degree is much more than 3.

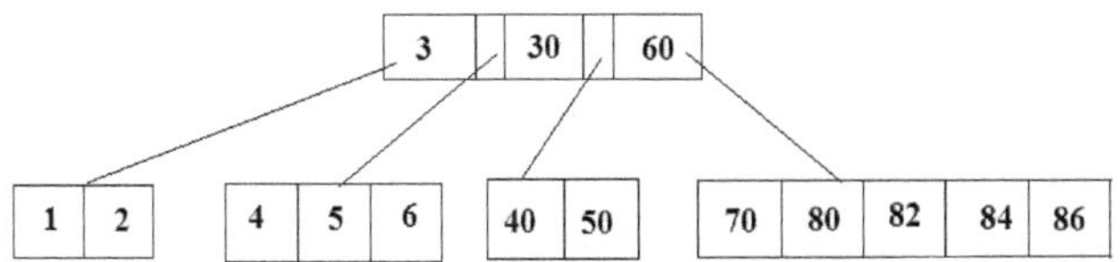

Search

Search is similar to search in Binary Search Tree. Let the key to be searched be k. We start from root and recursively traverse down. For every visited non-leaf node, if the node has key, we simply return the node. Otherwise we recur down to the appropriate child (The child which is just before the first greater key) of the node. If we reach a leaf node and don't find k in the leaf node, we return NULL.

Traverse

Traversal is also similar to Inorder traversal of Binary Tree. We start from the leftmost child, recursively print the leftmost child, then repeat the same process for remaining children and keys. In the end, recursively print the rightmost child.

7.11. B+ Trees

A B+ Tree combines features of B Trees. It contains index pages and data pages. The data pages always appear as leaf nodes in the tree. The root node and intermediate nodes are always index pages. The index pages in a B+ tree are constructed through the process of inserting and deleting records.

Thus, B+ trees grow and contract like their B Tree counterparts. The contents and the number of index pages reflects this growth and shrinkage. B+ Trees and B Trees use a "fill factor" to control the growth and the shrinkage. A 50% fill factor would be the minimum for any B+ or B tree.

As our example we use the smallest page structure. This means that our B+ tree conforms to the following guidelines.

Number of Keys/page	4
Number of Pointers/page	5
Fill Factor	50%
Minimum Keys in each page	2

As this table indicates each page must have a minimum of two keys. The root page may violate this rule. The following table shows a B+ tree. As the example illustrates this tree does not have a full index page. (We have room for one more key and pointer in the root page.) In addition, one of the data pages contains empty slots.

B+ Tree with four keys

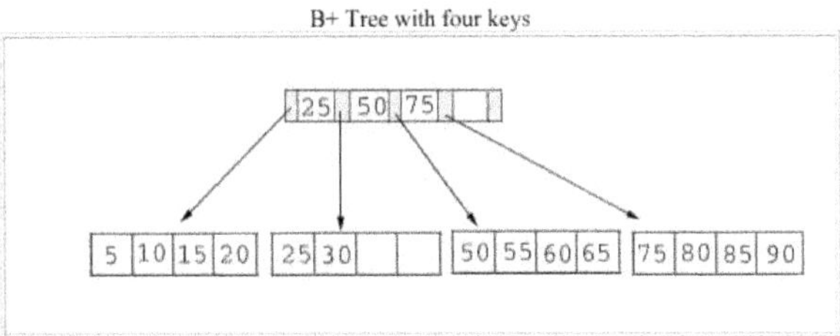

Adding Records to a B+ Tree

The key value determines a record's placement in a B+ tree. The leaf pages are maintained in sequential order AND a doubly linked list (not shown) connects each leaf page with its sibling page(s). This doubly linked list speeds data movement as the pages grow and contract. We must consider three scenarios when we add a record to a B+ tree. Each scenario causes a different action in the insert algorithm. The scenarios are:

The `insert` algorithm for B+ Trees

Leaf Page Full	Index Page FULL	Action
NO	NO	Place the record in sorted position in the appropriate leaf page
YES	NO	1. Split the leaf page 2. Place Middle Key in the index page in sorted order. 3. Left leaf page contains records with keys below the middle key. 4. Right leaf page contains records with keys equal to or greater than the middle key.
YES	YES	1. Split the leaf page. 2. Records with keys < middle key go to the left leaf page. 3. Records with keys >= middle key go to the right leaf page. 4. Split the index page. 5. Keys < middle key go to the left index page. 6. Keys > middle key go to the right index page. 7. The middle key goes to the next (higher level) index. IF the next level index page is full, continue splitting the index pages.

Illustrations of the Insert Algorithm

The following examples illlustrate each of the insert scenarios. We begin with the simplest scenario: inserting a record into a leaf page that is not full. Since only the leaf node containing 25 and 30 contains expansion room, we're going to insert a record with a key value of 28 into the B+ tree. The following figures shows the result of this addition.

Add Record with Key 28

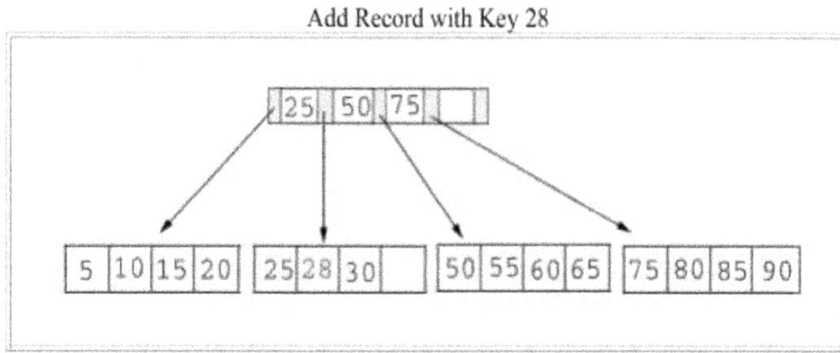

Adding a record when the leaf page is full but the index page is not.

Next, we're going to insert a record with a key value of 70 into our B+ tree. This record should go in the leaf page containing 50, 55, 60, and 65. Unfortunately this page is full. This means that we must split the page as follows:

Left Leaf Page	Right Leaf Page
50 55	60 65 70

The middle key of 60 is placed in the index page between 50 and 75. The following table shows the B+ tree after the addition of 70.

Add Record with Key 70

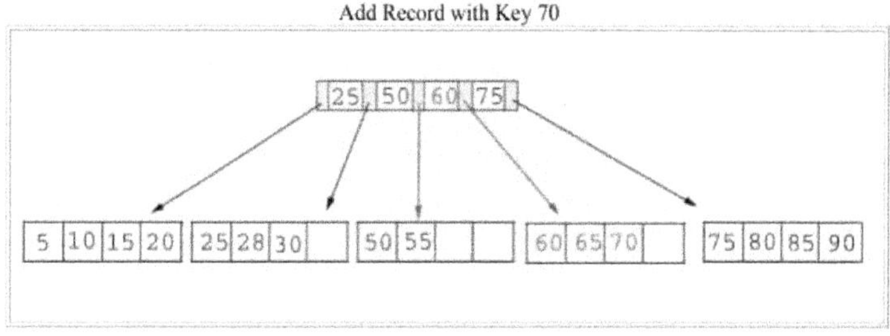

Adding a record when both the leaf page and the index page are full.

As our last example, we're going to add a record containing a key value of 95 to our B+ tree. This record belongs in the page containing 75, 80, 85, and 90. Since this page is full we split it into two pages:

Left Leaf Page	Right Leaf Page
75 80	85 90 95

The middle key, 85, rises to the index page. Unfortunately, the index page is also full, so we split the index page:

Left Index Page	Right Index Page	New Index Page
25 50	75 85	60

The following table illustrates the addition of the record containing 95 to the B+ tree.

Add Record with Key 95

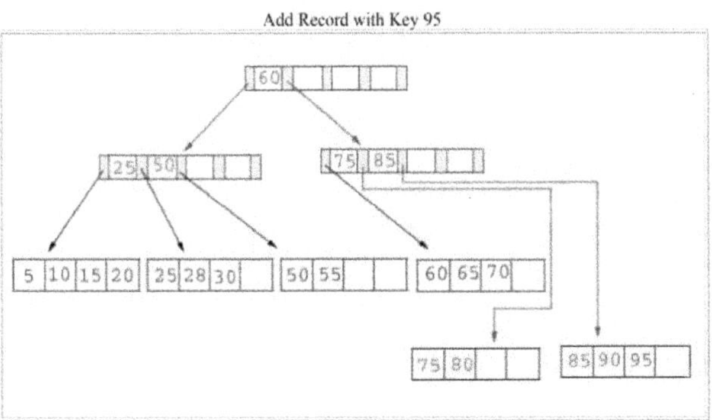

Rotation

B+ trees can incorporate rotation to reduce the number of page splits. A rotation occurs when a leaf page is full, but one of its sibling pages is not full. Rather than splitting the leaf page, we move a record to its sibling, adjusting the indices as necessary. Typically, the left sibling is checked first (if it exists) and then the right sibling. As an example, consider the B+ tree before the addition of the record containing a key of 70. As previously stated this record belongs in the leaf node containing 50 55 60 65. Notice that this node is full, but its left sibling is not.

Add Record with Key 28

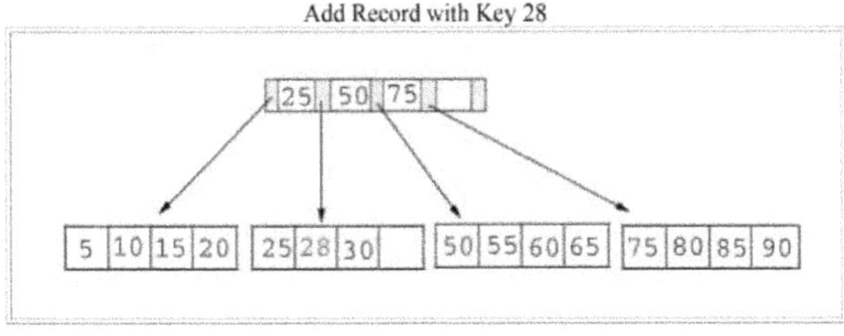

Using rotation we shift the record with the lowest key to its sibling. Since this key appeared in the index page we also modify the index page. The new B+ tree appears in the following table.

Illustration of Rotation

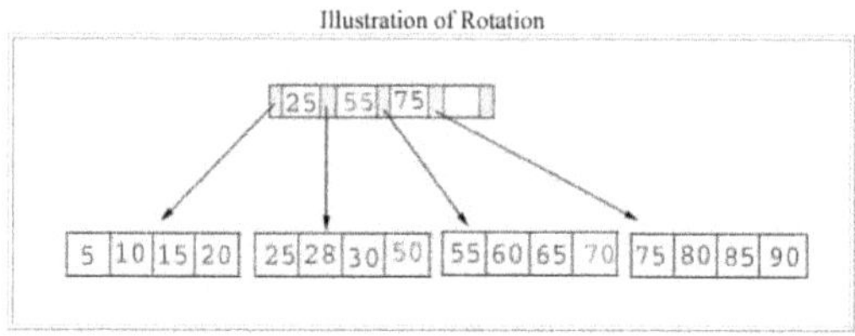

Deleting Keys from a B+ Tree

We must consider three scenarios when we delete a record from a B+ tree. Each scenario causes a different action in the delete algorithm. The scenarios are:

The `delete` algorithm for B+ Trees

Leaf Page Below Fill Factor	Index Page Below Fill Factor	Action
NO	NO	Delete the record from the leaf page. Arrange keys in ascending order to fill void. If the key of the deleted record appears in the index page, use the next key to replace it.
YES	NO	Combine the leaf page and its sibling. Change the index page to reflect the change.
YES	YES	1. Combine the leaf page and its sibling. 2. Adjust the index page to reflect the change. 3. Combine the index page with its sibling. Continue combining index pages until you reach a page with the correct fill factor or you reach the root page.

As our example, we consider the B+ tree after we added 95 as a key. As a refresher this tree is printed in the following table.

Add Record with Key 95

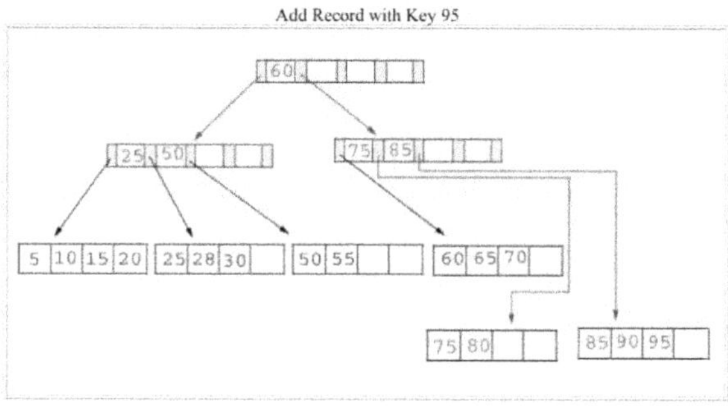

Delete 70 from the B+ Tree

We begin by deleting the record with key 70 from the B+ tree. This record is in a leaf page containing 60, 65 and 70. This page will contain 2 records after the deletion. Since our fill factor is 50% or (2 records) we simply delete 70 from the leaf node. The following table shows the B+ tree after the deletion.

Delete Record with Key 70

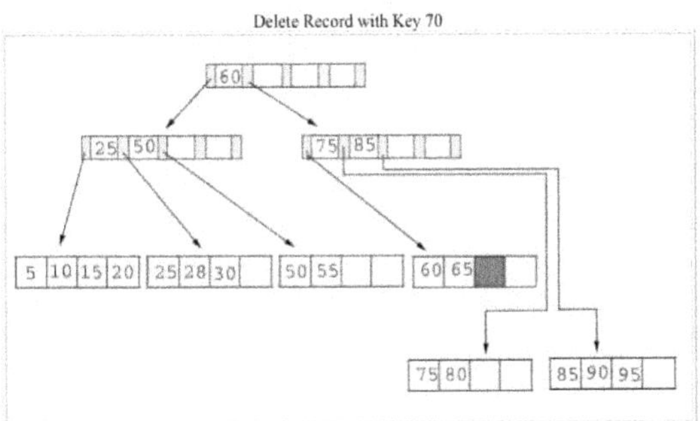

Delete 25 from the B+ Tree

Next, we delete the record containing 25 from the B+ tree. This record is found in the leaf node containing 25, 28, and 30. The fill factor will be 50% after the deletion; however, 25 appears in the index page. Thus, when we delete 25 we must replace it with 28 in the index page. The following table shows the B+ tree after this deletion.

Delete Record with Key 25

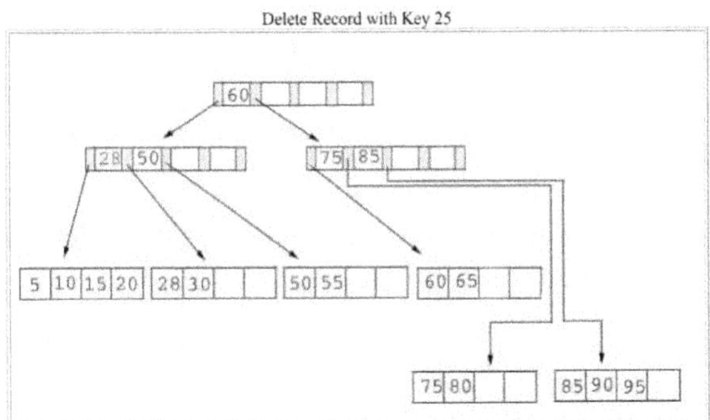

Delete 60 from the B+ Tree

As our last example, we're going to delete 60 from the B+ tree. This deletion is interesting for several resasons: The leaf page containing 60 (60 65) will be below the fill factor after the deletion. Thus, we must combine leaf pages. 1. With recombined pages, the index page will be reduced by one key. Hence, it will also fall below the fill factor. Thus, we must combine index pages. 2. 3. Sixty appears as the only key in the root index page. Obviously, it will be removed with the deletion. The following table shows the B+ tree after the deletion of 60. Notice that the tree contains a single index page.

Delete Record with Key 60

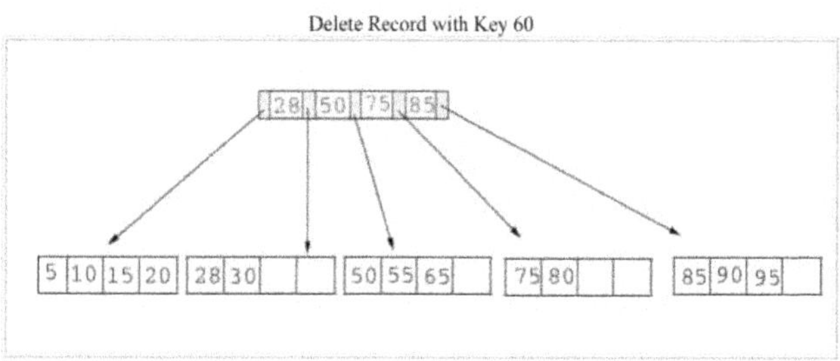

7.12. Heap

Heap data structure is a specialized binary tree based data structure. Heap is a binary tree with special characteristics. In a heap data structure, nodes are arranged based on thier value. A heap data structure, some time called as Binary Heap.

There are two types of heap data structures and they are as follows.

- Max Heap
- Min Heap

Every heap data structure has the following properties...

Property #1 (Ordering): Nodes must be arranged in a order according to values based on Max heap or Min heap.

Property #2 (Structural): All levels in a heap must full, except last level and nodes must be filled from left to right strictly.

Max heap data structure is a specialized full binary tree data structure except last leaf node can be alone. In a max heap nodes are arranged based on node value.

Max heap is defined as follows...

Max heap is a specialized full binary tree in which every parent node contains greater or equal value than its child nodes. And last leaf node can be alone.

Example

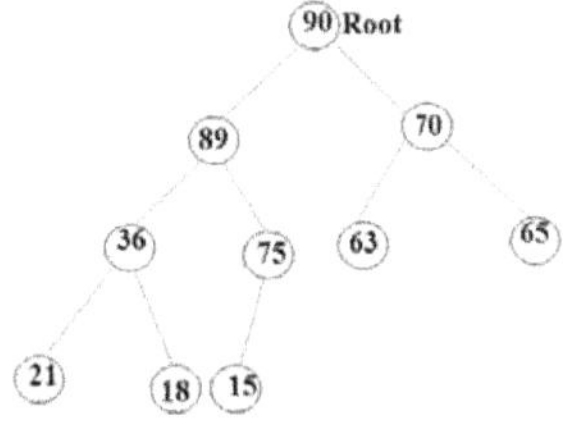

Above tree is satisfying both Ordering property and Structural property according to the Max Heap data structure.

Operations on Max Heap

The following operations are performed on a Max heap data structure...

- Finding Maximum
- Insertion
- Deletion

Finding Maximum Value Operation in Max Heap

Finding the node which has maximum value in a max heap is very simple. In max heap, the root node has the maximum value than all other nodes in the max heap. So, directly we can display root node value as maximum value in max heap.

Insertion Operation in Max Heap

Insertion Operation in max heap is performed as follows.

Step 1: Insert the newNode as last leaf from left to right.

Step 2: Compare newNode value with its Parent node.

Step 3: If newNode value is greater than its parent, then swap both of them.

Step 4: Repeat step 2 and step 3 until newNode value is less than its parent nede (or) newNode reached to root.

Example

Consider the above max heap. Insert a new node with value 85.

Step 1: Insert the newNode with value 85 as last leaf from left to right. That means newNode is added as a right child of node with value 75. After adding max heap is as follows:

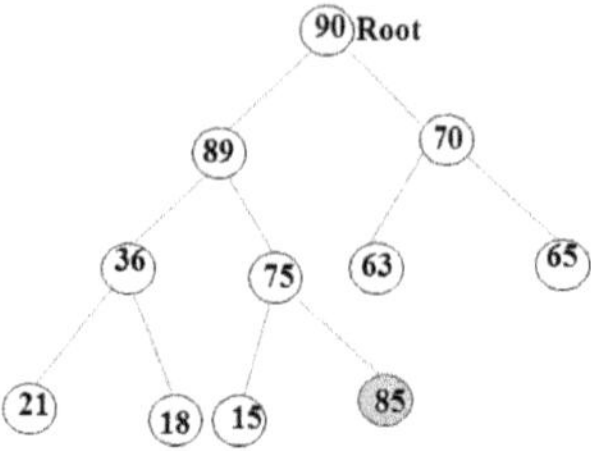

Step 2: Compare newNode value (85) with its Parent node value (75). That means 85 > 75.

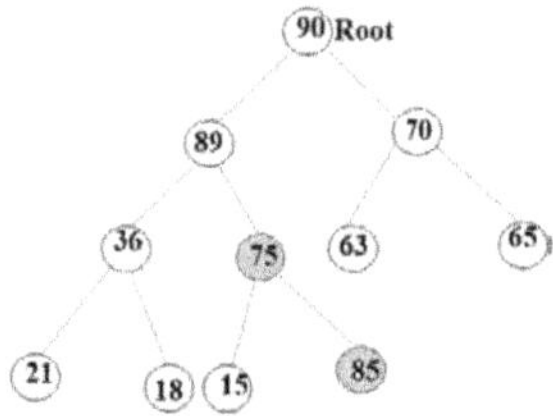

Step 3: Here new Node value (85) is greater than its parent value (75), then swap both of them. After swapping, max heap is as follows.

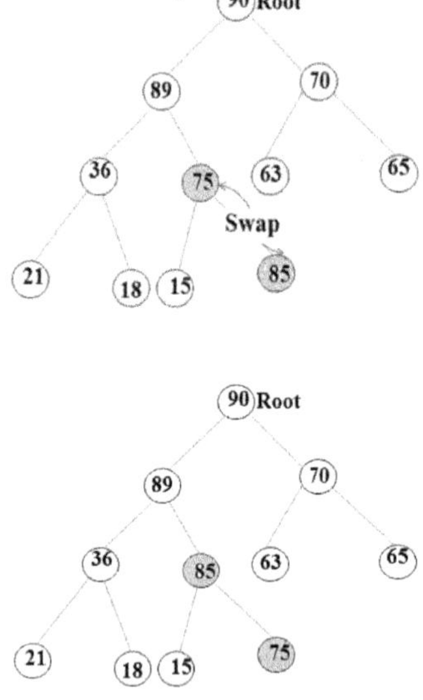

Step 4: Now, again compare newNode value (85) with its parent nede value (89).

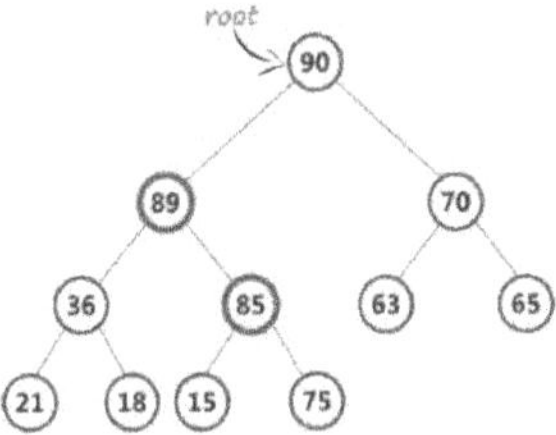

Here, newNode value (85) is smaller than its parent node value (89). So, we stop insertion process. Finally, max heap after insetion of a new node with value 85 is as follows

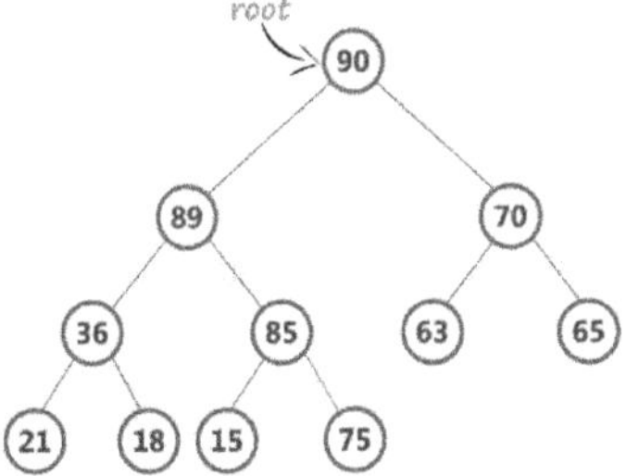

Deletion Operation in Max Heap

In a max heap, deleting last node is very simple as it is not disturbing max heap properties.

Deleting root node from a max heap is title difficult as it disturbing the max heap properties. We use the following steps to delete root node from a max heap...

Step 1: Swap the root node with last node in max heap

Step 2: Delete last node.

Step 3: Now, compare root value with its left child value.

Step 4: If root value is smaller than its left child, then compare left child with its right sibling. Else goto Step 6

Step 5: If left child value is larger than its right sibling, then swap root with left child. otherwise swap root with its right child.

Step 6: If root value is larger than its left child, then compare root value with its right child value.

Step 7: If root value is smaller than its right child, then swap root with rith child. otherwise stop the process.

Step 8: Repeat the same until root node is fixed at its exact position.

Example

Consider the above max heap. Delete root node (90) from the max heap.

Step 1: Swap the root node (90) with last node 75 in max heap After swapping max heap is as follows...

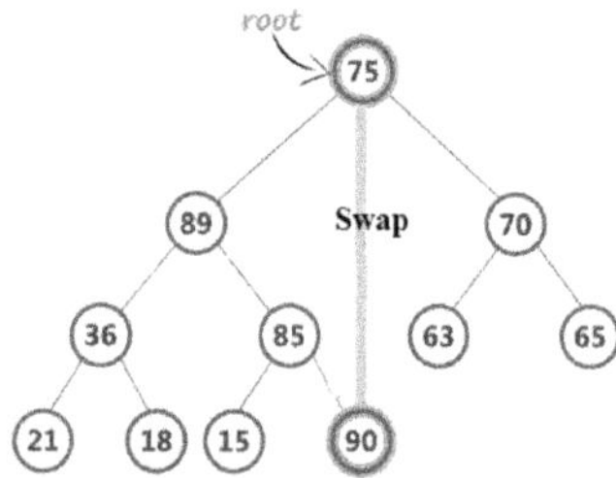

Step 2: Delete last node. Here node with value 90. After deleting node with value 90 from heap, max heap is as follows.

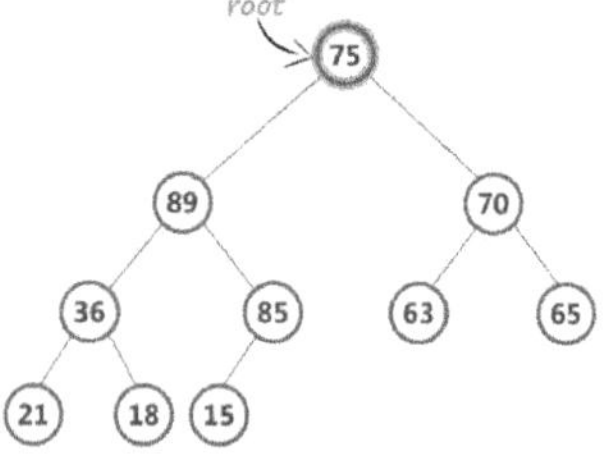

Step 3: Compare root node (75) with its left child (89).

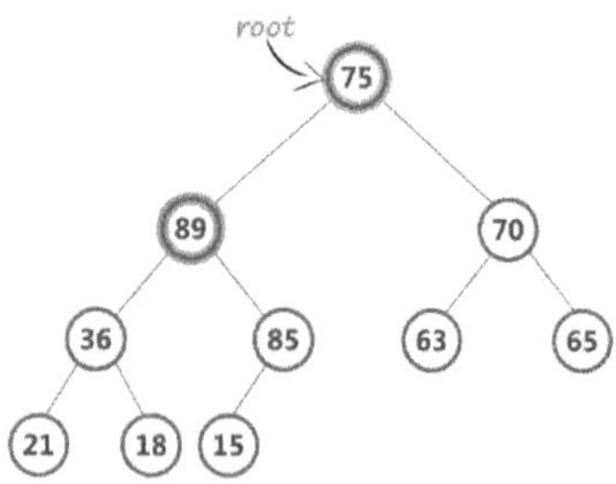

Here, root value (75) is smaller than its left child value (89). So, compare left child (89) with its right sibling (70).

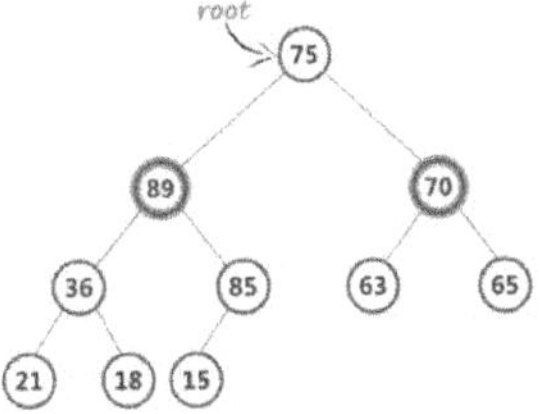

Step 4: Here, left child value (89) is larger than its right sibling (70), So, swap root (75) with left child (89).

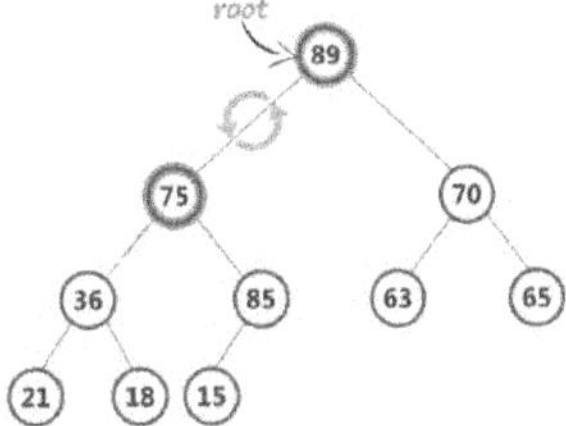

Step 5: Now, again compare 75 with its left child (36).

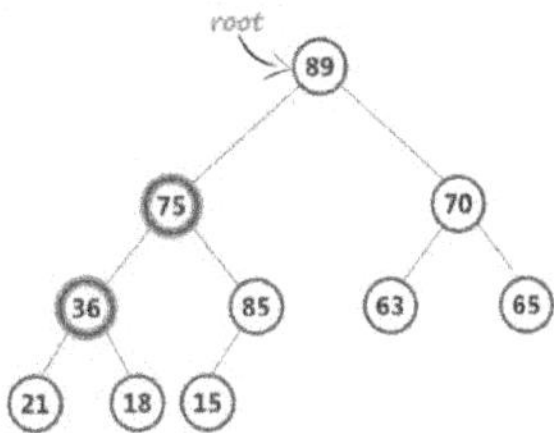

Here, node with value 75 is larger than its left child. So, we compare node with value 75 is compared with its right child 85.

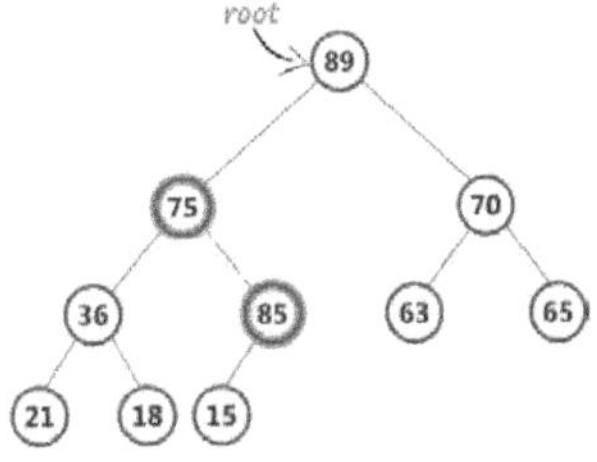

Step 6: Here, node with value 75 is smaller than its right child (85). So, we swap both of them. After swapping max heap is as follows.

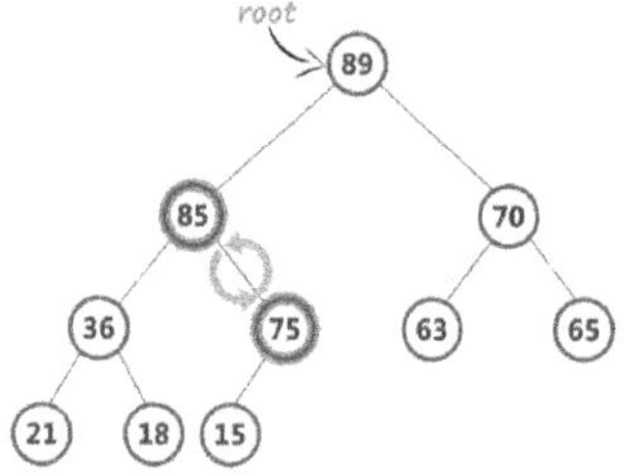

Step 7: Now, compare node with value 75 with its left child (15).

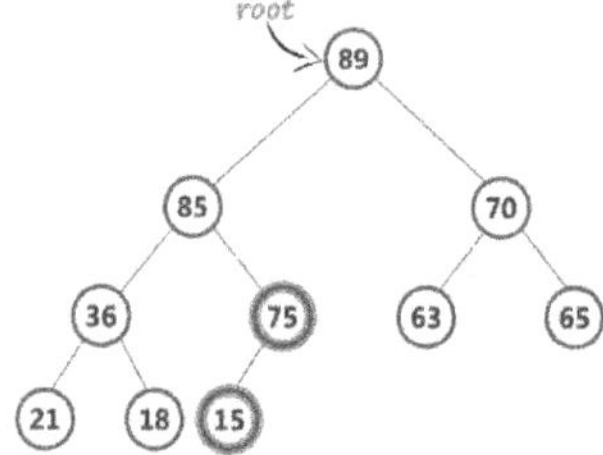

Here, node with value 75 is larger than its left child (15) and it does not have right child. So we stop the process.

Finally, max heap after deleting root node (90) is as follows...

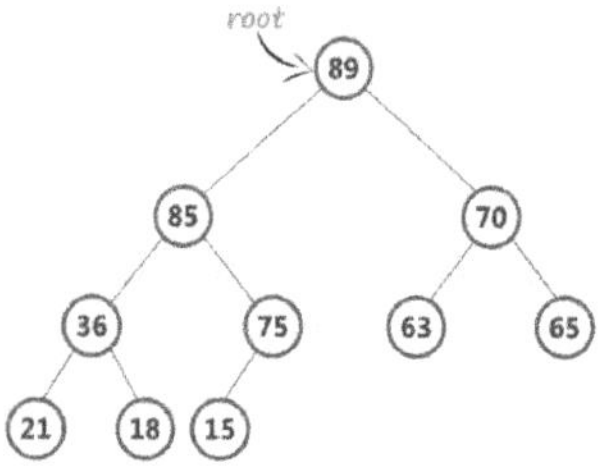

PART IV

- Definition – Representation of Graph
- Types of graph
- Breadth-first traversal
- Depth-first traversal
- Topological Sort
- Bi-connectivity
- Cut vertex
- Euler circuits
- Applications of graphs

CHAPTER 8

Non Linear Data Structures - Graphs

Definition – Representation of Graph – Types of graph - Breadth-first traversal - Depth-first traversal – Topological Sort – Bi-connectivity – Cut vertex – Euler circuits – Applications of graphs.

8.1. Definition

- Graph is a nonlinear data structure.
- It contains a set of points known as nodes (or vertices) and set of links known as edges (or Arcs) which connects the vertices.
- Generally, a graph G is represented as G = (V , E), where V is set of vertices and E is set of edges.

Example

The following is a graph with 5 vertices and 6 edges.

This graph G can be defined as G = (V , E)

Where V = {A,B,C,D,E} and E = {(A,B),(A,C)(A,D),(B,D),(C,D),(B,E),(E,D)}.

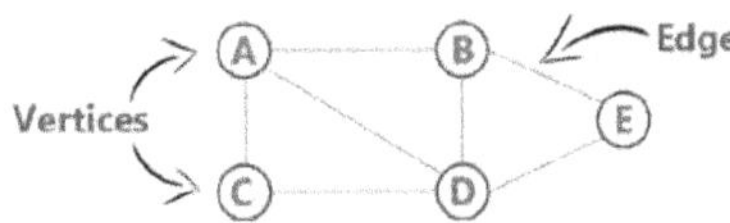

8.2. Graph Terminology

We use the following terms in graph data structure...

Vertex

A individual data element of a graph is called as Vertex. **Vertex** is also known as **node.** In above example graph, A, B, C, D & E are known as vertices.

Edge

An edge is a connecting link between two vertices. **Edge** is also known as **Arc**. An edge is represented as (startingVertex, endingVertex). For example, in above graph, the link between vertices A and B is represented as (A,B). In above example graph, there are 7 edges (i.e., (A,B), (A,C), (A,D), (B,D), (B,E), (C,D), (D,E)).

Edges are three types:

Undirected Edge - An undirected egde is a bidirectional edge. If there is a undirected edge between vertices A and B then edge (A , B) is equal to edge (B , A).

Directed Edge - A directed egde is a unidirectional edge. If there is a directed edge between vertices A and B then edge (A , B) is not equal to edge (B , A).

Weighted Edge - A weighted egde is an edge with cost on it.

Undirected Graph

A graph with only undirected edges is said to be undirected graph.

Directed Graph

A graph with only directed edges is said to be directed graph.

Mixed Graph

A graph with undirected and directed edges is said to be mixed graph.

End vertices or Endpoints

The two vertices joined by an edge are called the end vertices (or endpoints) of the edge.

Origin

If an edge is directed, its first endpoint is said to be origin of it.

Destination

If an edge is directed, its first endpoint is said to be origin of it and the other endpoint is said to be the destination of the edge.

Adjacent

If there is an edge between vertices A and B then both A and B are said to be adjacent. In other words, Two vertices A and B are said to be adjacent if there is an edge whose end vertices are A and B.

Incident

An edge is said to be incident on a vertex if the vertex is one of the endpoints of that edge.

Outgoing Edge

A directed edge is said to be outgoing edge on its orign vertex.

Incoming Edge

A directed edge is said to be incoming edge on its destination vertex.

Degree

Total number of edges connected to a vertex is said to be degree of that vertex.

Indegree

Total number of incoming edges connected to a vertex is said to be indegree of that vertex.

Outdegree

Total number of outgoing edges connected to a vertex is said to be outdegree of that vertex.

Parallel Edges or Multiple Edges

If there are two undirected edges to have the same end vertices, and for two directed edges to have the same origin and the same destination. Such edges are called parallel edges or multiple edges.

Self-Loop

An edge (undirected or directed) is a self-loop if its two endpoints coincide.

Simple Graph

A graph is said to be simple if there are no parallel and self-loop edges.

Path

A path is a sequence of alternating vertices and edges that starts at a vertex and ends at a vertex such that each edge is incident to its predecessor and successor vertex.

8.3. Graph Representations

Graph data structure is represented using following representations...

- Adjacency Matrix
- Adjacency List

8.3.1. Adjacency Matrix

Adjacency Matrix is a 2D array of size V x V where V is the number of vertices in a graph. Let the 2D array be adj[][], a slot adj[i][j] = 1 indicates that there is an edge from vertex i to vertex j. Adjacency matrix for undirected graph is always symmetric. Adjacency Matrix is also used to represent weighted graphs. If adj[i][j] = w, then there is an edge from vertex i to vertex j with weight w.

For example, consider the following undirected graph representation...

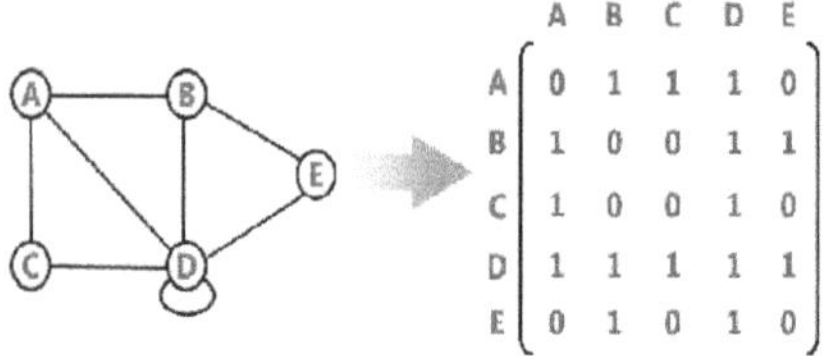

Directed graph representation...

	A	B	C	D	E
A	0	1	1	0	0
B	0	0	0	1	1
C	0	0	0	1	0
D	1	0	0	1	1
E	0	0	0	0	0

8.3.2. Adjacency List

An array of linked lists is used. Size of the array is equal to number of vertices. Let the array be array[]. An entry array[i] represents the linked list of vertices adjacent to the *i*th vertex. This representation can also be used to represent a weighted graph. The weights of edges can be stored in nodes of linked lists. Following is adjacency list representation of the above graph.

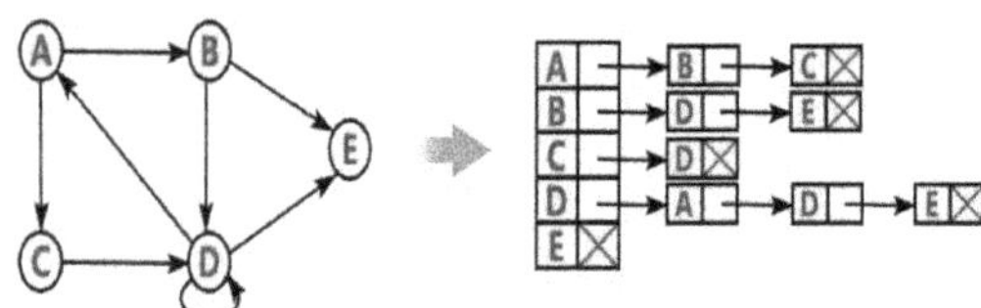

8.4. Types of Graphs

There are various types of graphs depending upon the number of vertices, number of edges, interconnectivity, and their overall structure. We will discuss only a certain few important types of graphs in this chapter.

8.4.1. Null Graph

A **graph having no edges** is called a Null Graph.

Example

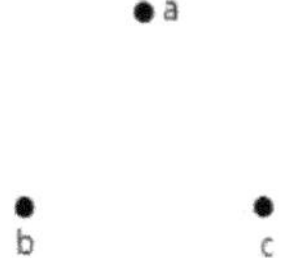

In the above graph, there are three vertices named 'a', 'b', and 'c', but there are no edges among them. Hence it is a Null Graph.

8.4.2. Trivial Graph

A **graph with only one vertex** is called a Trivial Graph.

Example

In the above shown graph, there is only one vertex 'a' with no other edges. Hence it is a Trivial graph.

8.4.3. Non-Directed Graph

A non-directed graph contains edges but the edges are not directed ones.

Example

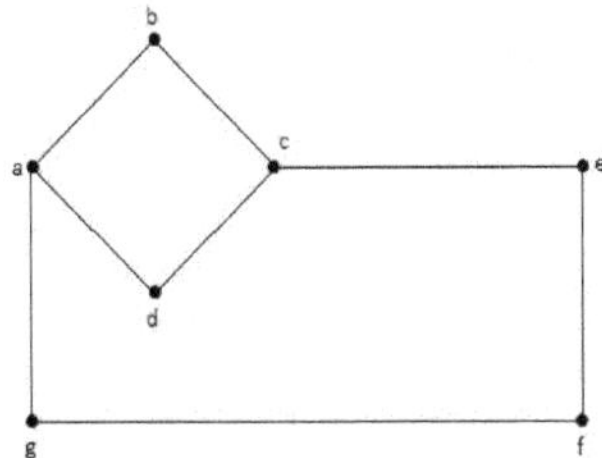

In this graph, 'a', 'b', 'c', 'd', 'e', 'f', 'g' are the vertices, and 'ab', 'bc', 'cd', 'da', 'ag', 'gf', 'ef' are the edges of the graph. Since it is a non-directed graph, the edges 'ab' and 'ba' are same. Similarly other edges also considered in the same way.

8.4.4. Directed Graph

In a directed graph, each edge has a direction.

Example

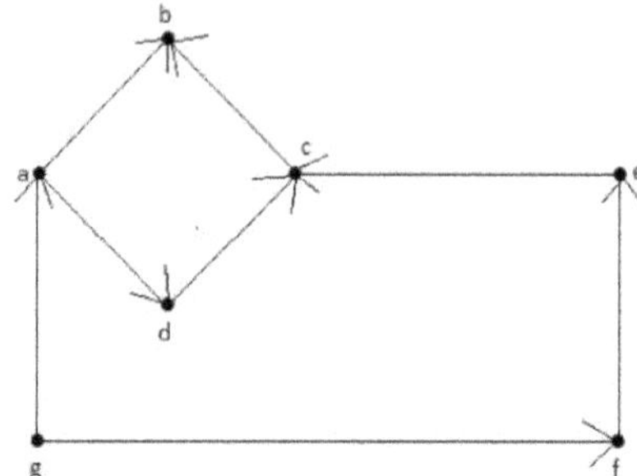

In the above graph, we have seven vertices 'a', 'b', 'c', 'd', 'e', 'f', and 'g', and eight edges 'ab', 'cb', 'dc', 'ad', 'ec', 'fe', 'gf', and 'ga'. As it is a directed graph, each edge bears an arrow mark that shows its direction. Note that in a directed graph, 'ab' is different from 'ba'.

8.4.5. Simple Graph

A graph **with no loops** and **no parallel edges** is called a simple graph.

- The maximum number of edges possible in a single graph with 'n' vertices is ${}^{n}C_2$ where ${}^{n}C_2 = n(n - 1)/2$.
- The number of simple graphs possible with 'n' vertices = $2^{{}^{n}c_2} = 2^{n(n-1)/2}$.

Example

In the following graph, there are 3 vertices with 3 edges which is maximum excluding the parallel edges and loops. This can be proved by using the above formulae.

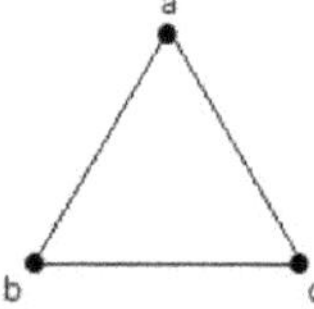

The maximum number of edges with n=3 vertices:

$${}^{n}C_2 = n(n-1)/2$$
$$= 3(3-1)/2$$
$$= 6/2$$
$$= 3 \text{ edges}$$

The maximum number of simple graphs with n=3 vertices:

$$2^{{}^{n}C_2} = 2^{n(n-1)/2}$$

$$= 2^{3(3-1)/2}$$

$$= 2^3$$

$$= 8$$

These 8 graphs are as shown below:

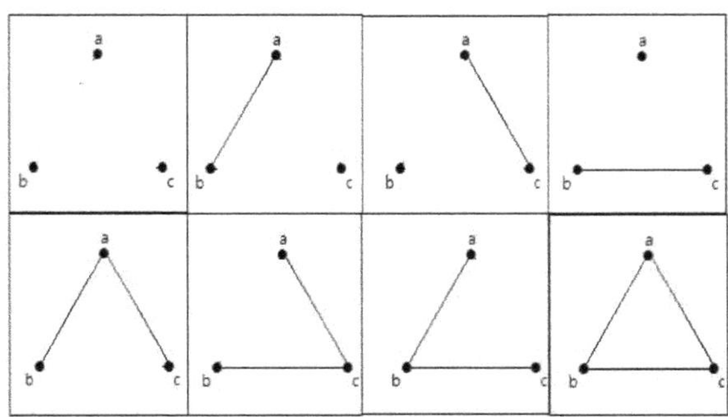

8.4.6. Connected Graph

A graph G is said to be connected **if there exists a path between every pair of vertices.** There should be at least one edge for every vertex in the graph. So that we can say that it is connected to some other vertex at the other side of the edge.

Example

In the following graph, each vertex has its own edge connected to other edge. Hence it is a connected graph.

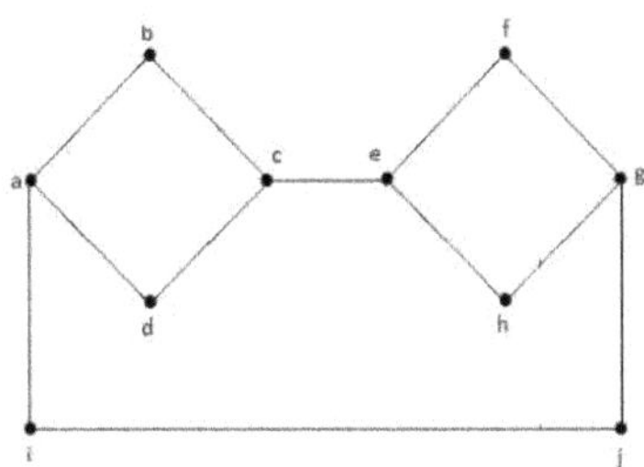

8.4.7. Disconnected Graph

A graph G is disconnected, if it does not contain at least two connected vertices.

Example 1

The following graph is an example of a Disconnected Graph, where there are two components, one with 'a', 'b', 'c', 'd' vertices and another with 'e', 'f', 'g', 'h' vertices.

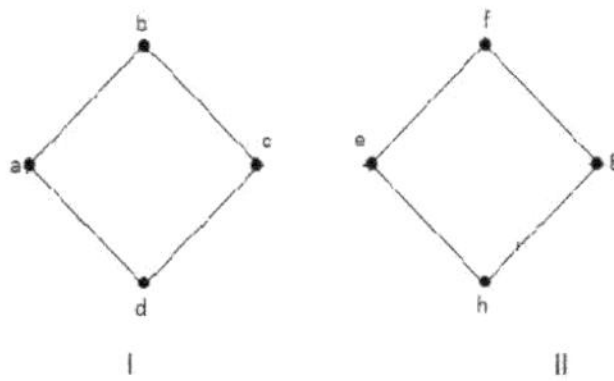

The two components are independent and not connected to each other. Hence it is called disconnected graph.

Example 2

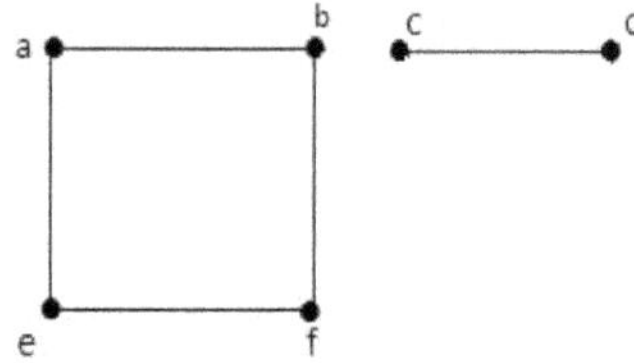

In this example, there are two independent components, a-b-f-e and c-d, which are not connected to each other. Hence this is a disconnected graph.

8.4.8. Regular Graph

A graph G is said to be regular, **if all its vertices have the same degree**. In a graph, if the degree of each vertex is 'k', then the graph is called a 'k-regular graph'.

Example

In the following graphs, all the vertices have the same degree. So these graphs are called regular graphs.

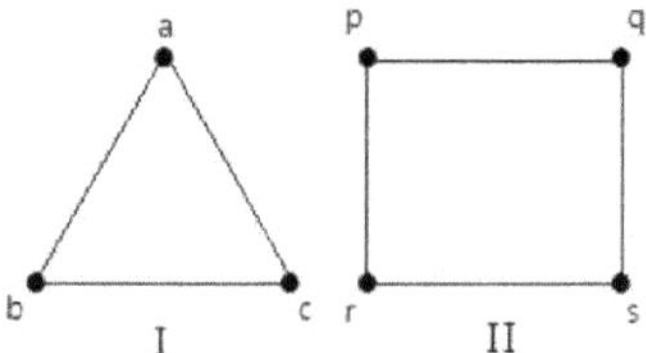

In both the graphs, all the vertices have degree 2. They are called 2-Regular Graphs.

8.4.9.Complete Graph

A simple graph with 'n' mutual vertices is called a complete graph and it is **denoted by 'K_n'**. In the graph, **a vertex should have edges with all other vertices,** then it called a complete graph.

In other words, if a vertex is connected to all other vertices in a graph, then it is called a complete graph.

Example

In the following graphs, each vertex in the graph is connected with all the remaining vertices in the graph except by itself.

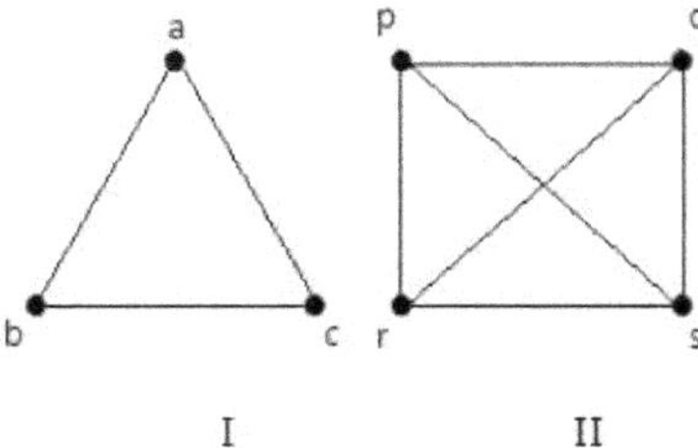

I II

In graph I,

	a	b	c
a	Not Connected	Connected	Connected
b	Connected	Not Connected	Connected
c	Connected	Connected	Not Connected

In graph II,

	p	q	r	s
p	Not Connected	Connected	Connected	Connected
q	Connected	Not Connected	Connected	Connected
r	Connected	Connected	Not Connected	Connected
s	Connected	Connected	Connected	Not Connected

8.4.10. Cycle Graph

A simple graph with 'n' vertices (n >= 3) and 'n' edges is called a cycle graph if all its edges form a cycle of length 'n'.

If the **degree of each vertex in the graph is two,** then it is called a Cycle Graph.

Notation – C_n

Example

Take a look at the following graphs:

- Graph I has 3 vertices with 3 edges which is forming a cycle 'ab-bc-ca'.
- Graph II has 4 vertices with 4 edges which is forming a cycle 'pq-qs-sr-rp'.
- Graph III has 5 vertices with 5 edges which is forming a cycle 'ik-km-ml-lj-ji'.

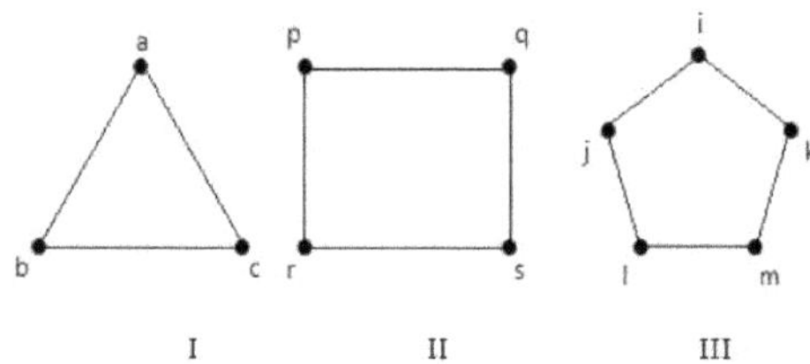

Hence all the given graphs are cycle graphs.

8.4.11. Wheel Graph

A wheel graph is obtained from a cycle graph C_{n-1} by adding a new vertex. That new vertex is called a **Hub** which is connected to all the vertices of C_n.

Notation – W_n

No. of edges in W_n = No. of edges from hub to all other vertices + No. of edges from all other nodes in cycle graph without a hub.

$= (n-1) + (n-1)$

$= 2(n-1)$

Example

Take a look at the following graphs. They are all wheel graphs.

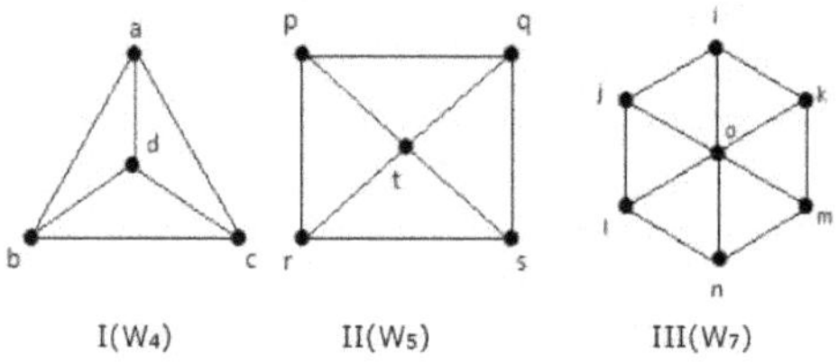

I(W_4) II(W_5) III(W_7)

In graph I, it is obtained from C_3 by adding an vertex at the middle named as 'd'. It is denoted as W_4.

Number of edges in W4 = 2(n-1) = 2(3) = 6

In graph II, it is obtained from C_4 by adding a vertex at the middle named as 't'. It is denoted as W5.

Number of edges in W5 = 2(n-1) = 2(4) = 8

In graph III, it is obtained from C6 by adding a vertex at the middle named as 'o'. It is denoted as W7.

Number of edges in W4 = 2(n-1) = 2(6) = 12

8.4.12. Cyclic Graph

A graph **with at least one** cycle is called a cyclic graph.

Example

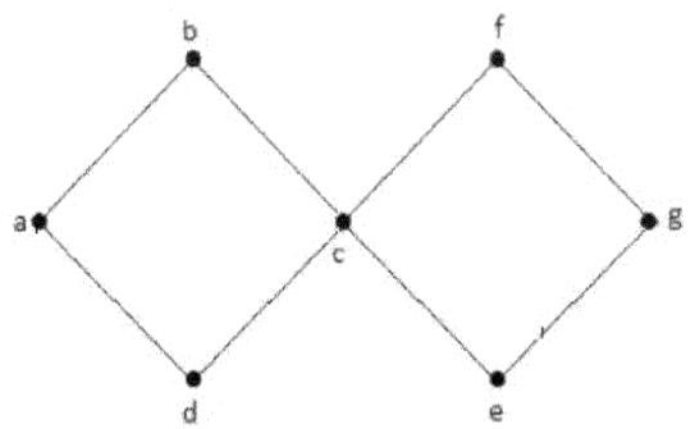

In the above example graph, we have two cycles a-b-c-d-a and c-f-g-e-c. Hence it is called a cyclic graph.

8.4.13. Acyclic Graph

A graph **with no cycles** is called an acyclic graph.

Example

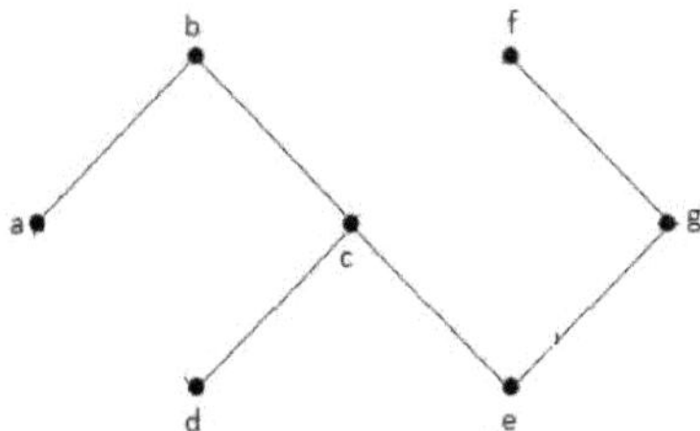

In the above example graph, we do not have any cycles. Hence it is a non-cyclic graph.

8.4.14. Bipartite Graph

A simple graph G = (V, E) with vertex partition V = {V_1, V_2} is called a bipartite graph **if every edge of E joins a vertex in V_1 to a vertex in V_2.**

In general, a Bipertite graph has two sets of vertices, let us say, V_1 and V_2, and if an edge is drawn, it should connect any vertex in set V_1 to any vertex in set V_2.

Example

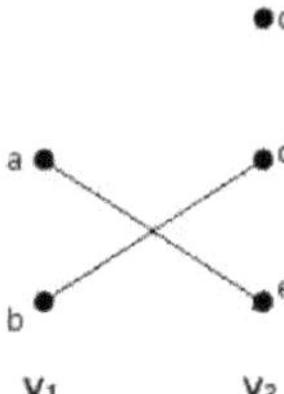

In this graph, you can observe two sets of vertices – V_1 and V_2. Here, two edges named 'ae' and 'bd' are connecting the vertices of two sets V_1 and V_2.

8.4.15. Complete Bipartite Graph

A bipartite graph 'G', G = (V, E) with partition V = {V_1, V_2} is said to be a complete bipartite graph if every vertex in V_1 is connected to every vertex of V_2.

In general, a complete bipartite graph connects each vertex from set V_1 to each vertex from set V_2.

Example

The following graph is a complete bipartite graph because it has edges connecting each vertex from set V_1 to each vertex from set V_2.

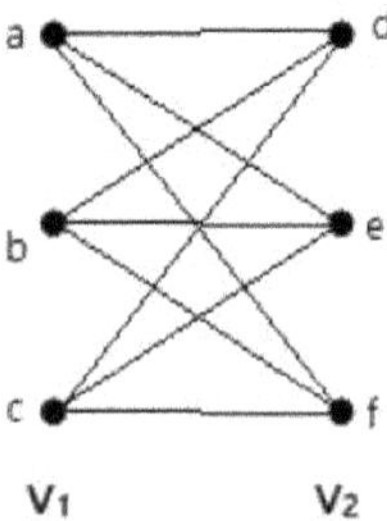

If $|V_1| = m$ and $|V_2| = n$, then the complete bipartite graph is denoted by $K_{m,n}$.

- $K_{m,n}$ has (m+n) vertices and (mn) edges.
- $K_{m,n}$ is a regular graph if m=n.

In general, **a complete bipartite graph is not a complete graph.**

$K_{m,n}$ is a complete graph if m=n=1.

The maximum number of edges in a bipartite graph with **n** vertices is

If n=10, k5, 5= ⌊n^2/4⌋ = ⌊10^2/4⌋ = 25

Similarly K6, 4=24

K7, 3=21

K8, 2=16

K9, 1=9

If n=9, k5, 4 = ⌊n^2/4⌋ = ⌊9^2/4⌋ = 20

Similarly K6, 3=18

K7, 2=14

K8, 1=8

'G' is a bipartite graph if 'G' has no cycles of odd length. A special case of bipartite graph is a **star graph.**

8.4.16. Star Graph

A complete bipartite graph of the form $K_{1, n-1}$ is a star graph with n-vertices. A star graph is a complete bipartite graph if a single vertex belongs to one set and all the remaining vertices belong to the other set.

Example

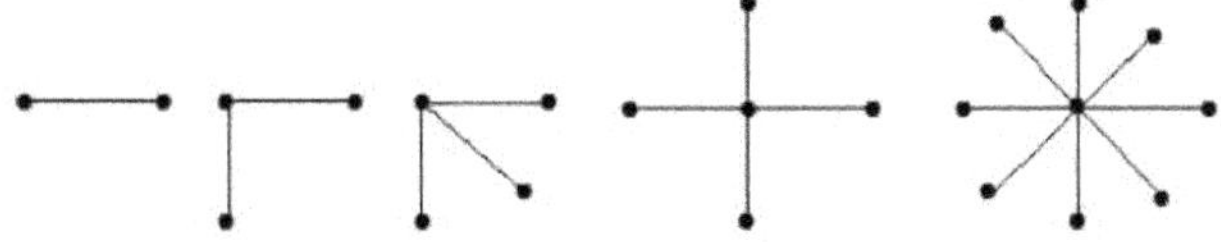

In the above graphs, out of 'n' vertices, all the 'n–1' vertices are connected to a single vertex. Hence it is in the form of $K_{1, n-1}$ which are star graphs.

8.4.17. Complement of a Graph

Let *'G–'* be a simple graph with some vertices as that of 'G' and an edge {U, V} is present in *'G–',* if the edge is not present in G. It means, two vertices are adjacent in *'G–'* if the two vertices are not adjacent in G.

If the edges that exist in graph I are absent in another graph II, and if both graph I and graph II are combined together to form a complete graph, then graph I and graph II are called complements of each other.

Example

In the following example, graph-I has two edges 'cd' and 'bd'. Its complement graph-II has four edges.

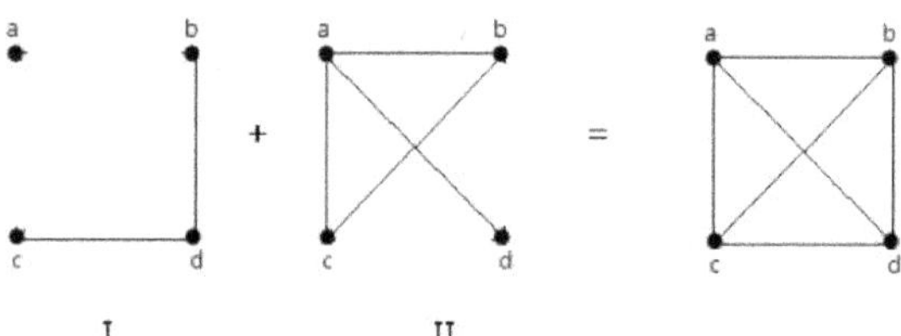

Note that the edges in graph-I are not present in graph-II and vice versa. Hence, the combination of both the graphs gives a complete graph of 'n' vertices.

Note – A combination of two complementary graphs gives a complete graph.

If 'G' is any simple graph, then

$|E(G)| + |E('G-')| = |E(K_n)|$, where n = number of vertices in the graph.

Example

Let 'G' be a simple graph with nine vertices and twelve edges, find the number of edges in *'G-'.*

You have, $|E(G)| + |E('G-')| = |E(K_n)|$

$12 + |E('G-')| =$

$9(9-1) / 2 = {}^9C_2$

$12 + |E('G-')| = 36$

$|E('G-')| = 24$

'G' is a simple graph with 40 edges and its complement 'G−' has 38 edges. Find the number of vertices in the graph G or 'G−'.

Let the number of vertices in the graph be 'n'.

We have, |E(G)| + |E('G-')| = $|E(K_n)|$

40 + 38 = n(n-1)|2|

156 = n(n-1)

13(12) = n(n-1)

n = 13

8.5. Graph Traversals

Graph traversal is technique used for searching a vertex in a graph. The graph traversal is also used to decide the order of vertices to be visit in the search process.

A graph traversal finds the egdes to be used in the search process without creating loops that means using graph traversal we visit all verticces of graph without getting into looping path.

There are two graph traversal techniques and they are as follows...

1. DFS (Depth First Search)
2. BFS (Breadth First Search)

8.5.1. Depth First Search

The DFS algorithm is a recursive algorithm that uses the idea of backtracking. It involves exhaustive searches of all the nodes by going ahead, if possible, else by backtracking.

Here, the word backtrack means that when you are moving forward and there are no more nodes along the current path, you move backwards on the same path to find nodes to traverse. All the nodes will be visited on the current path till all the unvisited nodes have been traversed after which the next path will be selected.

This recursive nature of DFS can be implemented using stacks. The basic idea is as follows: Pick a starting node and push all its adjacent nodes into a stack.

Pop a node from stack to select the next node to visit and push all its adjacent nodes into a stack. Repeat this process until the stack is empty.

However, ensure that the nodes that are visited are marked. This will prevent you from visiting the same node more than once.

If you do not mark the nodes that are visited and you visit the same node more than once, you may end up in an infinite loop.

Pseudocode

```
DFS-iterative (G, s):                    //Where G is graph and s is source vertex

    let S be stack

    S.push( s )                          //Inserting s in stack

    mark s as visited.

    while ( S is not empty):

                                         //Pop a vertex from stack to visit next

        v = S.top( )

        S.pop( )

                                         //Push all the neighbours of v in stack that are not visited

        for all neighbours w of v in Graph G:

            if w is not visited :

                S.push( w )

                mark w as visited

DFS-recursive(G, s):

    mark s as visited

    for all neighbours w of s in Graph G:

        if w is not visited:

            DFS-recursive(G, w)
```

Example

Step	Traversal	Description
1	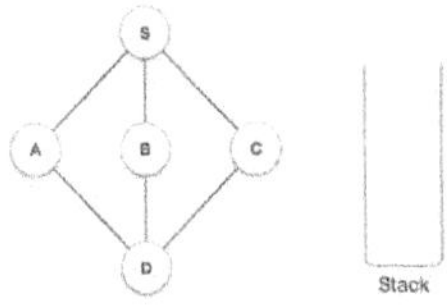	Initialize the stack.
2	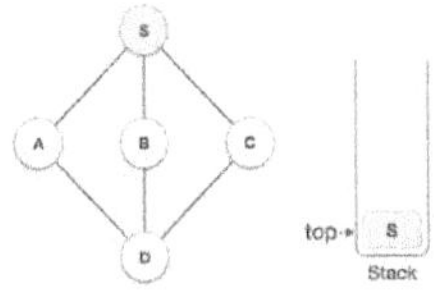	Mark **S** as visited and put it onto the stack. Explore any unvisited adjacent node from **S**. We have three nodes and we can pick any of them. For this example, we shall take the node in an alphabetical order.
3	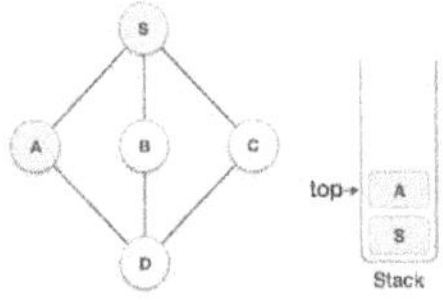	Mark **A** as visited and put it onto the stack. Explore any unvisited adjacent node from A. Both **S**and **D** are adjacent to **A** but we are concerned for unvisited nodes only.
4	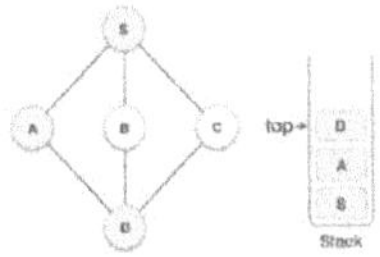	Visit **D** and mark it as visited and put onto the stack. Here, we have **B** and **C** nodes, which are adjacent to **D** and both are unvisited. However, we shall again choose in an alphabetical order.
5	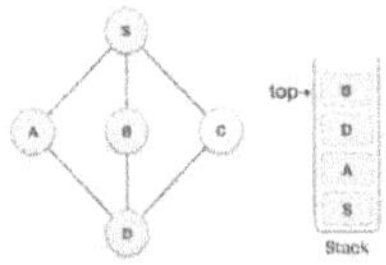	We choose **B**, mark it as visited and put onto the stack. Here **B**does not have any unvisited adjacent node. So, we pop **B**from the stack.
6	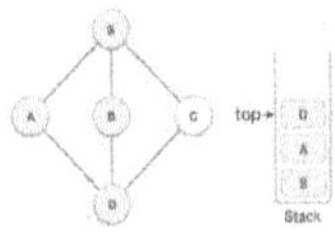	We check the stack top for return to the previous node and check if it has any unvisited nodes. Here, we find **D** to be on the top of the stack.
7	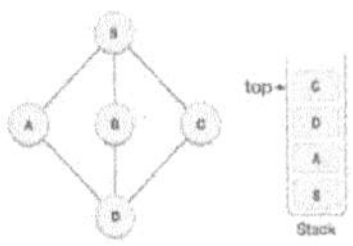	Only unvisited adjacent node is from **D** is **C** now. So we visit **C**, mark it as visited and put it onto the stack.

As **C** does not have any unvisited adjacent node so we keep popping the stack until we find a node that has an unvisited adjacent node. In this case, there's none and we keep popping until the stack is empty.

Implementation in C

```
#include <stdio.h>
#include <stdlib.h>
/*      ADJACENCY MATRIX                    */
int source,V,E,time,visited[20],G[20][20];
void DFS(int i)
{
        int j;
        visited[i]=1;
        printf(" %d->",i+1);
        for(j=0;j<V;j++)
        {
                if(G[i][j]==1&&visited[j]==0)
                        DFS(j);
        }
}
int main()
{
        int i,j,v1,v2;
        printf("\t\t\tGraphs\n");
        printf("Enter the no of edges:");
        scanf("%d",&E);
        printf("Enter the no of vertices:");
        scanf("%d",&V);
        for(i=0;i<V;i++)
        {
                for(j=0;j<V;j++)
                        G[i][j]=0;
        }
        /*  creating edges :P   */
```

```
        for(i=0;i<E;i++)
        {
                printf("Enter the edges (format: V1 V2) : ");
                scanf("%d%d",&v1,&v2);
                G[v1-1][v2-1]=1;
        }

        for(i=0;i<V;i++)
        {
                for(j=0;j<V;j++)
                printf(" %d ",G[i][j]);
                printf("\n");
        }
        printf("Enter the source: ");
        scanf("%d",&source);
        DFS(source-1);
        return 0;
}
```

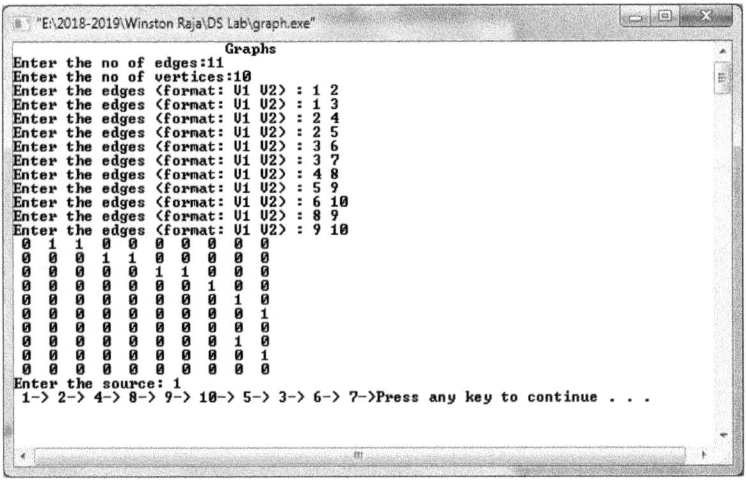

```
"E:\2018-2019\Winston Raja\DS Lab\graph.exe"
                              Graphs
Enter the no of edges:11
Enter the no of vertices:10
Enter the edges (format: V1 V2) : 1 2
Enter the edges (format: V1 V2) : 1 3
Enter the edges (format: V1 V2) : 2 4
Enter the edges (format: V1 V2) : 2 5
Enter the edges (format: V1 V2) : 3 6
Enter the edges (format: V1 V2) : 3 7
Enter the edges (format: V1 V2) : 4 8
Enter the edges (format: V1 V2) : 5 9
Enter the edges (format: V1 V2) : 6 10
Enter the edges (format: V1 V2) : 8 9
Enter the edges (format: V1 V2) : 9 10
 0  1  1  0  0  0  0  0  0  0
 0  0  0  1  1  0  0  0  0  0
 0  0  0  0  0  1  1  0  0  0
 0  0  0  0  0  0  0  1  0  0
 0  0  0  0  0  0  0  0  1  0
 0  0  0  0  0  0  0  0  0  1
 0  0  0  0  0  0  0  0  0  0
 0  0  0  0  0  0  0  0  1  0
 0  0  0  0  0  0  0  0  0  1
 0  0  0  0  0  0  0  0  0  0
Enter the source: 1
 1-> 2-> 4-> 8-> 9-> 10-> 5-> 3-> 6-> 7->Press any key to continue . . .
```

8.5.2. Breadth First Search

There are many ways to traverse graphs. BFS is the most commonly used approach.

BFS is a traversing algorithm where we start traversing from a selected node (source or starting node) and traverse the graph layerwise thus exploring the neighbour nodes (nodes which are directly connected to source node).

We must then move towards the next-level neighbour nodes.

As the name BFS suggests,

1. First move horizontally and visit all the nodes of the current layer
2. Move to the next layer

To make this process easy, use a queue to store the node and mark it as 'visited' until all its neighbours (vertices that are directly connected to it) are marked.

The queue follows the First In First Out (FIFO) queuing method, and therefore, the neigbors of the node will be visited in the order in which they were inserted in the node i.e. the node that was inserted first will be visited first, and so on.

Pseudocode

```
BFS (G, s)                  //Where G is the graph and s is the source node
    let Q be queue.
    Q.enqueue( s )    //Inserting s in queue until all its neighbour vertices are marked.

    mark s as visited.
    while ( Q is not empty)
                                //Removing that vertex from queue,whose neighbour will be visited
                                                                              now
     v  =  Q.dequeue( )

     //processing all the neighbours of v
     for all neighbours w of v in Graph G
         if w is not visited
                Q.enqueue( w )     //Stores w in Q to further visit its neighbour
                mark w as visited.
```

Example

Step	Traversal	Description
1	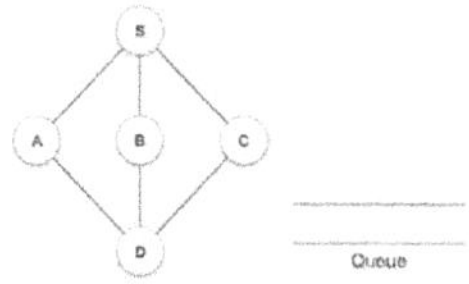	Initialize the queue.
2	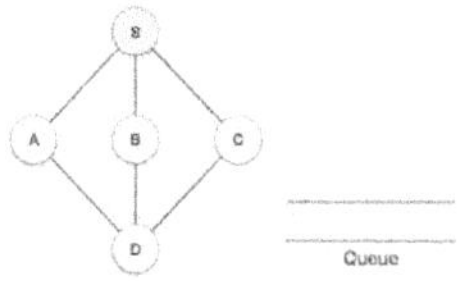	We start from visiting **S**(starting node), and mark it as visited.
3	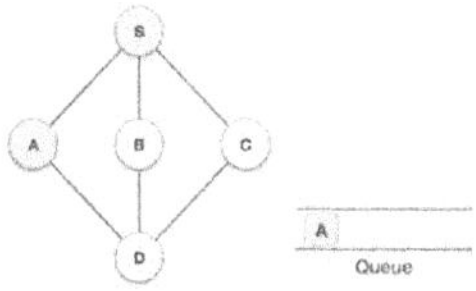	We then see an unvisited adjacent node from **S**. In this example, we have three nodes but alphabetically we choose **A**, mark it as visited and enqueue it.
4	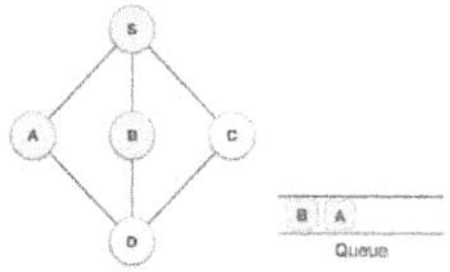	Next, the unvisited adjacent node from **S** is **B**. We mark it as visited and enqueue it.
5	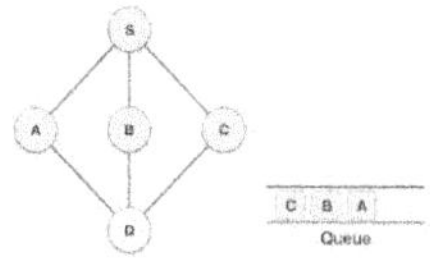	Next, the unvisited adjacent node from **S** is **C**. We mark it as visited and enqueue it.
6	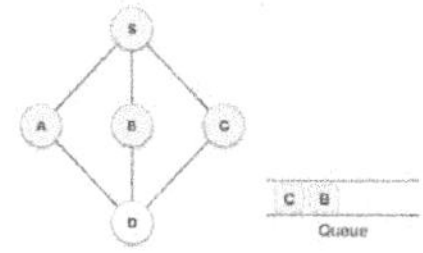	Now, **S** is left with no unvisited adjacent nodes. So, we dequeue and find **A**.
7	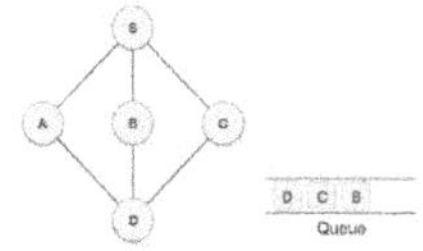	From **A** we have **D** as unvisited adjacent node. We mark it as visited and enqueue it.

At this stage, we are left with no unmarked (unvisited) nodes. But as per the algorithm we keep on dequeuing in order to get all unvisited nodes. When the queue gets emptied, the program is over.

Implementation in C

```
#include<stdio.h>
int G[20][20],q[20],visited[20],n,front = 1, rear = 0 ;
void bfs(int v)
{
	int i;
	visited[v] = 1;
	for(i=1;i<=n;i++)
		if(G[v][i] && !visited[i])
			q[++rear]=i;
	if(front <= rear)
		bfs(q[front++]);
}

int main()
{
	int v,i,j;
	printf("\n Enter the number of vertices:");
	scanf("%d",&n);
	for(i=1;i<=n;i++)
	{
		q[i]=0;
		visited[i]=0;
	}
	printf("\n Enter graph data in matrix form:\n");
	for(i=1;i<=n;i++)
		for(j=1;j<=n;j++)
			scanf("%d",&G[i][j]);
	printf("\n Enter the starting vertex:");
	scanf("%d",&v);
```

```
        bfs(v);
        printf("\n The nodes which are reachable are:\n");
        for(i=1;i<=n;i++)
                if(visited[i])
                        printf("%d\t",i);
                else
                        printf("\n %d is not reachable",i);

        return 0;
}
```

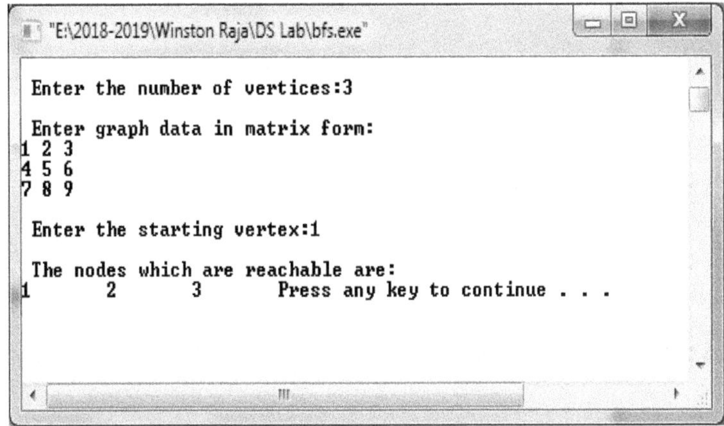

"E:\2018-2019\Winston Raja\DS Lab\bfs.exe"

```
Enter the number of vertices:3

Enter graph data in matrix form:
1 2 3
4 5 6
7 8 9

Enter the starting vertex:1

The nodes which are reachable are:
1       2       3       Press any key to continue . . .
```

8.6. Topological Sorting

8.6.1. Definition

Topological sorting for Directed Acyclic Graph (DAG) is a linear ordering of vertices such that for every directed edge uv, vertex u comes before v in the ordering. Topological Sorting for a graph is not possible if the graph is not a DAG.

For example, a topological sorting of the following graph is "5 4 2 3 1 0". There can be more than one topological sorting for a graph. For example, another topological sorting of the following graph is "4 5 2 3 1 0". The first vertex in topological sorting is always a vertex with in-degree as 0 (a vertex with no in-coming edges).

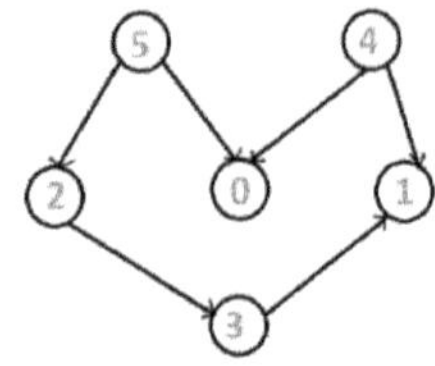

Topological Sort Example

Consider the following graph "D". Find the topological ordering of this graph "G".

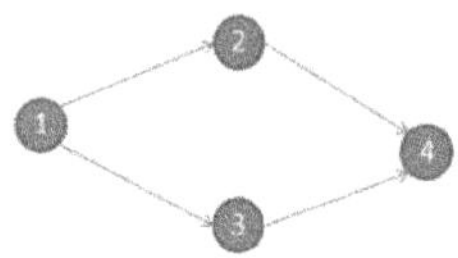

Step 1: Write in-degree of all vertices:

Vertex	in-degree
1	0
2	1
3	1
4	2

Step 2: Write the vertex which has in-degree 0 (zero) in solution. Here vertex 1 has in-degree 0.

So, solution is: 1 -> (not yet completed)

Step 3: Decrease in-degree count of vertices who are adjacent to the vertex which recently added to the solution. Here vertex 1 is recently added to the solution. Vertices 2 and 3 are adjacent to vertex 1. So decrease the in-degree count of those and update.

Updated result is:

Vertex	in-degree
1	Already added to solution
2	0
3	0
4	2

Step 4: Again repeat the same thing which we have done in step1 that is, write the vertices which have in-degree 0 in solution. Here we can observe that two vertices (2 and 3) havein-degree 0 (zero). Add any one vertex into the solution.

Note that, you may add vertex 2 into solution, and I may add vertex 3 to solution. That means the solution to topological sorting is not unique. Now add vertex 3.

Solution is: 1->3->

Step 5: Again decrease the in-degree count of vertices which are adjacent to vertex 3.

Updated result is:

Vertex	in-degree
1	Already added to solution
2	0
3	Already added to solution
4	1

Now add vertex 2 to solution because it only has in-degree 0.

Solution is: 1->3->2->

Updated result is:

Vertex	in-degree
1	Already added to solution
2	Already added to solution
3	Already added to solution
4	0

Finally add 4 to solution.

Final solution is: 1->3->2->4

Program for Topological Sort in C

```
#include <stdio.h>

int main(){
        int i,j,k,n,a[10][10],indeg[10],flag[10],count=0;

        printf("Enter the no of vertices:\n");
```

```
        scanf("%d",&n);

        printf("Enter the adjacency matrix:\n");
        for(i=0;i<n;i++){
                printf("Enter row %d\n",i+1);
                for(j=0;j<n;j++)
                        scanf("%d",&a[i][j]);
        }

        for(i=0;i<n;i++){
  indeg[i]=0;
  flag[i]=0;
}

for(i=0;i<n;i++)
  for(j=0;j<n;j++)
    indeg[i]=indeg[i]+a[j][i];

printf("\nThe topological order is:");

while(count<n){
  for(k=0;k<n;k++){
    if((indeg[k]==0) && (flag[k]==0)){
      printf("%d ",(k+1));
      flag [k]=1;
    }

    for(i=0;i<n;i++){
      if(a[i][k]==1)
        indeg[k]--;
    }
  }

  count++;
```

```
    }

    return 0;
}
```

Output

```
Enter the no of vertices:
4
Enter the adjacency matrix:
Enter row 1
0 1 1 0
Enter row 2
0 0 0 1
Enter row 3
0 0 0 1
Enter row 4
0 0 0 0
The topological order is:1 2 3 4
```

CHAPTER 9

Bi-Connectivity

9.1. Connectivity

Connectivity in an undirected graph means that every vertex can reach every other vertex via any path. If the graph is not connected the graph can be broken down into **Connected Components.**

9.2. Strong Connectivity

Strong Connectivity applies only to directed graphs. A directed graph is strongly connected if there is a **directed path** from any vertex to every other vertex. This is same as connectivity in an undirected graph, the only difference being strong connectivity applies to directed graphs and there should be directed paths instead of just paths. Similar to connected components, a directed graph can be broken down into **Strongly Connected Components.**

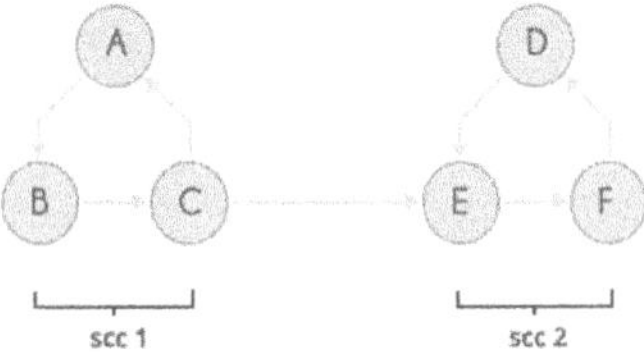

Articulation Point or Cut Vertex

A cut-vertex is a single vertex whose removal disconnects a graph.

In a graph, a vertex is called an **articulation point** if removing it and all the edges associated with it results in the increase of the number of connected components in the graph. For example consider the graph given in following figure.

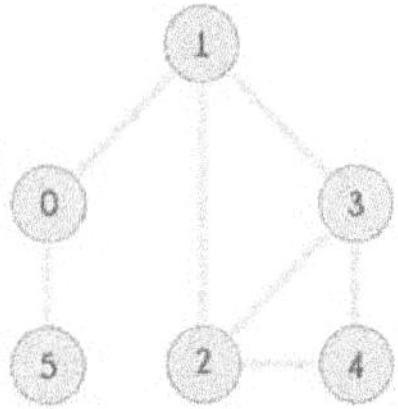

If in the above graph, vertex 1 and all the edges associated with it, i.e. the edges 1-0, 1-2 and 1-3 are removed, there will be no path to reach any of the vertices 2, 3 or 4 from the vertices 0 and 5, that means the graph will split into two separate components. One consisting of the vertices 0 and 5 and another one consisting of the vertices 2, 3 and 4 as shown in the following figure.

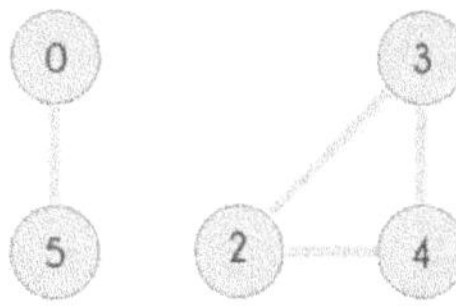

Likewise removing the vertex 0 will disconnect the vertex 5 from all other vertices. Hence the given graph has two articulation points: 0 and 1.

CHAPTER 10

Euler Circuits

10.1. Introduction

Euler Path

An Euler path is a path that uses every edge of a graph exactly once.

Euler Circuit

An Euler circuit is a circuit that uses every edge of a graph exactly once.

An Euler path starts and ends at different vertices. An Euler circuit starts and ends at the same vertex.

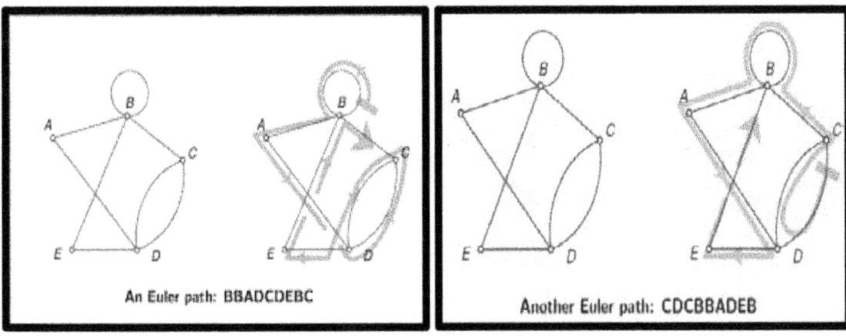

An Euler path: BBADCDEBC

Another Euler path: CDCBBADEB

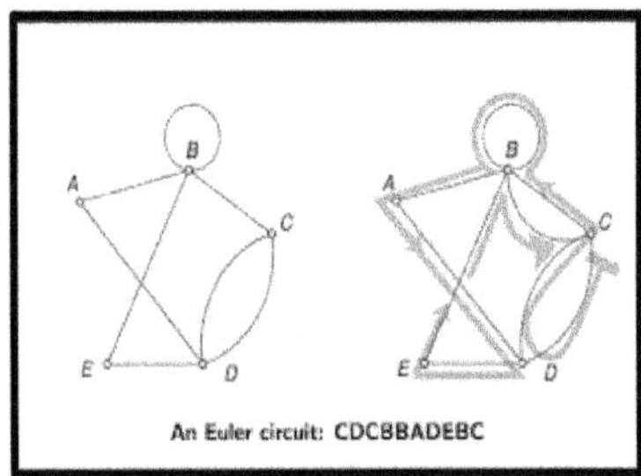

An Euler circuit: CDCBBADEBC

CHAPTER 11

Applications of Graphs

Graphs are nothing but connected nodes(vertex). So any network related, routing, finding relation, path etc related real life applications use graphs.

Since they are powerful abstractions, graphs can be very important in modeling data. In fact, many problems can be reduced to known graph problems. Here we outline just some of the many applications of graphs.

1. Social network graphs: to tweet or not to tweet. Graphs that represent who knows whom, who communicates with whom, who influences whom or other relationships in social structures. An example is the twitter graph of who follows whom. These can be used to determine how information flows, how topics become hot, how communities develop, or even who might be a good match for who, or is that whom.
2. Transportation networks. In road networks vertices are intersections and edges are the road segments between them, and for public transportation networks vertices are stops and edges are the links between them. Such networks are used by many map programs such as Google maps, Bing maps and now Apple IOS 6 maps (well perhaps without the public transport) to find the best routes between locations. They are also used for studying traffic patterns, traffic light timings, and many aspects of transportation.
3. Utility graphs. The power grid, the Internet, and the water network are all examples of graphs where vertices represent connection points, and edges the wires or pipes between them. Analyzing properties of these graphs is very important in understanding the reliability of such utilities under failure or attack, or in minimizing the costs to build infrastructure that matches required demands.
4. Document link graphs. The best known example is the link graph of the web, where each web page is a vertex, and each hyperlink a directed edge. Link graphs are used, for example, to analyze relevance of web pages, the best sources of information, and good link sites.
5. Protein-protein interactions graphs. Vertices represent proteins and edges represent interactions between them that carry out some biological function in the cell. These graphs can be used, for example, to study molecular pathways—chains of molecular

interactions in a cellular process. Humans have over 120K proteins with millions of interactions among them.

6. Network packet traffic graphs. Vertices are IP (Internet protocol) addresses and edges are the packets that flow between them. Such graphs are used for analyzing network security, studying the spread of worms, and tracking criminal or non-criminal activity.
7. Scene graphs. In graphics and computer games scene graphs represent the logical or spacial relationships between objects in a scene. Such graphs are very important in the computer games industry.
8. Finite element meshes. In engineering many simulations of physical systems, such as the flow of air over a car or airplane wing, the spread of earthquakes through the ground, or the structural vibrations of a building, involve partitioning space into discrete elements. The elements along with the connections between adjacent elements forms a graph that is called a finite element mesh.
9. Robot planning. Vertices represent states the robot can be in and the edges the possible transitions between the states. This requires approximating continuous motion as a sequence of discrete steps. Such graph plans are used, for example, in planning paths for autonomous vehicles.
10. Neural networks. Vertices represent neurons and edges the synapses between them. Neural networks are used to understand how our brain works and how connections change when we learn. The human brain has about 1011 neurons and close to 1015 synapses.
11. Graphs in quantum field theory. Vertices represent states of a quantum system and the edges the transitions between them. The graphs can be used to analyze path integrals and summing these up generates a quantum amplitude (yes, I have no idea what that means).
12. Semantic networks. Vertices represent words or concepts and edges represent the relationships among the words or concepts. These have been used in various models of how humans organize their knowledge, and how machines might simulate such an organization.
13. Graphs in epidemiology. Vertices represent individuals and directed edges the transfer of an infectious disease from one individual to another. Analyzing such graphs has become an important component in understanding and controlling the spread of diseases.

14. Graphs in compilers. Graphs are used extensively in compilers. They can be used for type inference, for so called data flow analysis, register allocation and many other purposes. They are also used in specialized compilers, such as query optimization in database languages.
15. Constraint graphs. Graphs are often used to represent constraints among items. For example the GSM network for cell phones consists of a collection of overlapping cells. Any pair of cells that overlap must operate at different frequencies. These constraints can be modeled as a graph where the cells are vertices and edges are placed between cells that overlap.
16. Dependence graphs. Graphs can be used to represent dependences or precedences among items. Such graphs are often used in large projects in laying out what components rely on other components and used to minimize the total time or cost to completion while abiding by the dependences.

PART V

- Sorting
- Searching
- Hashing
- Review Questions with solution

CHAPTER 12

Sorting

12.1. Introduction

A **sorting algorithm** is an algorithm that puts elements of a list in a certain order. It refers to ordering data in an increasing or decreasing fashion according to some linear relationship among the data items. It can be done on names, numbers and records.

For example, it is relatively easy to look up the phone number of a friend from a telephone dictionary because the names in the phone book have been sorted into alphabetical order.

12.2. Types of Sorting

- Internal Sorting
- External Sorting

(i) Internal Sorting

Internal Sorting takes place in the main memory of the computer. It is applicable when the number of elements in the list is small.

E.g. Bubble Sort, Inserting Sort, Shell Sort, Quick Sort.

(ii) External Sorting

External Sorting takes place in the Secondary memory of the computer. It is applicable when the number of elements in the list is large.

E.g. Merge Sort, Multiway Merge Sort.

12.3. Sorting algorithms

- **Insertion sort**
- **Selection sort**
- **Shell sort**
- **Bubble sort**
- **Quick sort**
- **Merge sort**
- **Radix sort**

12.3.1.Insertion Sort

- One of the simplest sorting algorithm is the Insertion sort.
- For "n" elements, it consist of "n – 1" passes.

How Insertion Sort Algorithm Works?

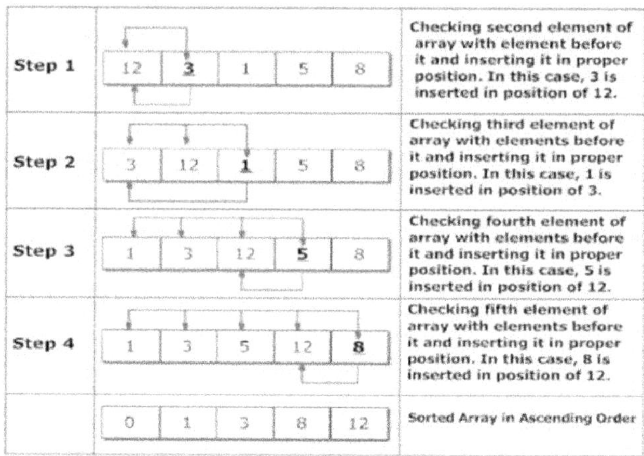

Sorting Array in Ascending Order using Insertion Sort Algorithm

Insertion Sort Routine

```
void Insertion_sort(int a[ ], int n)
{
  int i, j, temp;
  for ( i = 0 ; i < n -1  ;  i ++ )
  {
for ( j = i + 1 ; j > 0  && a [ j -1  ] >  a [ j ]  ;  j -- )
        {
            temp = a [ j ] ;
            a[ j ] = a [ j - 1 ] ;
            a[  j - 1 ]  = temp ;
        }
  }
}
```

Program for Insertion Sort

```
#include < stdio.h >
void main( )
{
 int n, a[ 25 ], i, j, temp;
 printf( "Enter number of elements \n" );
    scanf( "%d", &n );
  printf( "Enter %d integers \n", n );
  for ( i = 0; i < n; i++ )
     scanf( "%d", &a[i] );
  for ( i = 0 ; i < n - 1; i++ )
    {
      j = i + 1;
      while ( j > 0 && a[ j ] < a[ j-1 ])
      {
           temp  = a[ j ];
           a[ j ]   = a[ j - 1 ];
           a[ j - 1 ] = temp;
           j --;
      }
  }
  printf( "Sorted list in ascending order: \n ");
  for ( i = 0 ; i < n ; i++)
     printf ( "%d \n ", a[ i ] );
  }
```

Advantage of Insertion Sort

- Simple implementation.
- Efficient for (quite) small data sets.
- Efficient for data sets that are already substantially sorted.

Disadvantages of Insertion Sort

- It is less efficient on list containing more number of elements.
- As the number of elements increases the performance of the program would be slow.
- Insertion sort needs a large number of element shifts.

12.3.2. Selection Sort

Selection sort algorithm starts by comparing first two elements of an array and swapping if necessary, i.e., if you want to sort the elements of array in ascending order and if the first element is greater than second then, you need to swap the elements but, if the first element is smaller than second, leave the elements as it is. Then, again first element and third element are compared and swapped if necessary. This process goes on until first and last element of an array is compared. This completes the first step of selection sort.If there are n elements to be sorted then, the process mentioned above should be repeated n-1 times to get required result. But, for better performance, in second step, comparison starts from second element because after first step, the required number is automatically placed at the first (i.e., In case of sorting in ascending order, smallest element will be at first and in case of sorting in descending order, largest element will be at first.). Similarly, in third step, comparison starts from third element and so on.

Selection Sort Routine

```
void Selection_sort( int a[ ], int n )
{
int i , j , temp , position ;
    for ( i = 0 ; i < n – 1 ;  i ++ )
    {
            position = i ;
            for (  j = i + 1 ; j < n ;  j ++ )
            {
                    if ( a[ position ] > a[ j ] )
                            position = j;
            }
            temp = a[ i ];
            a[ i ] = a[ position ];
            a[ position ] = temp;
    }
}
```

- For "n" elements, (n-1) passes are required.
- At the end of the ith iteration, the ith smallest element will be placed in its correct position.

How Selection Sort Algorithm Works?

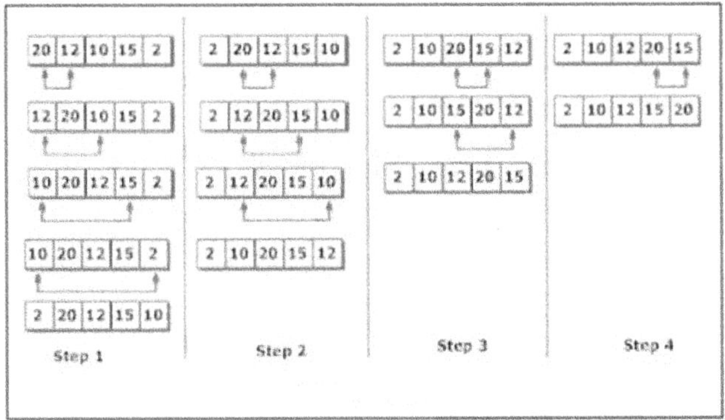

Selection Sort

Program for Selection Sort

```
#include <stdio.h>
void main( )
{
  int a [ 100 ] , n , i , j , position , temp ;
  printf ( "Enter number of elements \n" ) ;
     scanf ( "%d", &n ) ;
  printf ( " Enter %d integers \n ", n ) ;
  for ( i = 0 ; i < n ; i ++ )
     scanf ( "%d", & a[ i ] ) ;
  for ( i = 0 ; i < ( n - 1 ) ; i ++ )
    {
    position = i ;
    for ( j = i + 1 ; j < n ; j ++ )
    {
       if ( a [ position ] > a [ j ] )
       position = j ;
    }
    if ( position != i  )
    {
```

```
                temp = a [ i ] ;
                a [ i ] = a [ position ] ;
                a [ position ] = temp ;
            }
        }
        printf ( "Sorted list in ascending order: \n ") ;
        for ( i = 0 ; i < n ; i ++ )
            printf ( " %d \n ", a[ i ] ) ;
}
```

Advantages of Selection Sort

- Memory required is small.
- Selection sort is useful when you have limited memory available.
- Relatively efficient for small arrays.

Disadvantage of Selection Sort

- Poor efficiency when dealing with a huge list of items.
- The selection sort requires n-squared number of steps for sorting n elements.
- The selection sort is only suitable for a list of few elements that are in random order.

12.3.3. ShellSort

Shell sort works by comparing elements that are distant rather than adjacent elements in an array or list where adjacent elements are compared. Shell sort uses an increment sequence. The increment size is reduced after each pass until the increment size is 1. With an increment size of 1, the sort is a basic insertion sort, but by this time the data is guaranteed to be almost sorted, which is insertion sort's "best case".

The distance between comparisons decreases as the sorting algorithm runs until the last phase in which adjacent elements are compared hence, it is also known as diminishing increment sort.

Consider a list has nine items. If we use an increment of three, there are three sublist, each of which can be sorted by an insertion sort.

After completing these sorts, we get the list shown below. Although this list is not completely sorted, something very interesting has happened. By sorting the sublist, we have moved the items closer to where they actually belong.

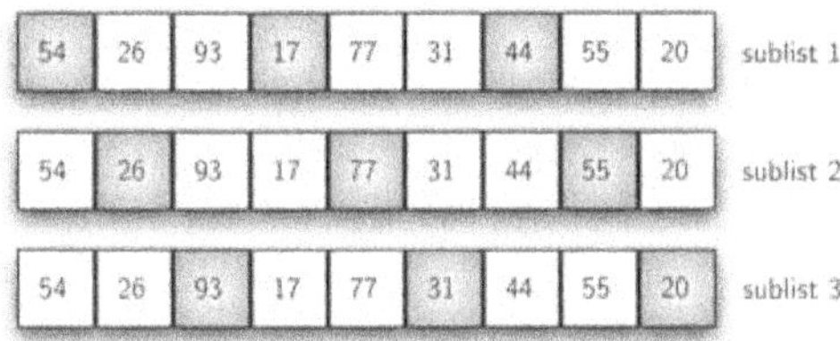

A Shell Sort with Increments of Three

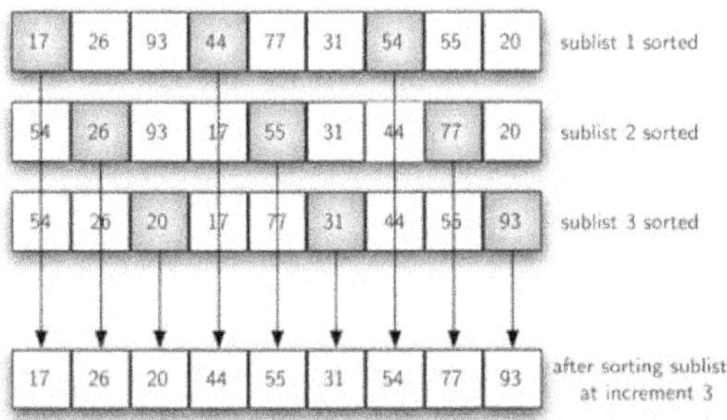

A Shell Sort after Sorting Each Sublist

Note that by performing the earlier sublist sorts, we have now reduced the total number of shifting operations necessary to put the list in its final order. For this case, we need only four more shifts to complete the process.

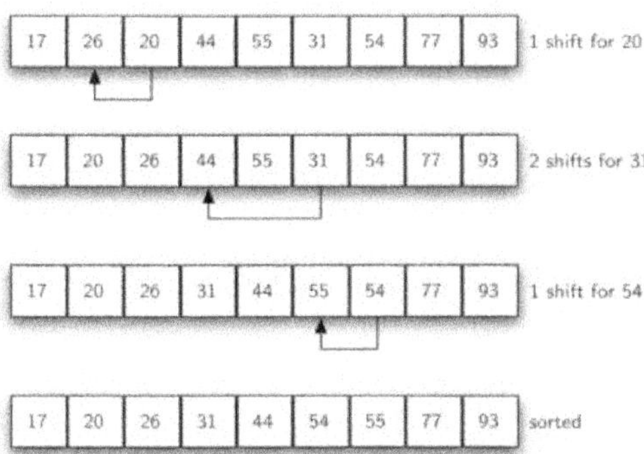

Shell Sort: A Final Insertion Sort with Increment of 1

Shell Sort Routine

```
void Shell_sort ( int a[ ], int n )
{
        int i, j, k, temp;
        for ( k = n / 2 ; k > 0 ;  k = k / 2 )
                for ( i = k ;  i < n ; i + + )
                {
                temp = a [ i ] ;
                for ( j = i ; j > = k && a [ j - k ]  > temp ; j  =  j - k )
                                {
                                        a [ j ] = a [ j - k ] ;
                                }
                        a [ j ] = temp ;
                }
}
```

Program for Shell Sort

```
#include  < stdio.h >
 void main( )
{
  int a [ 5 ] = { 4, 5, 2, 3, 6 } , i = 0  ;
  ShellSort ( a, 5 ) ;
  printf(  " After Sorting :" ) ;
  for ( i = 0 ; i < 5  ; i ++ )
     printf ( " %d ", a[ i ] ) ;
}
void ShellSort (int  a [ 5 ] , int n )
{
     int i , j , k , temp ;
     for ( k = n / 2 ; k  >  0 ;  k  / =  2)
     {
          for ( i = k ;  i < n ;  i ++ )
          {
              temp = a [ i ] ;
        for  ( j = i ; j > = k && a [ j - k ]  >  temp ; j =  j - k )
                                  {
                                             a [ j ] = a [ j - k ] ;
                                  }
                           a [ j ] = temp ;
          }
}
}
```

Advantages of Shell Sort

- Efficient for medium-size lists.

Disadvantages of Shell Sort

- Complex algorithm, not nearly as efficient as the merge, heap and quick sorts

12.3.4. Bubble Sort

This algorithm starts by comparing the first two elements of an array and swapping if necessary, i.e., if you want to sort the elements of array in ascending order and if the first element is greater than second then, you need to swap the elements but, if the first element is smaller than second, you mustn't swap the element.

Then, again second and third elements are compared and swapped if it is necessary and this process go on until last and second last element is compared and swapped. This completes the first step of bubble sort.

If there are *n* elements to be sorted then, the process mentioned above should be repeated *n-1* times to get required result. But, for better performance, in second step, last and second last elements are not compared because; the proper element is automatically placed at last after first step.

Similarly, in third step, last and second last and second last and third last elements are not compared and so on.

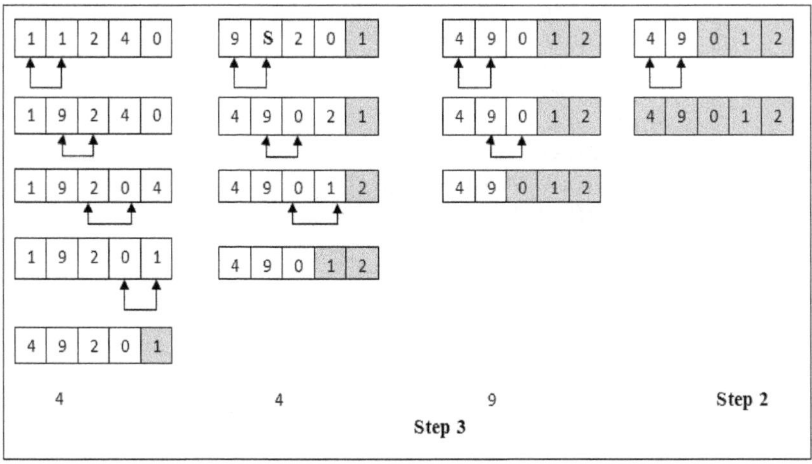

Bubble Sort Routine

```
  void Bubble_sort (int a [ ] , int n )
{
        int i, j, temp;
        for( i = 0; i < n - 1;  i++ )
    {
                for( j = 0; j < n – i - 1; j++ )
                {
                        if( a[ j ] > a [ j + 1 ] )
                        {
                                temp = a [ j ];
                                a[ j ] = a[ j + 1 ];
                                a[ j + 1 ] = temp;
                }       }
}}
```

- For "n" elements, (n-1) passes are required.
- At the end of ith pass, the ith largest element will be placed in its correct position.

Program for Bubble Sort

```
#include < stdio.h >
#include < conio.h >
void main( )
{
        int a [ 20 ], i, j, temp, n ;
        printf ( "\n Enter the number of elements \t " );
           scanf ( " %d ", &n );
        printf ( " \n Enter %d numbers \n " , n );
        for ( i = 0 ; i < n ; i++ )
           scanf ( " %d " , & a [ i ] );
        printf (" \n  Elements \t " );
        for ( i = 0 ; i < n ; i++ )
                printf ( " %d \t ", a [ i ] );
        for ( i = 0 ; i < n - 1 ; i++ )
        {
           for ( j = 0 ; j < n – i – 1 ; j++ )
           {
                if ( a [ j ] > a [ j + 1 ] )
                  {
               temp = a [ j ] ;
            a [ j ] = a [ j + 1 ] ;
            a [ j+ 1 ] = temp;
           }
```

```
        }
    }
            printf("\nSorted array\t");
            for(i=0;i<n;i++)
                printf("%d\t",a[i]);
    }
```

Advantage of Bubble Sort

- It is simple to write
- easy to understand
- it only takes a few lines of code.

Disadvantage of Bubble Sort

- The major drawback is the amount of time it takes to sort.
- The average time increases almost exponentially as the number of table elements increase.

12.3.5. Quick Sort

Quick sort algorithm is based on divide and conquer strategy. In a quick sort we take one element called as pivot, then we list all the smaller elements than pivot, and greater than pivot. After partitioning we have pivot in the final position. After recursively sorting the partition array, we get the sorted elements.

The basic steps to partition an array are:

1. Find a "pivot" item in the array. This item is the basis for comparison for a single round.
2. Start a pointer (the left pointer) at the first item in the array.
3. Start a pointer (the right pointer) at the last item in the array.
4. While the value at the left pointer in the array is less than the pivot value, move the left pointer to the right (add 1). Continue until the value at the left pointer is greater than or equal to the pivot value.
5. While the value at the right pointer in the array is greater than the pivot value, move the right pointer to the left (subtract 1). Continue until the value at the right pointer is less than or equal to the pivot value.
6. If the left pointer is less than or equal to the right pointer, then swap the values at these locations in the array.
7. Move the left pointer to the right by one and the right pointer to the left by one.
8. If the left pointer and right pointer don't meet, go to step 1.

Below figure shows that 54 will serve as our first pivot value. Since we have looked at this example a few times already, we know that 54 will eventually end up in the position currently holding 31. The **partition** process will happen next. It will find the split point and at the same time move other items to the appropriate side of the list, either less than or greater than the pivot value.

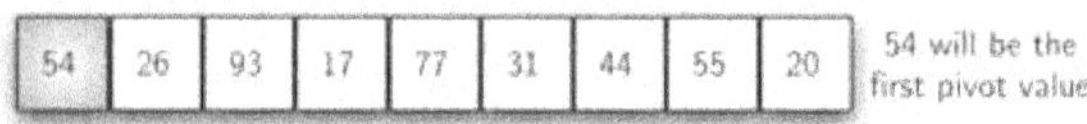

The First Pivot Value for a Quick Sort

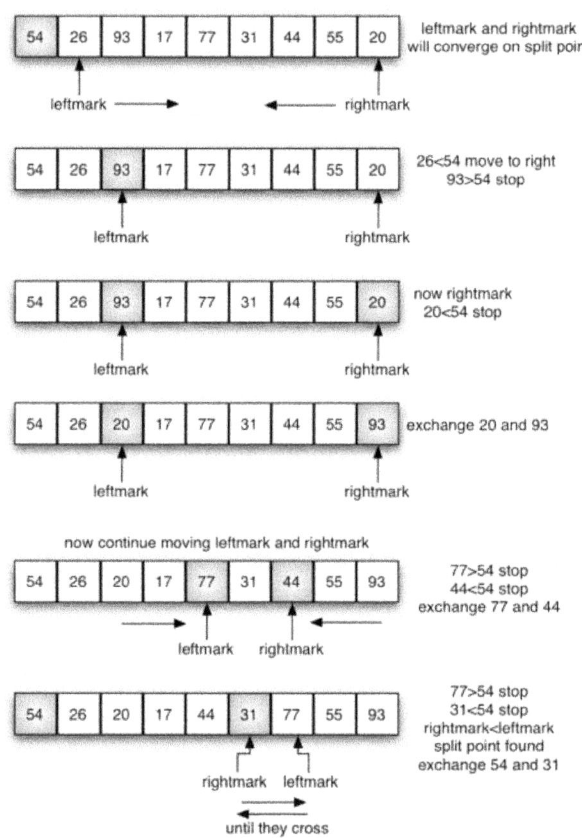

Finding the Split Point for 54At the point where rightmark becomes less than leftmark, we stop. The position of rightmark is now the split point. The pivot value can be exchanged with the contents of the split point and the pivot value is now in place. In addition, all the items to the left of the split point are less than the pivot value, and all the items to the right of the split point are greater than the pivot value. The list can now be divided at the split point and the quick sort can be invoked recursively on the two halves.

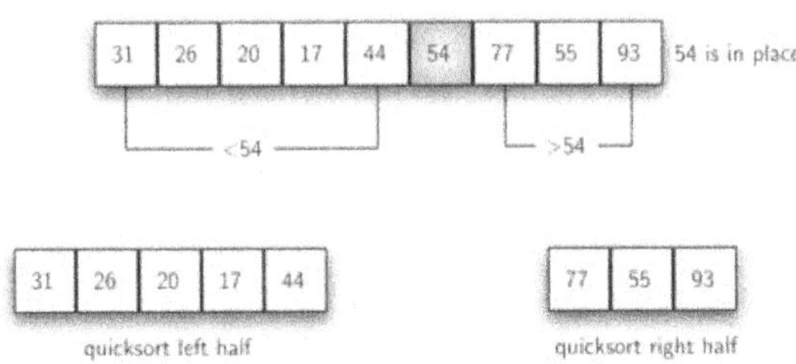

Completing the Partition Process to Find the Split Point for 54

Quick Sort Routine

```
void Quicksort ( int a [ ], int left, int right )
{
    int i, j, p, temp;
    if ( left < right )
    {
            p = left;
            i = left + 1;
            j = right;
            while ( i < j )
            {
                    while ( a [ i ] < = a [ p ] )
                            i = i + 1;
                    while ( a [ j ] > a [ p ] )
                            j = j - 1;
                    if ( i < j )
                    {
                            temp = a [ i ];
```

```
                    a [ i ] = a [ j ];
                    a [ j ] = temp;
               }
          }
          temp = a [ p ];
          a [ p ] =  a [ j ];
          a [ j ]  = temp;
          quicksort ( a, left, j - 1 );
          quicksort ( a, j + 1, right );
     }
}
```

Program for Quick Sort

```
#include < stdio.h >
void quicksort ( int [ 10 ], int, int ) ;
void main( )
{
        int a [ 20 ], n, i ;
        printf ( " Enter size of the array: " );
          scanf ( " %d ", & n );
        printf( " Enter % d elements : ", n );
        for ( i = 0 ; i < n ; i ++ )
          scanf ( " %d ", & a [ i  ]);
        quicksort ( a , 0  , n – 1 );
        printf ( " Sorted elements: " );
        for ( i = 0 ; i < n ; i ++ )
         printf ( " %d \ t ", a [ i ] );
}
void quicksort ( int  a [ 10 ], int left, int right )
{
int p, j, temp, i ;
if ( left < right )
{
 p = left ;
```

```
i = left ;
j = right ;
while ( i < j )
{
  while ( a [ i ]  < = a [ p ] && i <  right )
        i ++ ;
  while ( a [ j ] > a [  p ] )
        j - -;
  if ( i < j )
  {
        temp = a [ i ] ;
        a [ i ] = a [ j ] ;
        a[  j ] = temp ;
  }
}
        temp = a [ p ] ;
        a [ p ] = a [ j ] ;
        a [  j ] =temp ;
quicksort ( a , left ,  j – 1 ) ;
quicksort ( a , j + 1 , right ) ;
}
}
```

Advantages of Quick Sort

- Fast and efficient as it deals well with a huge list of items.
- No additional storage is required.

Disadvantages of Quick Sort

- The difficulty of implementing the partitioning algorithm.

12.3.6. Merge Sort

Merge sort is a recursive algorithm that continually splits a list in half. If the list has more than one item, we split the list and recursively invoke a merge sort on both halves. Once the two halves are sorted, the fundamental operation, called a **merge**, is performed. Merging is the process of taking two smaller sorted lists and combining them together into a single, sorted, new list. Below figure shows our familiar example list as it is being split by mergeSort. Below figure shows the simple lists, now sorted, as they are merged back together.

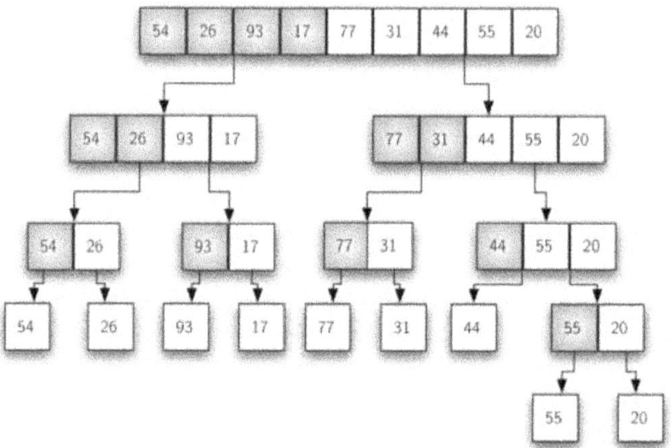

Splitting the List in a Merge Sort

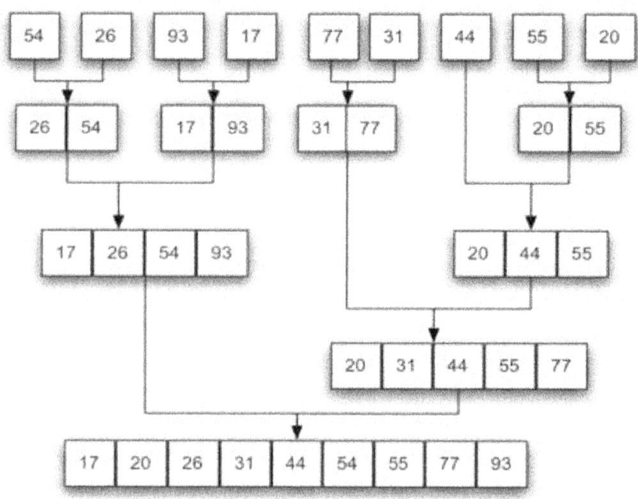

List, as they are Merged Together

Merge Sort Routine

```
void Merge_sort (int a [ ] , int temp [ ] , int n )
{
      msort ( a , temp , 0 , n - 1 ) ;
}
```

```
void msort ( int a[ ] , int temp [ ] , int left , int right )
{
      int center ;
      if( left < right )
      {
            center = ( left + right ) / 2 ;
            msort ( a , left , center ) ;
            msort ( a , temp , center + 1 , right ) ;
            merge ( a , temp , n , left , center , right ) ;
      }
}
```

```
void  merge ( int a [ ] , int temp [ ] , int n , int left , int center , int right )
{
      int i = 0 , j , left_end  = center , center = center + 1 ;
      while( ( left < = left_end ) && ( center < = right ) )
      {
            if( a [ left ] < = a [ center ]  )
            {
                  temp [ i ] = a [ left ] ;
                  i + + ;
                  left + + ;
            }
            else
            {
                  temp [ i ] = a [ center ] ;
                  i + + ;
```

```
                center + + ;
            }
    }
    while( left <= left_end )
    {
            temp [ I ] = a [ left ] ;
            left + + ;
            i + + ;
    }
    while( center < = right )
    {
            temp [ i ] = a [ center ] ;
            center + + ;
            i + + ;
    }
    for ( i = 0 ; i < n ;  i + + )
        print temp [ i ] ;
}
```

Program for Merge Sort

```
#include<stdio.h>
 void mergesort(int a[],int i,int j);
void merge(int a[],int i1,int j1,int i2,int j2);

int main()
{
  int a[30],n,i;
  printf("Enter no of elements:");
  scanf("%d",&n);
  printf("Enter array elements:");

  for(i=0;i<n;i++)
    scanf("%d",&a[i]);
```

```
    mergesort(a,0,n-1);

    printf("\nSorted array is :");
    for(i=0;i<n;i++)
        printf("%d ",a[i]);

    return 0;
}

void mergesort(int a[],int i,int j)
{
    int mid;

    if(i<j)
    {
        mid=(i+j)/2;
        mergesort(a,i,mid);        //left recursion
        mergesort(a,mid+1,j);    //right recursion
        merge(a,i,mid,mid+1,j);    //merging of two sorted sub-arrays
    }
}

void merge(int a[],int i1,int j1,int i2,int j2)
{
    int temp[50];    //array used for merging
    int i,j,k;
    i=i1;    //beginning of the first list
    j=i2;    //beginning of the second list
    k=0;

    while(i<=j1 && j<=j2)    //while elements in both lists
    {
        if(a[i]<a[j])
            temp[k++]=a[i++];
```

```
        else
            temp[k++]=a[j++];
    }

    while(i<=j1)    //copy remaining elements of the first list
        temp[k++]=a[i++];

    while(j<=j2)    //copy remaining elements of the second list
        temp[k++]=a[j++];

    //Transfer elements from temp[] back to a[]
    for(i=i1,j=0;i<=j2;i++,j++)
        a[i]=temp[j];
}
```

Advantages of Merge Sort

- Mergesort is well-suited for sorting really huge amounts of data that does not fit into memory.
- It is fast and stable algorithm.

Disadvantages of Merge Sort

- Merge sort uses a lot of memory.
- It uses extra space proportional to number of element n.
- This can slow it down when attempting to sort very large data.

12.3.7. Radix Sort

Radix sort is an unusual sorting algorithm. All the sorting algorithms discussed so far compare the elements being sorted to each other. The radix sort doesn't. A radix sort uses one or more keys to sort values. On a radix sort pass, a list of items to be sorted is processed from beginning to end. One at a time, the items in the list are placed at the end of a list of items with the same key value. After all items have been processed, the lists of key values are reassembled smallest key to largest key.

Radix sort passes should be performed from the last character to the first character. The first pass will use the Nth character, the second pass will use the (N - 1)th character, ..., the Nth pass will use the first Character.

Algorithm for Radix Sort

Step 1: Consider 10 buckets (1 for each digit 0 to 9).

Step 2: Consider the LSB (Least Significant Bit) of each number (numbers in the one's Place.... E.g., in 43 LSB = 3)

Step 3: place the elements in their respective buckets according to the LSB of each number.

Step 4: write the numbers from the bucket (0 to 9) bottom to top.

Step 5: repeat the same process with the digits in the 10's place (e.g. In 43 MSB =4).

Step 6: repeat the same step till all the digits of the given number are consider.

Consider the Following Numbers to be Sorted using Radix Sort

43 27 31 15 37 80 03

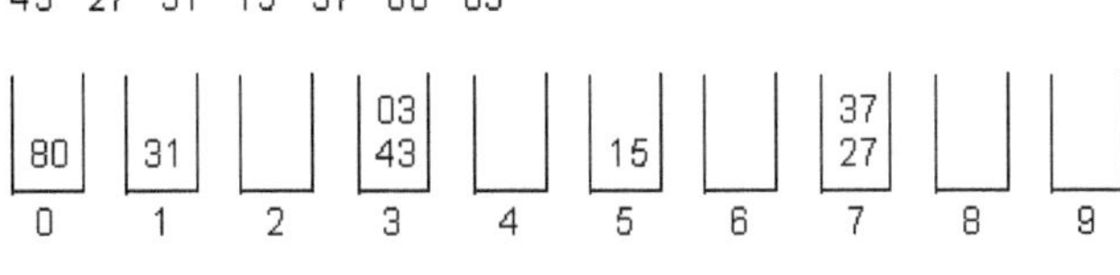

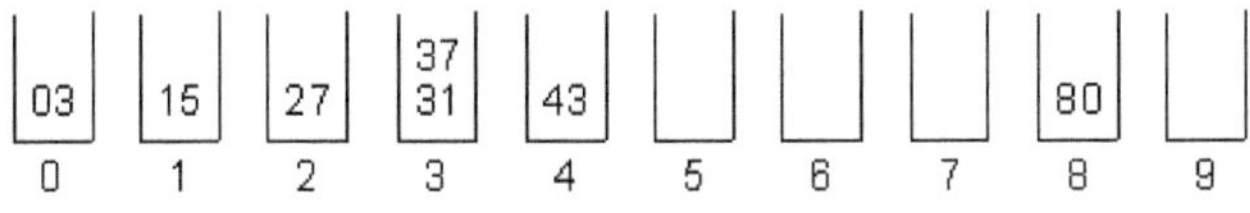

03 15 27 31 37 43 80

Sorted list of array : 3 15 27 31 37 43 80

```
void Radix_sort ( int a [ ] ,int n )
{
    int bucket [ 10 ] [ 5 ] , buck [ 10 ] , b [ 10 ] ;
    int i , j , k , l , num , div , large , passes ;
    div = 1 ;
    num = 0 ;
    large = a [ 0 ] ;
    for ( i = 0 ; i < n ; i ++ )
```

```
        {
                if ( a[ I ]> large )
                {
                        large = a [ i ] ;
                }
                while ( large >0 )
                {
                        num ++ ;
                        large = large / 10 ;
                }
                for ( passes = 0 ; passes < num ; passes ++ )
                {
                        for ( k = 0 ; k <10 ; k ++ )
                        {
                                buck [ k ]=0 ;
                        }
                        for ( i = 0 ; i < n ; i ++ )
                        {
                                l =( ( a [ i ] / div ) % 10 ) ;
                                bucket [ l ] [ buck [ l ] ++ ]= a [ i ] ;
                        }
                        i = 0 ;
                        for ( k = 0 ; k <10 ; k ++ )
                        {
                                for ( j = 0 ; j < buck [ k ] ; j ++ )
                                {
                                        a [ i ++ ]= bucket [ k ] [ j ] ;
                                }
                        }
                        div * = 10 ;
                }
        }
}
```

Advantages of Radix Sort

- Fast and complexity does not depend on the number of data.
- Radix Sort is very simple.

Disadvantages of Radix Sort

- It takes more space than other sorting algorithms, since in addition to the array that will be sorted, you need to have a sub list for each of the possible digits or letters.
- Since it depends on the digits or letters, Radix Sort is also much less flexible than other sorts.

CHAPTER 13

Searching

13.1. Introduction

Searching is an algorithmto check whether a particular element is present in the list.

13.2. Types of searching

- **Linear search**
- **Binary Search**

13.2.1.Linear Search

Linear search or sequential search is a method for finding a particular value in a list, that consists of checking every one of its elements, one at a time and in sequence, until the desired one is found. Linear search is the simplest search algorithm. For a list with n items, the best case is when the value is equal to the first element of the list, in which case only one comparison is needed. The worst case is when the value is not in the list (or occurs only once at the end of the list), in which case n comparisons are needed.

The worst case performance scenario for a linear search is that it has to loop through the entire collection, either because the item is the last one, or because the item is not found.

Linear Search Routine

```
void Linear_search ( int a[ ] , int n )
{
        int search , count = 0 ;
        for ( i = 0 ; i <  n ; I ++ )
        {
                if ( a [ i ] = = search )
                {
                        count ++ ;
                }
        }
        if ( count = = 0 )
                print        "Element    not
          Present" ;
        else
                print "Element is Present
          in list" ;
}
```

Program for Linear Search

```
#include < stdio.h >
void main( )
{
int a [ 10 ] , n , i , search, count = 0 ;
printf ( " Enter the number of elements \ t " ) ;
  scanf ( " %d " , & n ) ;
printf ( " \n Enter %d  numbers \n " , n ) ;
for ( i = 0 ;  i < n ; i ++ )
  scanf ( " %d " , & a [ i ] ) ;
printf ( " \n Array Elements \n " ) ;
for ( i = 0 ; i < n ; i ++ )
   printf ( " %d \t " , a [ i ] ) ;
printf ( " \ n \ n Enter the Element to be searched: \ t " ) ;

  scanf ( " % d " , & search ) ;
for ( i =0 ; i < n; i ++ )
 {
   if ( search = = a [ i ] )
          count ++ ;
 }
if ( count = = 0 )
  printf( " \n Element %d is not present in the array " , search ) ;
else
  printf ( " \n Element %d is present %d times in the array \n " , search , count ) ;
}
```

Advantages of Linear Search

- It is simple, very easy to understand and implement.
- It does not require the data in the array to be stored in any particular order.

Disadvantages of Linear Search

- Slower than many other search algorithms.
- It has a very poor efficiency.

13.2.2. Binary Search

It is possible to take greater advantage of the ordered list .Instead of searching the list in sequence, a binary search will start by examining the middle item. If that item is the one we are searching for, we are done. If it is not the correct item, we can use the ordered nature of the list to eliminate half of the remaining items. If the item we are searching for is greater than the middle item, we know that the entire lower half of the list as well as the middle item can be eliminated from further consideration. The item, if it is in the list, must be in the upper half.

We can then repeat the process with the upper half. Start at the middle item and compare it against what we are looking for. Again, we either find it or split the list in half, therefore eliminating another large part of our possible search space.

Working Principle

Algorithm is quite simple. It can be done either recursively or iteratively:

1. Get the middle element;
2. If the middle element equals to the searched value, the algorithm stops;
3. Otherwise, two cases are possible:
   - Search value is less than the middle element. In this case, go to the step 1 for the part of the array, before middle element.
   - Searched value is greater, than the middle element. In this case, go to the step 1 for the part of the array, after middle element.

First case is when search element is found. Second one is when subarray has no elements. In this case the search value is not present in the array.

Binary Search Routine

```
void Binary_search ( int a[ ] , int n , int search )
{
        int first, last, mid ;
        first = 0 ;
        last = n-1 ;
        mid = ( first + last ) / 2 ;
        while ( first < = last )
        {
                if ( Search > a [ mid ]  )
                        first = mid + 1 ;
                else if ( Search = = a [ mid ] )
                {
                        print "Element is present in
                   the list" ;
                        break ;
                }
                else
                        last = mid – 1 ;
                   mid = ( first + last ) / 2 ;
        }
        if( first > last )
                print "Element Not Found" ;
}
```

Example 1

Find 6 in {-1, 5, 6, 18, 19, 25, 46, 78, 102, 114}.

Step 1 (middle element is 19 > 6): -1 5 6 18 19 25 46 78 102 114

Step 2 (middle element is 5 < 6): -1 5 6 18 19 25 46 78 102 114

Step 3 (middle element is 6 == 6): -1 5 6 18 19 25 46 78 102 114

Advantages of Binary Search

- In Linear search, the search element is compared with all the elements in the array. Whereas in Binary search, the search element is compared based on the middle element present in the array.

Disadvantages of Binary Search

- It employs recursive approach and this approach requires more stack space.
- It requires the data in the array to be stored in sorted order.
- It involves additional complexity in computing the middle element of the array.

CHAPTER 14

Hashing

14.1. Introduction

Hashing is a technique that is used to store, retrieve and find data in the data structure called Hash Table. It is used to overcome the drawback of Linear Search (Comparison) & Binary Search (Sorted order list). It involves two important concepts-

- Hash Table
- Hash Function

Hash Table

- A **hash table** is a data structure that is used to store and retrieve data elements (keys) very quickly.
- It is an array of some fixed size, containing the keys.
- Hash table run from 0 to Tablesize – 1.
- Each key is mapped into some number in the range 0 to Tablesize – 1.
- This mapping is called Hash function.
- Insertion of the data in the hash table is based on the key value obtained from the hash function.
- Using same hash key value, the data can be retrieved from the hash table by few or more Hash key comparison.
- The **load factor** of a hash table is calculated using the formula:(Number of data elements in the hash table) / (Size of the hash table)

Factors Affecting Hash Table Design

- Hash function
- Table size.
- Collision handling scheme

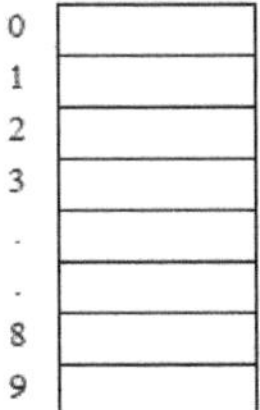

Simple Hash table with table size = 10

Hash Function

- It is a function, which distributes the keys evenly among the cells in the Hash Table.
- Using the same hash function we can retrieve data from the hash table.
- Hash function is used to implement hash table.
- **The integer value returned by the hash function is called hash key.**
- If the input keys are integer, the commonly used hash function is,

H (key) = key % Tablesize

```
typedef unsigned int index;
index Hash ( const char *key , int Tablesize )
{
   unsigned int Hashval = 0 ;
   while ( * key ! = '\0' )
        Hashval + = * key ++ ;
   return ( Hashval % Tablesize ) ;
}
```

A simple hash function

14.2. Types of Hash Functions

1. Division Method
2. Mid Square Method
3. Multiplicative Hash Function
4. Digit Folding

1. Division Method

- It depends on remainder of division.
- Divisor is Table Size.
- Formula is **(H (key) = key % table size)**

E.g. consider the following data or record or key (36, 18, 72, 43, 6) table size = 8

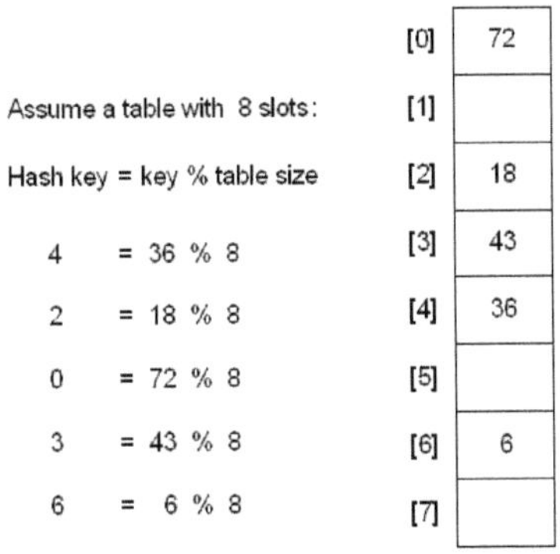

Assume a table with 8 slots:

Hash key = key % table size

Hash		Key % size	Index	Slot
			[0]	72
			[1]	
			[2]	18
4	=	36 % 8	[3]	43
2	=	18 % 8	[4]	36
0	=	72 % 8	[5]	
3	=	43 % 8	[6]	6
6	=	6 % 8	[7]	

2. Mid Square Method

We first square the item, and then extract some portion of the resulting digits. For example, if the item were 44, we would first compute 44^2=1,936. Extract the middle two digit 93 from the answer. Store the key 44 in the index 93.

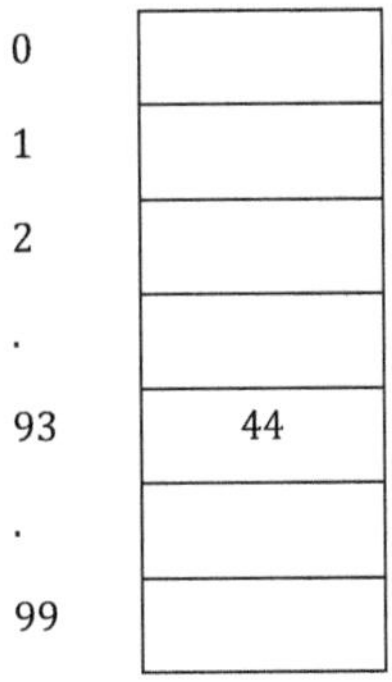

Index	Value
0	
1	
2	
.	
93	44
.	
99	

3. Multiplicative Hash Function

Key is multiplied by some constant value.

Hash function is given by,

H(key)=Floor (P * (key * A))

P = Integer constant [e.g. P=50]

A = Constant real number [A=0.61803398987]

E.g. Key 107

H(107)=Floor(50*(107*0.61803398987))

=Floor(3306.481845)

H(107)=3306

Consider table size is 5000

0	
1	
2	
.	
3306	107
.	
4999	

4. Digit Folding Method

The folding method for constructing hash functions begins by dividing the item into equal-size pieces (the last piece may not be of equal size). These pieces are then added together to give the resulting hash key value. For example, if our item was the phone number 436-555-4601, we would take the digits and divide them into groups of 2 (43, 65, 55, 46, 01). After the addition, 43+65+55+46+01, we get 210. If we assume our hash table has 11 slots, then we need to perform the extra step of dividing by 11 and keeping the remainder. In this case 210 % 11 is 1, so the phone number 436-555-4601 hashes to slot 1.

0	
1	436-555-4601
2	
3	
.	
8	
9	
10	

14.3. Collision

If two keys hashes to the same index, the corresponding records cannot be stored in the same location. So, if it's already occupied, we must find another location to store the new record.

Characteristics of Good Hashing Function

- It should be Simple to compute.
- Number of Collision should be less while placing record in Hash Table.
- **Hash function with no collision ➔ Perfect hash function.**
- Hash Function should produce keys which are distributed uniformly in hash table.

14.4. Collision Resolution Strategies / Techniques (CRT)

If collision occurs, it should be handled or overcome by applying some technique. Such technique is called CRT.

There are a number of collision resolution techniques, but the most popular are:

- **Separate chaining (**Open Hashing**)**
- **Open addressing**. (Closed Hashing)
  - **Linear Probing**
  - **Quadratic Probing**
  - **Double Hashing**

14.4.1. Separate Chaining (Open Hashing)

- Open hashing technique.
- Implemented using singly linked list concept.
- Pointer (ptr) field is added to each record.
- When collision occurs, a separate chaining is maintained for colliding data.
- Element inserted in front of the list.

H (key) =key % table size

Two operations are there:-

- Insert
- Find

Structure Definition for Node

```
typedef Struct node *Position;
Struct node
{
        int data;            ──> defines the nodes
        Position  next;
};
```

Structure Definition for Hash Table

```
typedef Position List;
struct Hashtbl
{
        int Tablesize;
        List * theLists;
};
```

→ Defines the hash table which contains array of linked list

Initialization for Hash Table for Separate Chaining

```
Hashtable initialize(int Tablesize)
{
        HashTable H;
        int i;
        H = malloc (sizeof(struct HashTbl));         →Allocates table
        H → Tablesize = NextPrime(Tablesize);
        H→the Lists=malloc(sizeof(List) * H→Tablesize);  → Allocates array of list
        for( i = 0; i < H → Tablesize; i++ )
        {
        H → TheLists[i] = malloc(Sizeof(Struct node));    → Allocates list headers
        H → TheLists[i] → next = NULL;
        }
        return H;
}
```

Insert Routine for Separate Chaining

```
void insert (int Key, Hashtable H)
{
  Position P, newnode;    *[Inserts element in the Front of the list always]*
  List L;
  P = find ( key, H );
  if(P = = NULL)
  {
        newnode = malloc(sizeof(Struct node));
        L = H → TheLists[Hash(key,Tablesize)];
```

```
            newnode → nex t= L → next;
            newnode → data = key;
            L → next = newnode;
    }
}
Position find( int key, Hashtable H)
{
  Position P, List L;
  L = H →TheLists[Hash(key,Tablesize)];
  P = L → next;
  while(P != NULL && P → data != key)
        P = P → next;
  return P;
}
```

If two keysmapto samevalue,the elements are chained together.

Initial configuration of the hash table with separate chaining. Here we use SLL(Singly Linked List) concept to chain the elements.

0		NULL
1		NULL
2		NULL
3		NULL
4		NULL
5		NULL
6		NULL
7		NULL
8		NULL
9		NULL

Insert the following four keys 22 84 35 62 into hash table of size 10 using separate chaining. The hash function is

H(key) = key % 10

1. H(22) = 22 % 10

   = 2

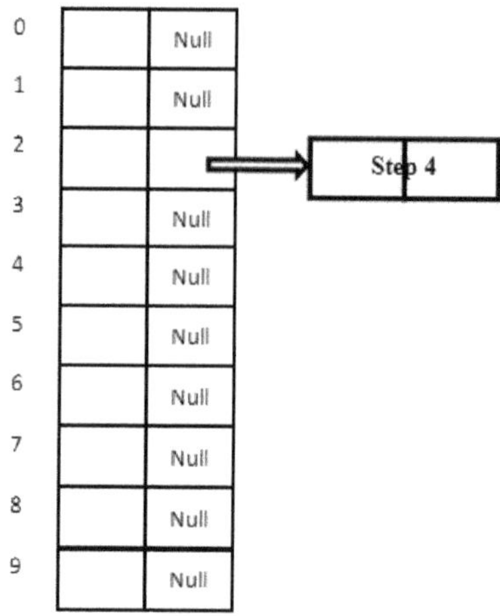

Insert the following four keys 22 84 3562 into hash table of size 10 using separate chaining

The hash function is key % 10

84 %10 =4

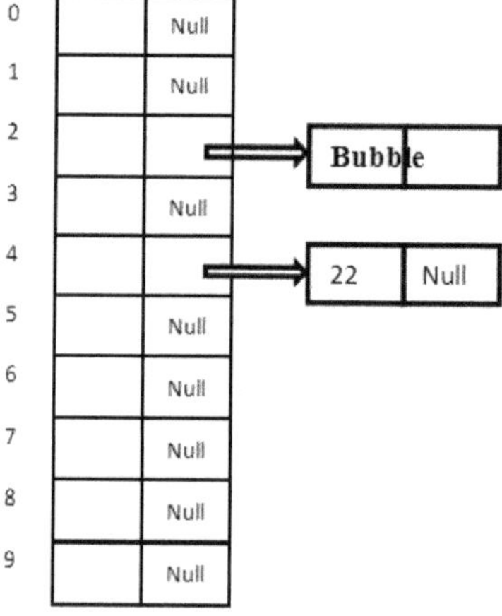

Insert the following four keys 22 84 3562 into hash table of size 10 using separate chaining.

The hash function is key % 10.

35 %10 =5

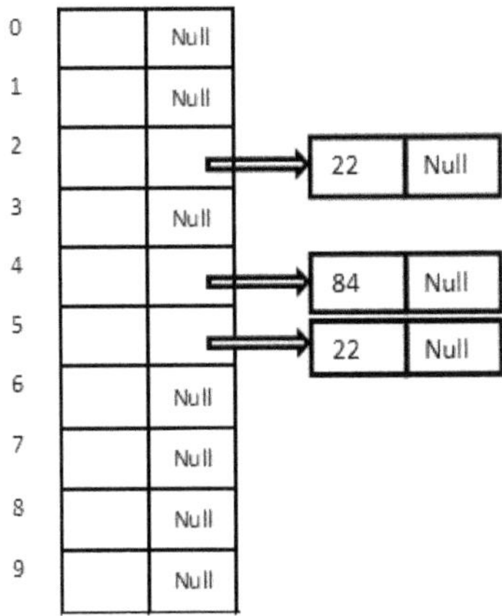

Insert the following four keys 22 84 3562 into hash table of size 10 using separate chaining.

The hash function is key % 10.

62 %10 =2.

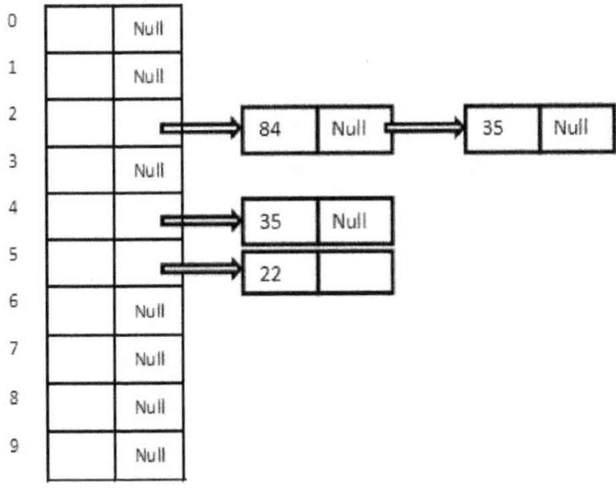

Advantage

1. more number of elements can be inserted using array of Link List.

Disadvantage

1. It requires more pointers, which occupies more memory space.
2. Search takes time. Since it takes time to evaluate Hash Function and also to traverse the List.

14.4.2. Open Addressing

- Closed Hashing
- Collision resolution technique
- When collision occurs, alternative cells are tried until empty cells are found.
- Types:-
  - Linear Probing
  - Quadratic Probing
  - Double Hashing
- Hash function
  - H(key) = key % table size.
- Insert Operation
  - To insert a key; Use the hash function to identify the list to which the element should be inserted.
  - Then traverse the list to check whether the element is already present.
  - If exists, increment the count.
  - Else the new element is placed at the front of the list.

14.4.3. Linear Probing

Easiest method to handle collision.

Apply the hash function H (key) = key % table size.

How to Probing

- first probe – given a key k, hash to H(key)
- second probe – if H(key)+f(1) is occupied, try H(key)+f(2)
- And so forth.

Probing Properties

- we force f(0)=0
- The ith probe is to (H (key) +f (i)) %table size.
- If I reach size-1, the probe has failed.
- Depending on f (), the probe may fail sooner.
- Long sequences of probe are costly.

Probe Sequence is

- H (key) % table size
- H (key)+1 % Table size
- H (Key)+2 % Table size

1. H(Key)=Key mod Tablesize

This is the common formula that you should apply for any hashing.

If collocation occurs use Formula 2.

2. H(Key)=(H(key)+i) Tablesize

Where i=1, 2, 3, ... etc

Example: - 89 18 49 58 69; Tablesize=10

1. H(89) =89%10
   =9
2. H(18) =18%10
   =8
3. H(49) =49%10
   =9 ((coloids with 89.So try for next free cell using formula 2))

   i=1 h1(49) = (H(49)+1)%10
   = (9+1)%10
   =10%10
   =0
4. H(58) =58%10
   =8 ((colloids with 18))

   i=1 h1(58) = (H(58) +1)%10
   = (8+1) %10
   =9%10
   =9 =>Again collision

   i=2 h2(58) =(H(58)+2)%10
   =(8+2)%10
   =10%10
   =0 =>Again collision

	EMPTY	89	18	49	58	69
0				49	49	49
1					58	58
2						69
3						
4						
5						
6						
7						
8			18	18	18	
9		89	89	89	89	

Linear Probing

14.4.4. Quadratic Probing

	insert(76) 76%7=6	Insert(93) 93%7=2	Insert(40) 40%7=5	Insert(47) 47%7=5	Insert(10) 10%7=3	Insert(55) 55%7=6
0				47	47	47
1						55
2		93	93	93	93	93
3					10	10
4						
5			40	40	40	40
6	76	76	76	76	76	76
	1	1	1	3	1	1

To resolve the primary clustering problem, quadratic probing can be used. With quadratic probing, rather than always moving one spot, move i2 spots from the point of collision, where i is the number of attempts to resolve the collision.

- Another collision resolution method which distributes items more evenly.
- From the original index H, if the slot is filled, try cells H+12, H+22, H+32,.., H + i2 with wrap-around.

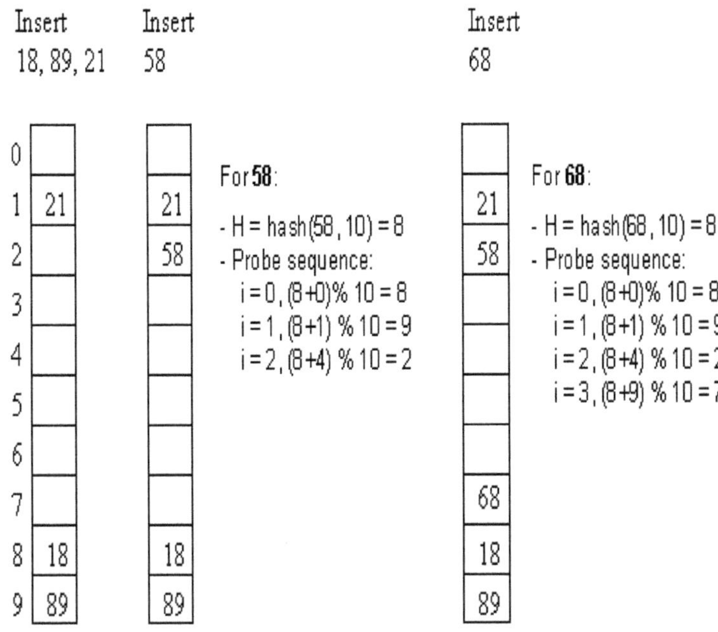

Limitation: at most half of the table can be used as alternative locations to resolve collisions.This means that once the table is more than half full, it's difficult to find an empty spot.

This new problem is known as secondary clustering because elements that hash to the same hash key will always probe the same alternative cells.

14.4.5.Double Hashing

Double hashing uses the idea of applying a second hash function to the key when a collision occurs. The result of the second hash function will be the number of positions forms the point of collision to insert.

There are a couple of requirements for the second function:

It must never evaluate to 0 must make sure that all cells can be probed

A popular second hash function is:

Hash2 (key) = R - (key % R) where R is a prime number that is smaller than the size of the table.

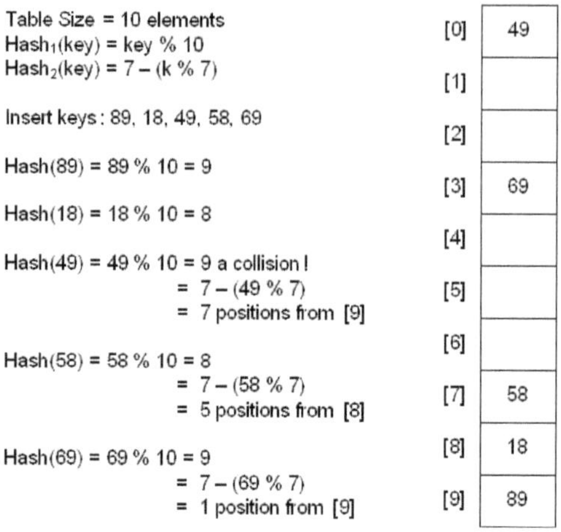

Table Size = 10 elements
$Hash_1(key)$ = key % 10
$Hash_2(key)$ = 7 – (k % 7)

Insert keys : 89, 18, 49, 58, 69

Hash(89) = 89 % 10 = 9

Hash(18) = 18 % 10 = 8

Hash(49) = 49 % 10 = 9 a collision !
= 7 – (49 % 7)
= 7 positions from [9]

Hash(58) = 58 % 10 = 8
= 7 – (58 % 7)
= 5 positions from [8]

Hash(69) = 69 % 10 = 9
= 7 – (69 % 7)
= 1 position from [9]

Index	Value
[0]	49
[1]	
[2]	
[3]	69
[4]	
[5]	
[6]	
[7]	58
[8]	18
[9]	89

14.5. Rehashing

Once the hash table gets too full, the running time for operations will start to take too long and may fail. To solve this problem, a table at least twice the size of the original will be built and the elements will be transferred to the new table.

Advantage

- A programmer doesn't worry about table system.
- Simple to implement
- Can be used in other data structure as well

The New Size of the Hash Table

- should also be prime
- will be used to calculate the new insertion spot (hence the name rehashing)
- This is a very expensive operation! O(N) since there are N elements to rehash and the table size is roughly 2N. This is ok though since it doesn't happen that often.

The Question becomes when Should the Rehashing be Applied?

Some possible answers:

- once the table becomes half full
- once an insertion fails
- once a specific load factor has been reached, where load factor is the ratio of the number of elements in the hash table to the table size

14.6. Extendible Hashing

Extendible Hashing is a mechanism for altering the size of the hash table to accommodate new entries when buckets overflow.

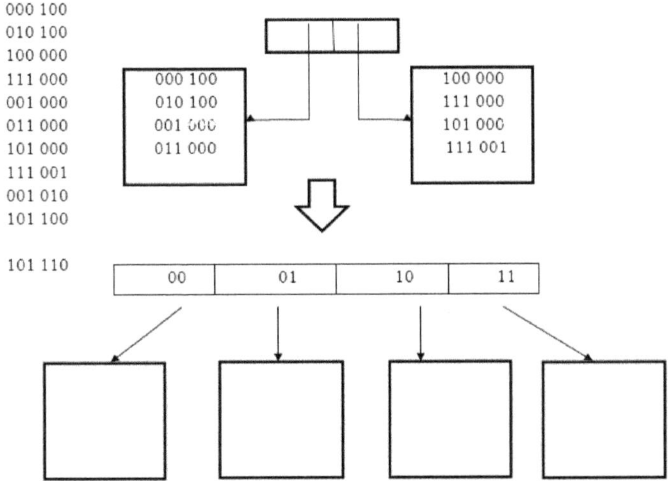

- Common strategy in internal hashing is to double the hash table and rehash each entry. However, this technique is slow, because writing all pages to disk is too expensive.
- Therefore, instead of doubling the whole hash table, we use a directory of pointers to buckets, and double the number of buckets by doubling the directory, splitting just the bucket that overflows.
- Since the directory is much smaller than the file, doubling it is much cheaper. Only one page of keys and pointers is split.

14.7. Applications of Hashing

- Construct a message authentication code (MAC)
- Digital signature
- Make commitments, but reveal message later
- Timestamping
- Key updating: key is hashed at specific intervals resulting in new key

B.E./B.TECH. DEGREE EXAMINATION, APRIL/MAY 2015

SECOND SEMESTER

COMPUTER SCIENCE AND ENGINEERING

CS 6202 – PROGRAMMING AND DATA STRUCTURES – I

(COMMON TO INFORMATION TECHNOLOGY)

(REGULATION 2013)

Time : Three hours **Maximum : 100 marks**

ANSWER ALL QUESTIONS

PART A-(10 × 2 = 20 MARKS)

1. Give two examples of C preprocessor with syntax.
2. What are function pointers in C ? Explain with example.
3. What is the difference between getc( ) and getchar( ) ? Explain.
4. Explain the syntax as given below:

   Fread(&my_record,sizeof(struct rec),ptr_myfile);
5. Define ADT.
6. What is static linked list ? State any two applications of it.
7. Write the syntax of calloc( ) and realloc( ) and mention its application in linked list.
8. Given the prefix for an expression, write its postfix

   - * - + a b c / e f – g / h i
9. What is meant by internal and external sorting ? Give four example of each type.
10. State the applications of linear and binary search techniques.

PART B (5 × 16 = 80 MARKS)

11. (a)

   1) Write a function that returns a pointer to the maximum value of an array of double's. If the array is empty, return NULL.Double * maximum(double *a, int size)(8)

   2) Write a C program to find all the roots of a quadratic equation. (8)

(or)

(b)

1) Write a C program using function to check if the given input number is palindrome or not (8)

2) Explain the C preprocessor operations, each with a neat example that is used to create macros. (8)

(or)

12. (a)

1) Write a C program that uses functions to perform the following operations using structure.

   1) Reading a complex number
   2) Writing a complex number
   3) Addition of two complex numbers
   4) Multiplication of two complex numbers (12)

2) State the advantage and disadvantage of structures and unions in C Programming.(4)

(b)

i. Perform the following to manipulate file handling using C.

   1) Define an input file handle called *input_file* , which is a pointer to a type FILE.
   2) Using *input_file,* open the file *results.dat* for read mode.
   3) Write C statements which tests to see if *input_file* has opened the data file successfully. If not,print and error message and exit the program.
   4) Write C code which will read a line of characters (terminated by a \n)from *input_file* into a character array called buffer. NULL terminate the nuffer upon reading a \n.
   5) Close the file associated with *input_file.* (12)

ii. Using C programming, display the contents of a file on screen . (4)

13.

a) Write a C program to perform addition,subtraction and multiplication operations on polynomial using linked list. (16)

(or)

b) Write C code for Circular link list with create, insert, delete,display operations using structure pointer. (16)

14. (a)

1) Write C program that checks if experssion is correctly parenthesized using stack(12)

2) Write the function to checkfor state status as Full ( ) or Empty ( ). (4)

(or)

(b) Write C program to implement Queue functions using Arrays and Macros. (16)

15. (a)

1) Sort the given integers and show the intermediate results using shell sort

35 , 12 , 14 , 9 , 15 , 45 , 32 , 95 , 40 , 5 (8)

2) Write C code to sort an integer array using shell sort. (8)

(or)

(b)

1) Explain a C code to perform binary search. (10)

2) Explain the Rehashing techniques. (6)

B.E./B.Tech. Degree Examination, November/December 2014

Second Semester

Computer Science and Engineering

CS 6202 – Programming and Data Structures – I

(Common to Information Technology)

(Regulation 2013)

Time : Three hours **Maximum : 100 marks**

Answer ALL Questions

Part A - (10 X 2 = 20 Marks)

1. Define an array. Give an example.
2. Give example on call by reference.
3. What are the statements used for reading a file.
4. Define the need for union in C.
5. What are abstract data type?
6. What is circular linked list?
7. Give the applications of stack.
8. What is double ended queue?
9. Define extendible hashing.
10. Differentiate internal and external sorting.

Part B – (5 X 16 = 80 Marks)

11.

a) Explain the various control statements in C language with example in detail. (16)

(Or)

b) Briefly discuss about:

1. Functions with number of arguments.
2. Function Pointers. (8 + 8)

12.

a) Explain the difference between structure and union with examples. (16)

(Or)

b) Explain about file manipulations in detail with suitable program. (16)

13.

a) Describe the creation of a doubly linked list and appending the list.
Give relevant coding in C. (16)

(Or)

b) Explain the following:

1. Applications of lists.
2. Polynomial manipulation (8 + 8)

14.

a) Discuss about Stack ADT in detail. Explain any one application of stack. (16)

(Or)

b) Explain about Queue ADT in detail. Explain any one application ofqueue with suitable example. (16)

15.

a) What are the different types of hashing techniques?
Explain them in detail with example. (8 + 8)

Or

b) Write an algorithm to sort a set of 'N' numbers using quick sort. Trace the algorithm for the following set of numbers:
88, 11, 22, 44, 66, 99, 32, 67, 54, 10. (16)

B.E./B.Tech. Degree Examination, May/June 2014

Second Semester

Computer Science and Engineering

CS 6202 – Programming and Data Structures – I

(Common to Computer and Communication Engineering and Information Technology)

(Regulation 2013)

Time : Three hours **Maximum : 100 marks**

Answer ALL Questions

Part A - (10 X 2 = 20 Marks)

1. With the help of the printf function show how C handles functions with variable number of arguments.
2. Define macro with an example.
3. Give applications in which union rather than structures can be used.
4. Will the following declaration work. Justify your answer.

```
Struct Student
{
        int rollno = 12;
        float marks[] = { 55, 60, 56 };
        char  gender;
};
```

5. Should arrays or linked lists be used for the following types of applications. Justify your answer.
   a) Many search operations in sorted list
   b) Many search operations in unsorted list
6. What is advantage of an ADT?
7. Define double ended queue.

8. List the applications of a Queue.
9. What is the time complexity of binary search?
10. List sorting algorithm which uses logarithmatic time complexity.

PART B – (5 X 16 = 80 MARKS)

11. (a)

1. write a c program to find the unique elements in an arrya using a function 'Unique". The function takes the array as a parameter and prints the unique elements (10)
2. Write a C program to print Fibonacci numbers. (6)

(Or)

(b) Write a C program to multiply two matrices that are represented as pointers. Use a function pointer to the function 'Multiply' which takes the two matrices as parameter and prints the result of the multiplication. (16)

12. (a)

1. Write a C program to read the contents of a file "in.txt" from last to first and write the contents to "out.txt". (8)
2. Write the function prototype and explain how files are manipulated in C. (8)

(Or)

(b)

1. Create a structure to store a complex number and write function (for addition) that handles this new structure. (8)
2. Write a program to perform the following operations for the customers of a bank using the concept of structures. (8)
    1. Input the customer details like name, account number and balance.
    2. When a withdrawal transaction is made the balance must change to reflect it.
    3. When a deposit transaction is made the balance must change to reflect it..

13.

a) Write an algorithm to perform insertion and deletion on a doubly linked list. (16)

(Or)

b) Consider an array A[1:n]. Given a position, write an algorithm to insert an element in the array. If the position is empty, the element is inserted easily. If the position is already occupied the element should be inserted with the minimum number of shifts.

(Note: The elements can shift to the left or right to make the minimum number of moves) (16)

14.

a) Write an algorithm to convert an infix expression to a postfix expression. Trace the algorithm to convert the infix expression "(a+b)*c/d+e/f" to a postfix expression.Explain the need for infix and postfix expressions. (16)

(Or)

b) Write an algorithm to perform the four operations in a double ended queue that is implemented as an array. (16)

15.

a) Write short notes on hashng and the various collision resolution techniques. (16)

(Or)

b) Write an algorithm to sort 'n' numbers using quicksort. Show how the following numbers are sorted using quicksort: 45, 28, 90, 1, 46, 39. 33, 87. (16)

A

B

C

Data Structures Laboratory

L T P C

0 0 4 2

Objectives

- To implement linear and non-linear data structures
- To understand the different operations of search trees
- To implement graph traversal algorithms
- To get familiarized to sorting and searching algorithms

1. Array implementation of Stack and Queue ADTs
2. Array implementation of List ADT
3. Linked list implementation of List, Stack and Queue ADTs
4. Applications of List, Stack and Queue ADTs
5. Implementation of Binary Trees and operations of Binary Trees
6. Implementation of Binary Search Trees
7. Implementation of AVL Trees
8. Implementation of Heaps using Priority Queues.
9. Graph representation and Traversal algorithms
10. Applications of Graphs
11. Implementation of searching and sorting algorithms
12. Hashing – any two collision techniques

Outcomes

At the end of the course, the students will be able to:

Total: 60 Periods

- Write functions to implement linear and non-linear data structure operations.
- Suggest appropriate linear/non-linear data structure operations for solving a given problem.
- Appropriately use the linear/non-linear data structure operations for a given problem
- Apply appropriate hash functions that result in a collision free scenario for data storage and retrieval.

Exp.No:1 **Array implementation of Stack ADT's**
Date:

A stack data structure can be implemented using one dimensional array. But stack implemented using array, can store only fixed number of data values. This implementation is very simple, just define a one dimensional array of specific size and insert or delete the values into that array by using **LIFO principle** with the help of a variable **'top'**. Initially top is set to -1. Whenever we want to insert a value into the stack, increment the top value by one and then insert. Whenever we want to delete a value from the stack, then delete the top value and decrement the top value by one.
Before implementing actual operations, first follow the below steps to create an empty stack.

- **Step 1:** Include all the **header files** which are used in the program and define a constant **'SIZE'** with specific value.
- **Step 2:** Declare all the **functions** used in stack implementation.
- **Step 3:** Create a one dimensional array with fixed size (**int stack[SIZE]**)
- **Step 4:** Define a integer variable **'top'** and initialize with **'-1'**. (**int top = -1**)
- **Step 5:** In main method display menu with list of operations and make suitable function calls to perform operation selected by the user on the stack.

push(value) - Inserting value into the stack
In a stack, push() is a function used to insert an element into the stack. In a stack, the new element is always inserted at **top** position. Push function takes one integer value as parameter and inserts that value into the stack. We can use the following steps to push an element on to the stack...

- **Step 1:** Check whether **stack** is **FULL**. (**top == SIZE-1**)
- **Step 2:** If it is **FULL**, then display **"Stack is FULL!!! Insertion is not possible!!!"** and terminate the function.
- **Step 3:** If it is **NOT FULL**, then increment **top** value by one (**top++**) and set stack[top] to value (**stack[top] = value**).

pop() - Delete a value from the Stack

In a stack, pop() is a function used to delete an element from the stack. In a stack, the element is always deleted from **top** position. Pop function does not take any value as parameter. We can use the following steps to pop an element from the stack...

- **Step 1:** Check whether **stack** is **EMPTY**. (**top == -1**)
- **Step 2:** If it is **EMPTY**, then display **"Stack is EMPTY!!! Deletion is not possible!!!"** and terminate the function.
- **Step 3:** If it is **NOT EMPTY**, then delete **stack[top]** and decrement **top** value by one (**top--**).

display() - Displays the elements of a Stack

We can use the following steps to display the elements of a stack...

- **Step 1:** Check whether **stack** is **EMPTY**. **(top == -1)**
- **Step 2:** If it is **EMPTY**, then display **"Stack is EMPTY!!!"** and terminate the function.
- **Step 3:** If it is **NOT EMPTY**, then define a variable **'i'** and initialize with top. Display **stack[i]** value and decrement **i** value by one (**i--**).
- **Step 4:** Repeat above step until **i** value becomes '0'.

Program:

```
#include<stdio.h>

#include<conio.h>
#define SIZE 10
void push(int);
void
pop();

void
display();
int stack[SIZE], top = -1;
void
main()

{

        int value, choice;
        while(1)

        {
                printf("\n\n***** MENU *****\n");

                printf("1. Push\n2. Pop\n3. Display\n4.

                Exit"); printf("\nEnter your choice: ");

                scanf("%d",&choice);

                switch(choice)

                {
                        case 1:
                                printf("Enter the value to be insert: ");

                                scanf("%d",&value);

                                push(value);

                                break;

                        case 2:

                                pop();

                                break;
```

```
                case 3:
                        display();
                         break;
                case 4:
                        exit(0);
                         default:
                         printf("\nWrong selection!!! Try again!!!");
            }
        }
}
void push(int value)
{
        if(top == SIZE-1)
        printf("\nStack is Full!!! Insertion is not possible!!!");
        else
        {
                top++;
                stack[top] = value;
                printf("\nInsertion success!!!");
        }
}
void pop()
{
        if(top == -1)
        printf("\nStack is Empty!!! Deletion is not possible!!!");
        else
        {
                printf("\nDeleted : %d", stack[top]);
                top--;
        }
}
void display()
{
        if(top == -1)
        printf("\nStack is Empty!!!");
        else
```

```
    {
        int i;
        printf("\nStack elements
        are:\n"); for(i=top; i>=0; i--)
        printf("%d\n",stack[i]);
    }
}
```

Output:

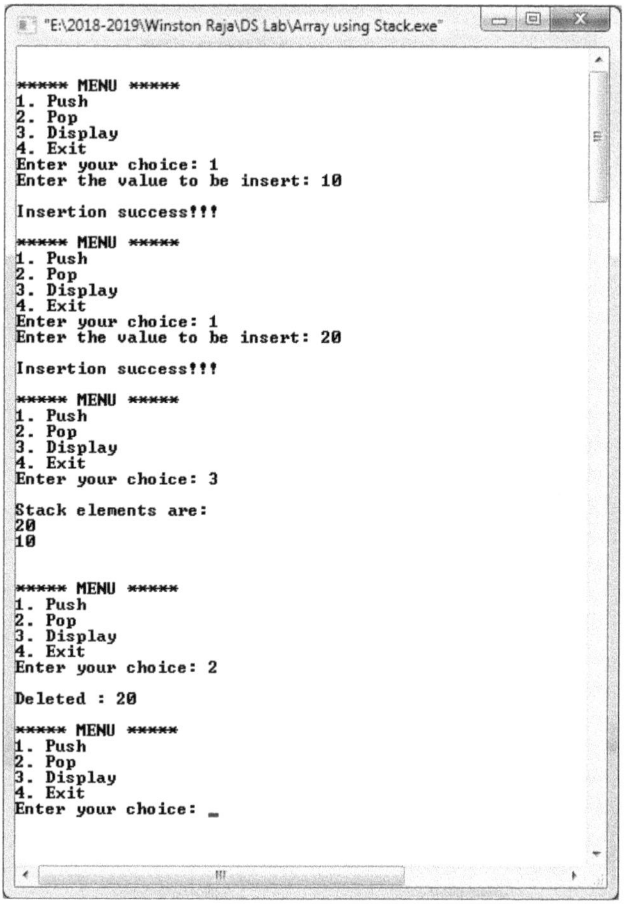

```
"E:\2018-2019\Winston Raja\DS Lab\Array using Stack.exe"

***** MENU *****
1. Push
2. Pop
3. Display
4. Exit
Enter your choice: 1
Enter the value to be insert: 10

Insertion success!!!

***** MENU *****
1. Push
2. Pop
3. Display
4. Exit
Enter your choice: 1
Enter the value to be insert: 20

Insertion success!!!

***** MENU *****
1. Push
2. Pop
3. Display
4. Exit
Enter your choice: 3

Stack elements are:
20
10


***** MENU *****
1. Push
2. Pop
3. Display
4. Exit
Enter your choice: 2

Deleted : 20

***** MENU *****
1. Push
2. Pop
3. Display
4. Exit
Enter your choice: _
```

Result:

Thus the program is completed successfully and the Result is verified.

Exp.No:2 **Array implementation of Queue ADT's**

Date :

A queue data structure can be implemented using one dimensional array. But, queue implemented using array can store only fixed number of data values. The implementation of queue data structure using array is very simple, just define a one dimensional array of specific size and insert or delete the values into that array by using **FIFO (First In First Out) principle** with the help of variables **'front'** and **'rear'**. Initially both **'front'** and **'rear'** are set to -

1. Whenever, we want to insert a new value into the queue, increment **'rear'** value by one and then insert at that position. Whenever we want to delete a value from the queue, then increment

'front' value by one and then display the value at **'front'** position as deleted element.

Before we implement actual operations, first follow the below steps to create an empty queue.

- **Step 1:** Include all the **header files** which are used in the program and define a constant **'SIZE'** with specific value.
- **Step 2:** Declare all the **user defined functions** which are used in queue implementation.
- **Step 3:** Create a one dimensional array with above defined SIZE (**int queue[SIZE]**)
- **Step 4:** Define two integer variables **'front'** and **'rear'** and initialize both with **'-1'**. (**int front = -1, rear = -1**)
- **Step 5:** Then implement main method by displaying menu of operations list and make suitable function calls to perform operation selected by the user on queue.

enQueue(value) - Inserting value into the queue

In a queue data structure, enQueue() is a function used to insert a new element into the queue. In a queue, the new element is always inserted at **rear** position. The enQueue() function takes one integer value as parameter and inserts that value into the queue. We can use the following steps to insert an element into the queue...

- **Step 1:** Check whether **queue** is **FULL.** (**rear == SIZE-1**)
- **Step 2:** If it is **FULL,** then display **"Queue is FULL!!! Insertion is not possible!!!"** and terminate the function.
- **Step 3:** If it is **NOT FULL,** then increment **rear** value by one (**rear++**) and set **queue[rear]** = **value.**

deQueue() - Deleting a value from the Queue

In a queue data structure, deQueue() is a function used to delete an element from the queue. In a queue, the element is always deleted from **front** position. The deQueue() function does not take any value as parameter. We can use the following steps to delete an element from the queue...

- **Step 1:** Check whether **queue** is **EMPTY**. (**front == rear**)
- **Step 2:** If it is **EMPTY**, then display **"Queue is EMPTY!!! Deletion is not possible!!!"** and terminate the function.
- **Step 3:** If it is **NOT EMPTY**, then increment the **front** value by one (**front ++**). Then display **queue[front]** as deleted element. Then check whether both **Front** and **rear** are equal (**front == rear**), if it **TRUE**, then set both **front** and **rear** to '**-1**' (**front = rear = -1**).

display() - Displays the elements of a Queue

We can use the following steps to display the elements of a queue...

- **Step 1:** Check whether **queue** is **EMPTY**. (**front == rear**)
- **Step 2:** If it is **EMPTY**, then display **"Queue is EMPTY!!!"** and terminate the function.
- **Step 3:** If it is **NOT EMPTY**, then define an integer variable '**i**' and set '**i = front+1**'.
- **Step 4:** Display '**queue[i]**' value and increment '**i**' value by one (**i++**). Repeat the same until '**i**' value is equal to **rear** (**i <= rear**)

Program:

```
#include<stdio.h>
#include<conio.h>
#define SIZE 10
void
enQueue(int);
void deQueue();
void display();
int queue[SIZE], front = -1, rear = -1;
void main()
{
        int value, choice;
        while(1)
        {
                printf("\n\n***** MENU *****\n");
                printf("1. Insertion\n2. Deletion\n3. Display\n4. Exit");
                printf("\nEnter your choice:
                "); scanf("%d",&choice);
                switch(choice)
                {
                                case 1:
                                                printf("Enter the value to be insert: ");
                                                scanf("%d",&value);
```

```
                    enQueue(value);
                    break;

            case 2:
                    deQueue();
                    break;
            case 3:
                    display();
                    break;
            case 4:
                    exit(0);

            default:
                    printf("\nWrong selection!!! Try again!!!");

            }
        }
}
void enQueue(int value)
{
    if(rear == SIZE-1)
    printf("\nQueue is Full!!! Insertion is not possible!!!");
    else
    {
        if(front == -1) front = 0; rear++;
        queue[rear] = value;
        printf("\nInsertion success!!!");
    }
}
void deQueue()
{
    if(front == rear)
    printf("\nQueue is Empty!!! Deletion is not possible!!!");
    else
    {
        printf("\nDeleted : %d", queue[front]);
        front++;
        if(front == rear)
        front = rear = -1;
    }
```

```
}
void display()
{
        if(rear == -1)
        printf("\nQueue is Empty!!!");
        else
        {
                int i;
                printf("\nQueue elements
                are:\n"); for(i=front; i<=rear;
                i++) printf("%d\t",queue[i]);
        }
}
```

Output:

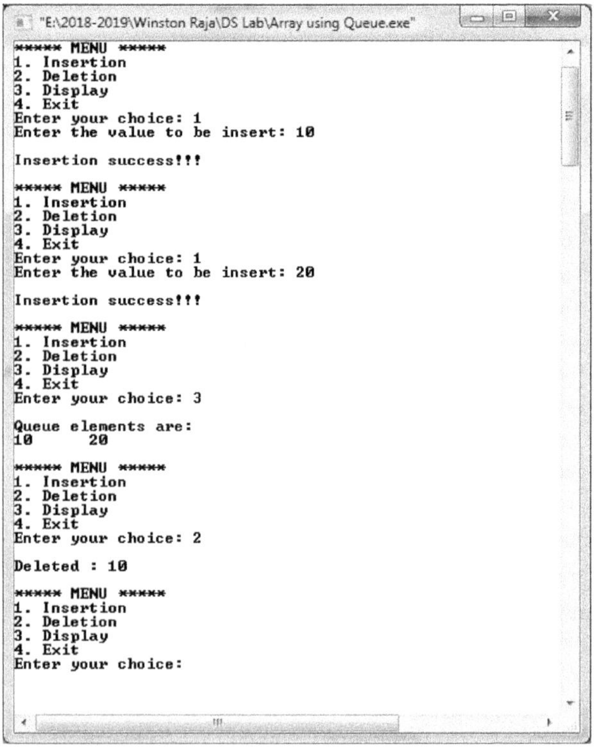

```
"E:\2018-2019\Winston Raja\DS Lab\Array using Queue.exe"
***** MENU *****
1. Insertion
2. Deletion
3. Display
4. Exit
Enter your choice: 1
Enter the value to be insert: 10

Insertion success!!!

***** MENU *****
1. Insertion
2. Deletion
3. Display
4. Exit
Enter your choice: 1
Enter the value to be insert: 20

Insertion success!!!

***** MENU *****
1. Insertion
2. Deletion
3. Display
4. Exit
Enter your choice: 3

Queue elements are:
10      20

***** MENU *****
1. Insertion
2. Deletion
3. Display
4. Exit
Enter your choice: 2

Deleted : 10

***** MENU *****
1. Insertion
2. Deletion
3. Display
4. Exit
Enter your choice:
```

Result:

Thus the program is completed successfully and the Result is verified.

Exp.No:3 **Array implementation of List ADT's**

Date :

To implement stack using linked list, we need to set the following things before implementing actual operations.

Create - Inserting an element into the List

- **Step 1:** Include all the **header files** which are used in the program. And declare all the **user defined functions**.
- **Step 2:** Define maxsize.
- **Step 3:** Implement the **main** method by displaying Menu with list of operations and make suitable function calls in the **main** method.

Insert - Inserting an element into the List

- **Step 1:** Read data from keyboard.
- **Step 2:** Read possession from keyboard
- **Step 3:** list[i+1] = list[i];
  list[pos-1] = data;
- **Step 4:** Finally data placed in the correct position.

Delete - Deleting an Element from a List

- **Step 1:** Read position from keyboard.
- **Step 2:** list[i]=list[i+1];
  n=n-1;
- **Step 3:** Data deleted from memory

Display - Displaying stack of elements

- **Step 1:** Display the data items present in the list using **list[i];**

Program:

```
#include<stdio.h>
#include<conio.h>
#define    maxsize
10int
list[maxsize],n;
void Create();
void Insert();
void Delete();
void
Display();
void Search();
void main()
```

```
{
    int choice;
    do
    {
        printf("\n Array Implementation of List\n");
        printf("\t1.create\n");
        printf("\t2.Insert\n");
        printf("\t3.Delete\n");
        printf("\t4.Display\n");
        printf("\t5.Search\n");
        printf("\t6.Exit\n");
        printf("\nEnter your
        choice:\t");
        scanf("%d",&choice);
        switch(choice)
        {
            case 1:
                Create();
                break;
            case 2:
                Insert();
                break;
            case 3:
                Delete();
                break;
            case 4:
                Display();
                break;
            case 5:
                Search();
                break;
            case 6:
                exit(1);
            default:
```

```
                    printf("\nEnter option between 1 -  6\n");
                    break;
                                        }
    }while(choice<7);
}
void Create()
{
    int i;
    printf("\nEnter the number of elements to be added in the list:\t");
    scanf("%d",&n);
    printf("\nEnter the array elements:\t");
    for(i=0;i<n;i++) scanf("%d",&list[i]); Display();
}
void Insert()
{
    int i,data,pos;
    printf("\nEnter the data to be inserted:\t");
    scanf("%d",&data);
    printf("\nEnter the position at which element to be inserted:\t");
    scanf("%d",&pos);
    for(i = n-1 ; i >= pos-1 ; i--)
    list[i+1] =
    list[i]; list[pos-
    1] = data; n+=1;
    Display();
}
void Delete( )
{
    int i,pos;
    printf("\nEnter the position of the data to be deleted:\t");
    scanf("%d",&pos);
    printf("\nThe data deleted is:\t %d", list[pos-1]);
    for(i=pos-1;i<n-1;i++)
    list[i]=list[i+1];
    n=n-1; Display();
}
void Display()
{
    int i;
```

```
    printf("\n**********Elements in the array**********\n");
    for(i=0;i<n;i++)
            printf("%d\t",list[i]);
}
void Search()
{
    int search,i,count = 0;
    printf("\nEnter the element to be searched:\t");
    scanf("%d",&search);
    for(i=0;i<n;i++)
    {
            if(search == list[i])
            {
            count++;
            }
    }
                    if(count == 0)

                    printf("\nElement not present in the list");

                    else

                    printf("\nElement present in the list");

}
```

Output:

```
"E:\2018-2019\Winston Raja\DS Lab\Array using List.exe"

 Array Implementation of List
        1.create
        2.Insert
        3.Delete
        4.Display
        5.Search
        6.Exit

Enter your choice:      1

Enter the number of elements to be added in the list:   5

Enter the array elements:       10
20
30
40
50

**********Elements in the array**********
10      20      30      40      50
 Array Implementation of List
        1.create
        2.Insert
        3.Delete
        4.Display
        5.Search
        6.Exit

Enter your choice:      2

Enter the data to be inserted:  60

Enter the position at which element to be inserted:     2

**********Elements in the array**********
10      60      20      30      40      50
 Array Implementation of List
        1.create
        2.Insert
        3.Delete
        4.Display
        5.Search
        6.Exit

Enter your choice:      3

Enter the position of the data to be deleted:   2

The data deleted is:    60
**********Elements in the array**********
10      20      30      40      50
 Array Implementation of List
        1.create
        2.Insert
        3.Delete
        4.Display
        5.Search
        6.Exit

Enter your choice:
```

Result:

Thus the program is completed successfully and the Result is verified.

Exp.No:4 **Linked list implementation of List ADT's**

Date :

In a single linked list we perform the following operations...

1. Insertion
2. Deletion
3. Display

Before we implement actual operations, first we need to setup empty list. First perform the following steps before implementing actual operations.

- **Step 1:** Include all the **header files** which are used in the program.
- **Step 2:** Declare all the **user defined** functions.
- **Step 3:** Define a **Node** structure with two members **data** and **next**
- **Step 4:** Define a Node pointer '**head**' and set it to **NULL**.
- **Step 5:** Implement the **main** method by displaying operations menu and make suitable function calls in the main method to perform user selected operation.

Insertion

In a single linked list, the insertion operation can be performed in three ways. They are as follows...

1. Inserting At Beginning of the list
2. Inserting At End of the list
3. Inserting At Specific location in the list

Inserting At Beginning of the list

We can use the following steps to insert a new node at beginning of the single linked list...

- **Step 1:** Create a **newNode** with given value.
- **Step 2:** Check whether list is **Empty (head == NULL)**
- **Step 3:** If it is **Empty** then, set **newNode→next = NULL** and **head = newNode**.
- **Step 4:** If it is **Not Empty** then, set **newNode→next = head** and **head = newNode**.

Inserting At End of the list

We can use the following steps to insert a new node at end of the single linked list...

- **Step 1:** Create a **newNode** with given value and **newNode → next** as **NULL**.
- **Step 2:** Check whether list is **Empty (head == NULL)**.
- **Step 3:** If it is **Empty** then, set **head = newNode**.
- **Step 4:** If it is **Not Empty** then, define a node pointer **temp** and initialize with **head**.
- **Step 5:** Keep moving the **temp** to its next node until it reaches to the last node in the list (until **temp → next** is equal to **NULL**).
- **Step 6:** Set **temp → next = newNode**.

Inserting At Specific location in the list (After a Node)

We can use the following steps to insert a new node after a node in the single linked list...

- **Step 1:** Create a **newNode** with given value.
- **Step 2:** Check whether list is **Empty (head == NULL)**

- **Step 3:** If it is **Empty** then, set **newNode → next = NULL** and **head = newNode**.
- **Step 4:** If it is **Not Empty** then, define a node pointer **temp** and initialize with **head**.
- **Step 5:** Keep moving the **temp** to its next node until it reaches to the node after which we want to insert the newNode (until **temp1 → data** is equal to **location**, here location is the node value after which we want to insert the newNode).
- **Step 6:** Every time check whether **temp** is reached to last node or not. If it is reached to last node then display **'Given node is not found in the list!!! Insertion not possible!!!'** and terminate the function. Otherwise move the **temp** to next node.
- **Step 7:** Finally, Set '**newNode → next = temp → next**' and '**temp → next = newNode**'

Deletion

In a single linked list, the deletion operation can be performed in three ways. They are as follows...

1. Deleting from Beginning of the list
2. Deleting from End of the list
3. Deleting a Specific Node

Deleting from Beginning of the list

We can use the following steps to delete a node from beginning of the single linked list...

- **Step 1:** Check whether list is **Empty** (**head == NULL**)
- **Step 2:** If it is **Empty** then, display **'List is Empty!!! Deletion is not possible'** and terminate the function.
- **Step 3:** If it is **Not Empty** then, define a Node pointer **'temp'** and initialize with **head**.
- **Step 4:** Check whether list is having only one node (**temp → next == NULL**)
- **Step 5:** If it is **TRUE** then set **head = NULL** and delete **temp** (Setting **Empty** list conditions)
- **Step 6:** If it is **FALSE** then set **head = temp → next**, and delete **temp**.

Deleting from End of the list

We can use the following steps to delete a node from end of the single linked list...

- **Step 1:** Check whether list is **Empty** (**head == NULL**)
- **Step 2:** If it is **Empty** then, display **'List is Empty!!! Deletion is not possible'** and terminate the function.
- **Step 3:** If it is **Not Empty** then, define two Node pointers **'temp1'** and **'temp2'** and initialize **'temp1'** with **head**.
- **Step 4:** Check whether list has only one Node (**temp1 → next == NULL**)
- **Step 5:** If it is **TRUE**. Then, set **head = NULL** and delete **temp1**. And terminate the function. (Setting **Empty** list condition)
- **Step 6:** If it is **FALSE**. Then, set '**temp2 = temp1** ' and move **temp1** to its next node. Repeat the same until it reaches to the last node in the list. (until **temp1 → next == NULL**)
- **Step 7:** Finally, Set **temp2 → next = NULL** and delete **temp1**.

Deleting a Specific Node from the list

We can use the following steps to delete a specific node from the single linked list...

- **Step 1:** Check whether list is **Empty** (**head** == **NULL**)
- **Step 2:** If it is **Empty** then, display **'List is Empty!!! Deletion is not possible'** and terminate the function.
- **Step 3:** If it is **Not Empty** then, define two Node pointers **'temp1'** and **'temp2'** and initialize **'temp1'** with **head**.
- **Step 4:** Keep moving the **temp1** until it reaches to the exact node to be deleted or to the last node. And every time set '**temp2 = temp1**' before moving the '**temp1**' to its next node.
- **Step 5:** If it is reached to the last node then display **'Given node not found in the list! Deletion not possible!!!'**. And terminate the function.
- **Step 6:** If it is reached to the exact node which we want to delete, then check whether list is having only one node or not
- **Step 7:** If list has only one node and that is the node to be deleted, then set **head** = **NULL** and delete **temp1** (**free(temp1)**).
- **Step 8:** If list contains multiple nodes, then check whether **temp1** is the first node in the list (**temp1 == head**).
- **Step 9:** If **temp1** is the first node then move the **head** to the next node (**head = head →next**) and delete **temp1**.
- **Step 10:** If **temp1** is not first node then check whether it is last node in the list (**temp1 →next** == **NULL**).
- **Step 11:** If **temp1** is last node then set **temp2 → next** = **NULL** and delete **temp1** (**free(temp1)**).
- **Step 12:** If **temp1** is not first node and not last node then set **temp2 → next** = **temp1 →next** and delete **temp1** (**free(temp1)**).

Displaying a Single Linked List

We can use the following steps to display the elements of a single linked list...

- **Step 1:** Check whether list is **Empty** (**head** == **NULL**)
- **Step 2:** If it is **Empty** then, display **'List is Empty!!!'** and terminate the function.
- **Step 3:** If it is **Not Empty** then, define a Node pointer **'temp'** and initialize with **head**.
- **Step 4:** Keep displaying **temp → data** with an arrow (**--->**) until **temp** reaches to the last node
- **Step 5:** Finally display **temp → data** with arrow pointing to **NULL** (**temp → data ---> NULL**).

Program:

```
#include<stdio.h>
#include<conio.h>
#include<stdlib.h>
void create();
```

```
void
display();
void insert();
void find();
void delete();
typedef struct node *position;
position L,p,newnode;
struct node
{
        int data;
        position next;
};
void main()
{
        int choice;
        clrscr();
        do
        {
                printf("1.create\n2.display\n3.insert\n4.find\n5.delete\n\n\n");
                printf("Enter your
                choice\n\n");
                scanf("%d",&choice);
                switch(choice)
                {

                        case 1:
                                create();
                                break;

                        case 2:
                                display();
                                break;

                        case 3:

                                insert();
                                break;

                        case 4:

                                find();
                                break;
```

```
                    case 5:
                            delete();
                            break;

                    case 6:

                            exit(0);
}

}

          while(choice<7);
          getch();
 }
 void create()
 {
          int i,n;
          L=NULL;
          newnode=(struct node*)malloc(sizeof(struct
          node)); printf("\n Enter the number of nodes to be
          inserted\n"); scanf("%d",&n);
          printf("\n Enter the
          data\n");
          scanf("%d",&newnode-
          >data); newnode-
          >next=NULL; L=newnode;
          p=L;
          for(i=2;i<=n;i++)
          {
                newnode=(struct node *)malloc(sizeof(struct node));
                scanf("%d",&newnode->data);
                newnode-
                >next=NULL; p-
                >next=newnode;
                p=newnode;
 }

  }
  void display()
  {
           p=L;
```

```
		while(p!=NULL)
		{
			printf("%d -> ",p->data);
			p=p->next;
		}
		printf("Null\n");
}
void insert()
{
		int ch;
		printf("\nEnter ur choice\n");
		printf("\n1.first\n2.middle\n3.end
		\n"); scanf("%d",&ch);
		switch(ch)
		{
			case 2:
			{
				int pos,i=1;
				p=L;
				newnode=(struct node*)malloc(sizeof(struct
				node)); printf("\nEnter the data to be
				inserted\n"); scanf("%d",&newnode->data);
				printf("\nEnter the position to be inserted\n");
				scanf("%d",&pos);
				newnode-
				>next=NULL;
				while(i<pos-1)
				{
				p=p->next;
				i++;
				}
				newnode->next=p-
				>next; p-
				>next=newnode;
				p=newnode;
				display();
				break;
				}
```

```
case 1:
{
        p=L;
        newnode=(struct node*)malloc(sizeof(struct
        node)); printf("\nEnter the data to be
        inserted\n"); scanf("%d",&newnode->data);
        newnode-
        >next=L;
        L=newnode;
        display();
}       break;
case 3:
{

        p=L;
        newnode=(struct node*)malloc(sizeof(struct
        node)); printf("\nEnter the data to be
        inserted\n"); scanf("%d",&newnode->data);
        while(p->next!=NULL)
        p=p->next;
        newnode-
        >next=NULL; p-
        >next=newnode;
        p=newnode;
}       display();
    }           break;
}
void find()
{
    int search,count=0;
    printf("\n Enter the element to be found:\n");
    scanf("%d",&search);
    p=L;
    while(p!=NULL)
    {
        if(p->data==search)
        {
            count++;
            break;
        }
```

```
            p=p->next;
        }
        if(count==0)
            printf("\n Element Not present\n");
        else
            printf("\n Element present in the list \n\n");
}
void delete()
{
        position p,temp;
        int x; p=L;
        if(p==NULL)
        {
            printf("empty list\n");
        }
        else
        {
            printf("\nEnter the data to be deleted\n");
            scanf("%d",&x);
            if(x==p->data)
            {
                temp=p;
                L=p->next;
                free(temp)
                ; display();
            }
            else
            {
                while(p->next!=NULL && p->next->data!=x)
                {
                    p=p->next;
                }
                temp=p->next;
                p->next=p->next->next;
                free(temp);
                display();
            }
        }
}
```

Output:

```
"E:\2018-2019\Winston Raja\DS Lab\Linked list implementation ...
1.create
2.display
3.insert
4.find
5.delete


Enter your choice

1

 Enter the number of nodes to be inserted
4

 Enter the data
10 20 30 40
1.create
2.display
3.insert
4.find
5.delete


Enter your choice

2
10 -> 20 -> 30 -> 40 -> Null
1.create
2.display
3.insert
4.find
5.delete


Enter your choice

3

Enter ur choice

1.first
2.middle
3.end
1

Enter the data to be inserted
60
60 -> 10 -> 20 -> 30 -> 40 -> Null
1.create
2.display
3.insert
4.find
5.delete
```

Result:

Thus the program is completed successfully and the Result is verified.

Exp.No:5 Linked list implementation of Stack ADT's

Date :

In linked list implementation of a stack, every new element is inserted as '**top**' element. That means every newly inserted element is pointed by '**top**'. Whenever we want to remove an element from the stack, simply remove the node which is pointed by '**top**' by moving '**top**' to its next node in the list. The **next** field of the first element must be always **NULL**.

To implement stack using linked list, we need to set the following things before implementing actual operations.

- **Step 1:** Include all the **header files** which are used in the program. And declare all the **user defined functions**.
- **Step 2:** Define a '**Node**' structure with two members **data** and **next**.
- **Step 3:** Define a **Node** pointer '**top**' and set it to **NULL**.
- **Step 4:** Implement the **main** method by displaying Menu with list of operations and make suitable function calls in the **main** method.

push(value) - Inserting an element into the Stack

We can use the following steps to insert a new node into the stack...

- **Step 1:** Create a **newNode** with given value.
- **Step 2:** Check whether stack is **Empty** (**top == NULL**)
- **Step 3:** If it is **Empty**, then set **newNode → next = NULL**.
- **Step 4:** If it is **Not Empty**, then set **newNode → next = top**.
- **Step 5:** Finally, set **top = newNode**.

pop() - Deleting an Element from a Stack

We can use the following steps to delete a node from the stack...

- **Step 1:** Check whether **stack** is **Empty** (**top == NULL**).
- **Step 2:** If it is **Empty**, then display **"Stack is Empty!!! Deletion is not possible!!!"** and terminate the function
- **Step 3:** If it is **Not Empty**, then define a **Node** pointer '**temp**' and set it to '**top**'.
- **Step 4:** Then set '**top = top → next**'.
- **Step 5:** Finally, delete '**temp**' (**free(temp)**).

display() - Displaying stack of elements

We can use the following steps to display the elements (nodes) of a stack...

- **Step 1:** Check whether stack is **Empty** (**top** == **NULL**).
- **Step 2:** If it is **Empty**, then display **'Stack is Empty!!!'** and terminate the function.
- **Step 3:** If it is **Not Empty**, then define a Node pointer **'temp'** and initialize with **top**.
- **Step 4:** Display '**temp → data** --->' and move it to the next node. Repeat the same until **temp** reaches to the first node in the stack (**temp → next** != **NULL**).
- **Step 5:** Finally! Display '**temp → data** ---> **NULL**'.

Program:

```
#include<stdio.h>
#include<conio.h>
struct Node
{
int data;
struct Node *next;
}*top = NULL;

void
push(int);
void pop();
void
display();

void main()
{
        int choice, value;
        printf("\n:: Stack using Linked List ::\n");
        while(1)
        {
                printf("\n****** MENU ******\n");
                printf("1. Push\n2. Pop\n3. Display\n4.
                Exit\n"); printf("Enter your choice: ");
                scanf("%d",&choice);
                switch(choice)
                {
                        case 1: printf("Enter the value to be insert: ");
                                scanf("%d", &value);
                                push(value);
                                break;
```

```
			case 2:
				pop();
				break;
			case 3:
				display();
				break;
			case 4:
				exit(0);
			default:
				printf("\nWrong selection!!! Please try again!!!\n");
		}
	}
}
void push(int value)
{
	struct Node *newNode;
	newNode = (struct Node*)malloc(sizeof(struct Node));
	newNode->data = value;
	if(top == NULL)
		newNode->next = NULL;
	else
		newNode->next = top;
		top = newNode;
		printf("\nInsertion is Success!!!\n");
}
void pop()
{
	if(top == NULL)
		printf("\nStack is Empty!!!\n");
	else
	{

			struct Node *temp = top;
		printf("\nDeleted element: %d", temp->data);
		top = temp->next;
		free(temp);
		}
}
```

```
void display()
{
	if(top == NULL)
		printf("\nStack is Empty!!!\n");
	else
	{
		struct Node *temp = top;
		while(temp->next != NULL)
		{
			printf("%d--->",temp->data);
			temp = temp -> next;
		}
		printf("%d--->NULL",temp->data);
	}
}
```

Output:

```
"E:\2018-2019\Winston Raja\DS Lab\Linked list implementation of Stack.exe"

:: Stack using Linked List ::

****** MENU ******
1. Push
2. Pop
3. Display
4. Exit
Enter your choice: 1
Enter the value to be insert: 10

Insertion is Success!!!

****** MENU ******
1. Push
2. Pop
3. Display
4. Exit
Enter your choice: 1
Enter the value to be insert: 20

Insertion is Success!!!

****** MENU ******
1. Push
2. Pop
3. Display
4. Exit
Enter your choice: 3
20--->10--->NULL
****** MENU ******
1. Push
2. Pop
3. Display
4. Exit
Enter your choice: 2

Deleted element: 20
****** MENU ******
1. Push
2. Pop
3. Display
4. Exit
Enter your choice: 3
10--->NULL
****** MENU ******
1. Push
2. Pop
3. Display
4. Exit
Enter your choice:
```

Result:

Thus the program is completed successfully and the Result is verified.

Exp.No: 6 Linked list implementation of Queue ADTs

Date :

To implement queue using linked list, we need to set the following things before implementing actual operations.

- **Step 1:** Include all the **header files** which are used in the program. And declare all the **user defined functions**.
- **Step 2:** Define a '**Node**' structure with two members **data** and **next**.
- **Step 3:** Define two **Node** pointers '**front**' and '**rear**' and set both to **NULL**.
- **Step 4:** Implement the **main** method by displaying Menu of list of operations and make suitable function calls in the **main** method to perform user selected operation.

enQueue(value) - Inserting an element into the Queue

We can use the following steps to insert a new node into the queue...

- **Step 1:** Create a **newNode** with given value and set '**newNode → next**' to **NULL**.
- **Step 2:** Check whether queue is **Empty** (**rear == NULL**)
- **Step 3:** If it is **Empty** then, set **front = newNode** and **rear = newNode**.
- **Step 4:** If it is **Not Empty** then, set **rear → next = newNode** and **rear = newNode**.

deQueue() - Deleting an Element from Queue

We can use the following steps to delete a node from the queue...

- **Step 1:** Check whether **queue** is **Empty** (**front == NULL**).
- **Step 2:** If it is **Empty**, then display **"Queue is Empty!!! Deletion is not possible!!!"** and terminate from the function
- **Step 3:** If it is **Not Empty** then, define a Node pointer '**temp**' and set it to '**front**'.
- **Step 4:** Then set '**front = front → next**' and delete '**temp**' (**free(temp)**).

display() - Displaying the elements of Queue

We can use the following steps to display the elements (nodes) of a queue...

- **Step 1:** Check whether queue is **Empty** (**front == NULL**).
- **Step 2:** If it is **Empty** then, display **'Queue is Empty!!!'** and terminate the function.
- **Step 3:** If it is **Not Empty** then, define a Node pointer **'temp'** and initialize with **front**.
- **Step 4:** Display '**temp → data** --->' and move it to the next node. Repeat the same until '**temp**' reaches to '**rear**' (**temp → next** != **ULL**).
- **Step 5:** Finally! Display '**temp → data** ---> **NULL**'.

Program:

```
#include<stdio.h>
#include<conio.h
> void enqueue();
void dequeue();
void display();
typedef struct node *position;
position front=NULL,rear=NULL,newnode,temp,p;
struct node
{
	int data;
	position next;
};
void main()
{
	int choice;
	do
	{
		printf("1.Enqueue\n2.Dequeue\n3.display\n4.exit\n");
		printf("Enter your
		choice\n\n");
		scanf("%d",&choice);
		switch(choice)
		{

			case 1:
				enqueue();
				break;
			case 2:
				dequeue();
				break;

			case 3:
				display();
				break;
			case 4:
				exit(0);
		}
	}
```

```
        while(choice<5);
}
void enqueue()
{
        newnode=(struct node*)malloc(sizeof(struct
        node)); printf("\n Enter the data to be
        enqueued\n"); scanf("%d",&newnode->data);
        newnode->next=NULL;
        if(rear==NULL)
          front=rear=newnod
                  e;
        else
        {
          rear->next=newnode;
          rear=newnode;
        }
  display();
}
void dequeue()
{
        if(front==NULL)
                printf("\nEmpty queue!!!!! Deletion not possible\n");
        else if(front==rear)
          {
                printf("\nFront element %d is deleted from queue!!!! now
                      queue is empty!!!! no more deletion possible!!!!\n",front-
                      >data);
                front=rear=NULL;
          }
        else
          {       temp=front;
                  front=front->next;
                  printf("\nFront element %d is deleted from queue!!!!\n",temp->data);
                  free(temp);
```

```
        }
    display();
}
void display()
{
        p=front;
        while(p!=NULL)
        {
                printf("%d -> ",p->data);
                p=p->next;
        }
        printf("Null\n");
}
```

Output:

```
"E:\2018-2019\Winston Raja\DS Lab\Linked list implementation of Queue.exe"
1.Enqueue
2.Dequeue
3.display
4.exit
Enter your choice

1

 Enter the data to be enqueued
10
10 -> Null
1.Enqueue
2.Dequeue
3.display
4.exit
Enter your choice

1

 Enter the data to be enqueued
20
10 -> 20 -> Null
1.Enqueue
2.Dequeue
3.display
4.exit
Enter your choice

2

Front element 10 is deleted from queue!!!!
20 -> Null
1.Enqueue
2.Dequeue
3.display
4.exit
Enter your choice

3
20 -> Null
1.Enqueue
2.Dequeue
3.display
4.exit
Enter your choice
```

Result:

Thus the program is completed successfully and the Result is verified.

Exp.No:7 **Applications of List - Polynomial Addition**

Date :

Algorithm Steps:

Step 1: Read the coefficient and power of the polynomial equation one and assign it's elements into a linked list.

Step 2: Read the coefficient and power of the polynomial equation two and assign it's elements into a linked list.

Step 3: Sorting the first polynomial in power order wise. Compare the first node's power with next nodes power, if second node's power is greater than first Node then swap. Repeat the process until we get the proper order.

Step 4: Sorting the second polynomial in power order wise. Compare the first node's power with next nodes power, if second node's power is greater than first Node then swap. Repeat the process until we get the proper order.

Step 5: Add the two polynomial.

If power part of the two list is equal than add the coefficient

Program:

```
#include <stdio.h>
#include <conio.h>
#include <stdlib.h>
struct poly
{
        int coeff;
        int exp;
        struct poly *next;
}*head1=NULL,*head2=NULL,*head3=NULL,*head4=NULL,*temp,*ptr;

void create();
void makenode(int,int);
struct poly *insertend(struct poly *);
```

```
void display(struct poly );
struct poly *addtwopoly(struct poly *,struct poly *,struct poly *);
struct poly *subtwopoly(struct poly *,struct poly *,struct poly *);
struct poly *multwopoly(struct poly *,struct poly *,struct poly *);
struct poly *dispose(struct poly *);
int search(struct poly *,int);

void
main()
{
        int ch,coefficient,exponent;
        int listno;
        while(1)
        {
                printf("\n\tMenu");
                printf("\n\t1. Create First Polynomial.");
                printf("\n\t2. Display First Polynomial.");
                printf("\n\t3. Create Second Polynomial.");
                printf("\n\t4. Display Second
                Polynomial."); printf("\n\t5. Add Two
                Polynomials."); printf("\n\t6. Display
                Result of Addition."); printf("\n\t7.
                Subtract Two Polynomials."); printf("\n\t8.
                Display Result of Subtraction.");
                printf("\n\t9. Multiply Two Polynomials.");
                printf("\n\t10. Display Result of
                Product."); printf("\n\t11. Dispose List.");
                printf("\n\t12. Exit");
                printf("\n\nEnter your
                choice?"); scanf("%d",&ch);
                switch(ch)
                {
                                case 1:
                                        printf("\nGenerating first polynomial:");
                                        printf("\nEnter coefficient?");
                                        scanf("%d",&coefficient);
                                        printf("\nEnter exponent?");
                                        scanf("%d",&exponent);
                                        makenode(coefficient,exponent);
                                        head1 = insertend(head1);
                                        break;
```

```
case 2:
        display(head1);
        break;

case 3:
        printf("\nGenerating second polynomial:");
        printf("\nEnter coefficient?");
         scanf("%d",&coefficient);
        printf("\nEnter exponent?");
        scanf("%d",&exponent);
        makenode(coefficient,exponent);
        head2 = insertend(head2);
        break;

case 4:
        display(head2);
        break;

case 5:
        printf("\nDisposing result list.");
        head3=dispose(head3);
        head3=addtwopoly(head1,head2,head3);
        printf("Addition successfully done!");
        break;
case 6:
        display(head3);
        break;
case 7:
        head3=dispose(head3);
        head3=subtwopoly(head1,head2,head3);
        printf("Subtraction successfully done!");
        getch();
        break;
case 8:
        display(head3);
        break;
case 9:
        head3=dispose(head3);
        head4=dispose(head4);
        head4=multwopoly(head1,head2,head3);
        break;
case 10:
        display(head4);
        break;
```

```
                case 11:
                        printf("Enter list number to dispose(1 to 4)?");
                        scanf("%d",&listno);
                        if(listno==1)
                                head1=dispose(head1);
                        else if(listno==2)
                                head2=dispose(head2);
                        else if(listno==3)
                                head3=dispose(head3);
                        else if(listno==4)
                                head4=dispose(head4);
                        else
                                printf("Invalid number specified.");
                                break;
                case 12:
                        exit(0);
                default:
                        printf("Invalid Choice!");
                        break;
        }}}

void create()
{
        ptr=(struct poly *)malloc(sizeof(struct poly));
        if(ptr==NULL)
        {
                printf("Memory Allocation Error!");
                exit(1);
        }}

void makenode(int c,int e)
{
        create();
        ptr->coeff = c;
        ptr->exp = e;
        ptr->next = NULL;
}
```

```
struct poly *insertend(struct poly *head)
{
	if(head==NULL)
		head = ptr;
	else
	{
		temp=head;
		while(temp->next != NULL)
		temp = temp->next;
		temp->next = ptr;
	}
	return head;
}

void display(struct poly *head)
{
	if(head==NULL)
		printf("List is empty!");
	else
	{
		temp=head;
		while(temp!=NULL)
		{
			printf("(%d,%d)->",temp->coeff,temp->exp);
			temp=temp->next;
		}
		printf("bb ");
	}
	getch();
}

struct poly *addtwopoly(struct poly *h1,struct poly *h2,struct poly *h3)
{
	/*
	(5,3)->(6,1) + (7,3)->(9,2) = (12,3)->(6,1)->(9,2)
	*/
	struct poly *temp1,*temp2,*temp3;
	temp1=h1;
	temp2=h2;
```

```
	while(temp1!=NULL || temp2!=NULL)
	{
		if(temp1->exp==temp2->exp)
		{
			makenode(temp1->coeff+temp2->coeff,temp1->exp);
			h3=insertend(h3);
		}
		else
		{
			makenode(temp1->coeff,temp1->exp);
				h3=insertend(h3);
				makenode(temp2->coeff,temp2->exp);
				h3=insertend(h3);
			}
			temp1=temp1->next;
			temp2=temp2->next;
		}
		if(temp1==NULL && temp2!=NULL)
		{
			while(temp2!=NULL)
			{
				makenode(temp2->coeff,temp2->exp);
				h3=insertend(h3);
				temp2=temp2->next;
			}
		}
		if(temp2==NULL && temp1!=NULL)
		{
			while(temp1!=NULL)
			{
				makenode(temp2->coeff,temp2->exp);
				h3=insertend(h3);
				temp1=temp1->next;
			}
		}
		return h3;
}
struct poly *subtwopoly(struct poly *h1,struct poly *h2,struct poly *h3)
{
```

```
/*
(5,3)->(6,1) – (7,3)->(9,2) = (-2,3)+(6,1)-(9,2)
*/
struct poly *temp1,*temp2,*temp3;
temp1=h1;
temp2=h2;
while(temp1!=NULL || temp2!=NULL)
{
	if(temp1->exp==temp2->exp)
	{
		makenode(temp1->coeff-temp2->coeff,temp1->exp);
		h3=insertend(h3);
	}
	else
	{
		makenode(temp1->coeff,temp1->exp);
		h3=insertend(h3);
		makenode(-temp2->coeff,temp2->exp);
		h3=insertend(h3);
	}
	temp1=temp1->next;
	temp2=temp2->next;
}
if(temp1==NULL && temp2!=NULL)
{
	while(temp2!=NULL)
	{
		makenode(temp2->coeff,temp2->exp);
		h3=insertend(h3);
		temp2=temp2->next;
	}
}
if(temp2==NULL && temp1!=NULL)
{
	while(temp1!=NULL)
	{
		makenode(-temp2->coeff,temp2->exp);
		h3=insertend(h3);
		temp1=temp1->next;
	}
```

```
        }
        return h3;
}
struct poly *multwopoly(struct poly *h1,struct poly *h2,struct poly *h3)
{
        /*
        h1=(5,3)->(6,1) * h2=(7,3)->(9,2) (5,3)->(7,3),(9,2) = (35,6),(45,5) (6,1)-
        >(7,3),(9,2) = (42,4),(54,3) h3->(35,6)->(45,5)->(42,4)->(54,3)
        (35,6)+(45,5)+(42,4)+(54,3)=Result
        */
        int res=0;
        struct poly *temp1,*temp2,*temp3;
        printf("nDisplaying First
        Polynomial:ntt"); display(h1);
        printf("nDisplaying Second Polynomial:ntt");
        display(h2);

        temp1=h1;
        while(temp1!=NULL)
        {
                temp2=h2;
                while(temp2!=NULL)
                {
                        makenode(temp1->coeff*temp2->coeff,temp1->exp+temp2->exp);
                        h3=insertend(h3);
                        temp2=temp2->next;
                }
                temp1=temp1->next;
        }

        printf("nDisplaying Initial Result of Product:ntt");
        display(h3);
        getch();

        temp1=h3;
        while(temp1!=NULL)
        {
                temp2=temp1->next;
```

```
{
                while(temp2!=NULL)
                 res=0;
                 {
                         if(temp1->exp==temp2-
                         >exp) res += temp2->coeff;
                         temp2=temp2->next;
                 }
                 if(search(head4,temp1->exp)==1)
                 {
                         makenode(res+temp1->coeff,temp1->exp);
                         head4=insertend(head4);
                 }
                 temp1=temp1->next;
         }
         return head4;
 }

 int search(struct poly *h,int val)
 {
         struct poly *tmp;
         tmp=h;
         while(tmp!=NULL)
         {
                 if(tmp->exp==val)
                         return 0;
                 tmp=tmp->next;
         }
return 1;
 }

 struct poly *dispose(struct poly *list)
 {
         if(list==NULL)
         {
                 printf("List is already empty.");
                 return list;
         }
         else
```

```
{
                    temp=list;
                   while(list!=NULL)
                   free(temp);
                   list=list->next;
                   temp=list;

}
          return list;
         }
 }
```

Output:

Menu
1. Create First Polynomial.
2. Display First Polynomial.
3. Create Second Polynomial.
4. Display Second Polynomial.
5. Add Two Polynomials.
6. Display Result of Addition.
7. Subtract Two Polynomials.
8. Display Result of Subtraction.
9. Multiply Two Polynomials.
10. Display Result of Product.
11. Dispose List.
12. Exit

Enter your choice?1

Enter exponent?3

Menu

1. Create First Polynomial.
2. Display First Polynomial.
3. Create Second Polynomial.
4. Display Second Polynomial.
5. Add Two Polynomials.
6. Display Result of Addition.
7. Subtract Two Polynomials.
8. Display Result of Subtraction.
9. Multiply Two Polynomials.
10. Display Result of Product.
11. Dispose List.
12. Exit

Enter your choice?1

Generating first

polynomial: Enter

coefficient?5

Enter exponent?2

1. Create First Polynomial.
2. Display First Polynomial.
3. Create Second Polynomial.
4. Display Second Polynomial.
5. Add Two Polynomials.
6. Display Result of Addition.
7. Subtract Two Polynomials.
8. Display Result of Subtraction.
9. Multiply Two Polynomials.
10. Display Result of Product.
11. Dispose List.
12. Exit

Enter your Choice?2 (4,3)->(5,2)->bb

Menu

1. Create First Polynomial.
2. Display First Polynomial.
3. Create Second Polynomial.
4. Display Second Polynomial.
5. Add Two Polynomials.
6. Display Result of Addition.
7. Subtract Two Polynomials.

10. Display Result of Product.
11. Dispose List.
12. Exit

Enter your choice?3

Generating second

polynomial: Enter

coefficient?7

Enter exponent?4

Menu

1. Create First Polynomial.
2. Display First Polynomial.
3. Create Second Polynomial.
4. Display Second Polynomial.
5. Add Two Polynomials.
6. Display Result of Addition.
7. Subtract Two Polynomials.
8. Display Result of Subtraction.
9. Multiply Two Polynomials.
10. Display Result of Product.
11. Dispose List.
12. Exit

Enter your choice?3

Generating second

polynomial: Enter

coefficient?4

Enter exponent?2

Menu

1. Create First Polynomial.
2. Display First Polynomial.
3. Create Second Polynomial.
4. Display Second Polynomial.
5. Add Two Polynomials.
6. Display Result of Addition.
7. Subtract Two Polynomials.
8. Display Result of Subtraction.
9. Multiply Two Polynomials.
10. Display Result of Product.
11. Dispose List.
12. Exit

Enter your choice?4 (7,4)->(4,2)->bb

Menu

1. Create First Polynomial.
2. Display First Polynomial.
3. Create Second Polynomial.

```
    4. Display Second Polynomial.
    5. Add Two Polynomials.
    6. Display Result of Addition.
    7. Subtract Two Polynomials.
    8. Display Result of Subtraction.
    9. Multiply Two Polynomials.
    10. Display Result of Product.
    11. Dispose List.
    12. Exit

Enter your choice?5

Disposing result list.List is already empty.Addition successfully done!

    Menu
    1. Create First Polynomial.
    2. Display First Polynomial.
    3. Create Second Polynomial.
    4. Display Second Polynomial.
    5. Add Two Polynomials.
    6. Display Result of Addition.
    7. Subtract Two Polynomials.
    8. Display Result of Subtraction.
    9. Multiply Two Polynomials.
    10. Display Result of Product.
    11. Dispose List.
    12. Exit

Enter your choice?6 (4,3)->(7,4)->(9,2)->bb

    Menu
    1. Create First Polynomial.
    2. Display First Polynomial.
    3. Create Second Polynomial.
    4. Display Second Polynomial.
    5. Add Two Polynomials.
    6. Display Result of Addition.
    7. Subtract Two Polynomials.
    8. Display Result of Subtraction.
    9. Multiply Two Polynomials.
    10. Display Result of Product.
    11. Dispose List.
    12. Exit

Enter your choice?
```

Exp.No:8 **Applications of Stack - Infix to Postfix**

Date :

Algorithm to convert Infix to Postfix

Let, X is an arithmetic expression written in infix notation. This algorithm finds the equivalent postfix expression Y.

1. Push "("onto Stack, and add ")" to the end of X.
2. Scan X from left to right and repeat Step 3 to 6 for each element of X until the Stack is empty.
3. If an operand is encountered, add it to Y.
4. If a left parenthesis is encountered, push it onto Stack.
5. If an operator is encountered ,then:
   1. Repeatedly pop from Stack and add to Y each operator (on the top of Stack) which has the same precedence as or higher precedence than operator.
   2. Add operator to Stack. [End of If]
6. If a right parenthesis is encountered ,then:
   1. Repeatedly pop from Stack and add to Y each operator (on the top of Stack) until a left parenthesis is encountered.
   2. Remove the left Parenthesis. [End of If]
      [End of If]
7. END.

Program:

```
#include<stdio.h>

#include<stdlib.h>

#include<ctype.h>

#include<string.h>

#define SIZE 100 char stack[SIZE];

int top = -1;

void push(char item)

{

if(top >= SIZE-1)

{
```

```
                printf("\nStack Overflow.");
        }
        else
        {
                top = top+1;
                stack[top] = item;
        }
}
char pop()
{
        char item ;

        if(top <0)
        {
                printf("stack under flow: invalid infix expression");
                getchar();
                exit(1);
        }
        else
        {
                item =
                stack[top]; top =
                top-1;
        }       return(item);
}
int is_operator(char symbol)
{
        if(symbol == '^' || symbol == '*' || symbol == '/' || symbol == '+' || symbol =='-')
        {
                return 1;
        }
        else
        {
        return 0;
        }
}
int precedence(char symbol)
```

```
{
        if(symbol == '^')
        {
                return(3);
        }
        else if(symbol == '*' || symbol == '/')
        {
                return(2);
        }
        else if(symbol == '+' || symbol == '-')
        {
                return(1);
        }
        else
        {
                return(0);
        }}
void InfixToPostfix(char infix_exp[], char postfix_exp[])
{
        int i, j;
        char
        item;
        char x;
        push('(');
        strcat(infix_exp,")");

        i=0; j=0;
        item=infix_exp[i];

        while(item != '\0')
        {
                if(item == '(')
                {
                        push(item);
                }
else if( isdigit(item) || isalpha(item))
{
```

```
            postfix_exp[j] = item;
            j++;
        }
        else if(is_operator(item) == 1)
        {
            x=pop();
            while(is_operator(x) == 1 && precedence(x)>= precedence(item))
            {
                postfix_exp[j] = x;
                j++;
                x = pop();
            }
            push(x);
            push(item);
        }
        else if(item == ')')
        {
            x = pop();
            while(x != '(')
            {
                postfix_exp[j] = x;
                j++;
                x = pop();
            }}
        else
        {
            printf("\nInvalid infix Expression.\n");
            getchar();
            exit(1);
        }
        i++;

        item = infix_exp[i];
    }
    if(top>0)
    {
        printf("\nInvalid infix Expression.\n");
        getchar();
      exit(1);
```

```
	}
	if(top>0)
	{
		printf("\nInvalid infix Expression.\n");
		getchar();
		exit(1);
	}


	postfix_exp[j] = '\0';
}
int main()
{
	char infix[SIZE], postfix[SIZE];	/* declare infix string and postfix string */
	printf("ASSUMPTION: The infix expression contains single letter variables and
single digit constants only.\n");
	printf("\nEnter Infix expression : ");
	gets(infix);
	InfixToPostfix(infix,postfix);		/* call to convert */
	printf("Postfix Expression: ");
	puts(postfix);			/* print postfix expression */
	return 0;
}
```

Output:

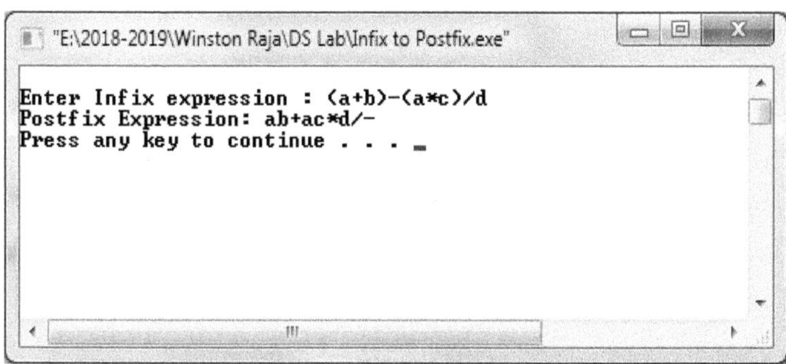

Result:

Thus the program is completed successfully and the Result is verified.

Exp.No:9 **Applications of Queue ADTs**

Date : **First Come First Serve Scheduling**

In the "First come first serve" scheduling algorithm, as the name suggests, the process which arrives first, gets executed first, or we can say that the process which requests the CPU first, gets the CPU allocated first.

- First Come First Serve, is just like **FIFO**(First in First out) Queue data structure, where the data element which is added to the queue first, is the one who leaves the queue first.
- This is used in Batch Systems.
- It's **easy to understand and implement** programmatically, using a Queue data structure, where a new process enters through the **tail** of the queue, and the scheduler selects process from the **head** of the queue.
- A perfect real life example of FCFS scheduling is **buying tickets at ticket counter**.

Calculating Average Waiting Time

- For every scheduling algorithm, **Average waiting time** is a crucial parameter to judge it's performance.
- AWT or Average waiting time is the average of the waiting times of the processes in the queue, waiting for the scheduler to pick them for execution.
- Lower the Average Waiting Time, better the scheduling algorithm.
- Consider the processes P1, P2, P3, P4 given in the below table, arrives for execution in the same order, with **Arrival Time** 0, and given **Burst Time**, let's find the average waiting time using the FCFS scheduling algorithm.

PROCESS	BURST TIME
P1	21
P2	3
P3	6
P4	2

The average waiting time will be = (0 + 21 + 24 + 30)/4 = 18.75 ms

P1	P2	P3	P4

0 21 24 30 32

This is the GANTT chart for the above processes

The average waiting time will be 18.75 ms

For the above given processes, first **P1** will be provided with the CPU resources,

- Hence, waiting time for **P1** will be 0
- **P1** requires 21 ms for completion, hence waiting time for **P2** will be 21 ms
- Similarly, waiting time for process **P3** will be execution time of **P1** + execution time for **P2**, which will be (21 + 3) ms = 24 ms.
- For process **P4** it will be the sum of execution times of **P1**, **P2** and **P3**.

The **GANTT chart** above perfectly represents the waiting time for each process.

Program:

```
#include<stdio.h>
int main()
{
        int n,bt[20],wt[20],tat[20],avwt=0,avtat=0,i,j;
        printf("Enter total number of processes(maximum
        20):"); scanf("%d",&n);
        printf("\nEnter Process Burst Time\n");
        for(i=0;i<n;i++)
        {
                printf("P[%d]:",i+1);
                scanf("%d",&bt[i]);
        }

        wt[0]=0;   //waiting time for first process is 0
                              //calculating waiting time
        for(i=1;i<n;i++)
        {
                wt[i]=0;
                for(j=0;j<i;j++)
                wt[i]+=bt[j];
        }

        printf("\nProcess\t\tBurst Time\tWaiting Time\tTurnaround Time");
                //calculating turnaround
        time for(i=0;i<n;i++)
        {
                tat[i]=bt[i]+wt[i
                ]; avwt+=wt[i];
                avtat+=tat[i];
                printf("\nP[%d]\t\t%d\t\t%d\t\t%d",i+1,bt[i],wt[i],tat[i]);
        }

                avwt/=i;
```

```
        avtat/=i;
        printf("\n\nAverage Waiting Time:%d",avwt);
        printf("\nAverage Turnaround Time:%d",avtat);
        return 0;
}
```

Output:

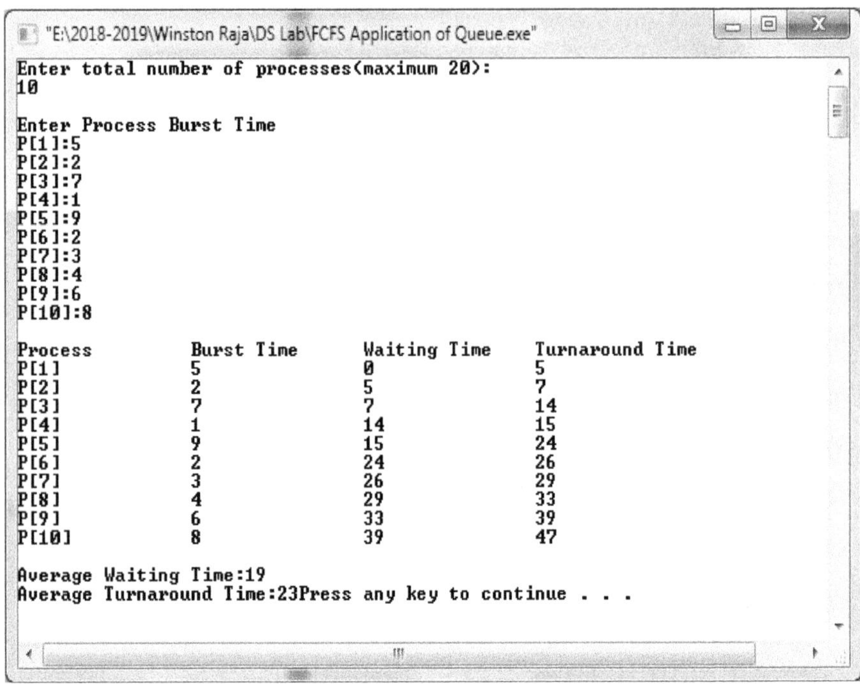

```
"E:\2018-2019\Winston Raja\DS Lab\FCFS Application of Queue.exe"
Enter total number of processes(maximum 20):
10

Enter Process Burst Time
P[1]:5
P[2]:2
P[3]:7
P[4]:1
P[5]:9
P[6]:2
P[7]:3
P[8]:4
P[9]:6
P[10]:8

Process         Burst Time      Waiting Time    Turnaround Time
P[1]            5               0               5
P[2]            2               5               7
P[3]            7               7               14
P[4]            1               14              15
P[5]            9               15              24
P[6]            2               24              26
P[7]            3               26              29
P[8]            4               29              33
P[9]            6               33              39
P[10]           8               39              47

Average Waiting Time:19
Average Turnaround Time:23Press any key to continue . . .
```

Result:

Thus the program is completed successfully and the Result is verified.

Exp.No:10 Implementation of Binary Trees and operations of Binary Trees

Date :

Procedure:

Traversing a tree means visiting every node in the tree. You might for instance want to add all the values in the tree or find the largest one. For all these operations, you will need to visit each node of the tree.

Linear data structures like arrays, stacks, queues and linked list have only one way to read the data. But a hierarchical data structure like a tree can be traversed in different ways.

Let's think about how we can read the elements of the tree in the image shown above. Starting from top, Left to right

1 -> 12 -> 9 -> 5 -> 6

Starting from bottom, Left to right
5 -> 6 -> 12 -> 9 -> 1

Although this process is somewhat easy, it doesn't respect the hierarchy of the tree, only the depth of the nodes.

Instead, we use traversal methods that take into account the basic structure of a tree i.e.

```
struct node
{
   int data;
   struct node* left;
   struct node* right;
}
```

The struct node pointed to by left and right might have other left and right children so we should think of them as sub-trees instead of sub-nodes.

According to this structure, every tree is a combination of

- A node carrying data
- Two subtrees

Remember that our goal is to visit each node, so we need to visit all the nodes in the subtree, visit the root node and visit all the nodes in the right subtree as well.

Depending on the order in which we do this, there can be three types of traversal.

Inorder traversal

1. First, visit all the nodes in the left subtree
2. Then the root node
3. Visit all the nodes in the right subtree

```
inorder(root->left)
display(root->data)
```

```
inorder(root->right)
```

Preorder traversal

1. Visit root node
2. Visit all the nodes in the left subtree
3. Visit all the nodes in the right subtree

```
display(root->data)
preorder(root->left)
preorder(root->right)
```

Postorder traversal

1. visit all the nodes in the left subtree
2. visit the root node
3. visit all the nodes in the right subtree

```
postorder(root->left)
postorder(root->right)
display(root->data)
```

Program:

```
#include <stdio.h>
#include <stdlib.h>
struct node
{
        int data;
        struct node* left;
        struct node* right;
};
void inorder(struct node* root)
{
        if(root == NULL)
                return; inorder(root->left);
                printf("%d ->", root->data);
                 inorder(root->right);
}
struct node* createNode(value)
{
void preorder(struct node* root)
{
```

```
        if(root == NULL)
                return;
        printf("%d ->", root-
        >data); preorder(root-
        >left); preorder(root-
        >right);
}

void postorder(struct node* root)
{
        if(root == NULL)
                return;
        postorder(root->left);
        postorder(root->right);
        printf("%d ->", root-
        >data);
}
        struct node* newNode = malloc(sizeof(struct node));
        newNode->data = value;
        newNode->left = NULL;
        newNode->right = NULL;
        return newNode;
}
struct node* insertLeft(struct node *root, int value)
{
        root->left = createNode(value);
        return root->left;
}
struct node* insertRight(struct node *root, int value)
{
        root->right = createNode(value);
        return root->right;
}

int main()
{
        struct node* root =
        createNode(1); insertLeft(root,
```

```
        12); insertRight(root, 9);
        insertLeft(root->left, 5);
        insertRight(root->left, 6);
        printf("Inorder traversal
        \n"); inorder(root);
        printf("\nPreorder traversal
        \n"); preorder(root);
        printf("\nPostorder traversal
        \n"); postorder(root);
}
```

Output:

```
"E:\2018-2019\Winston Raja\DS Lab\Binary tree traverse.exe"
Inorder traversal
5 ->12 ->6 ->1 ->9 ->
Preorder traversal
1 ->12 ->5 ->6 ->9 ->
Postorder traversal
5 ->6 ->12 ->9 ->1 ->Press any key to continue . . .
```

Result:

Thus the program is completed successfully and the Result is verified.

Exp.No:11 **Implementation of Binary Search Trees**

Date :

Operations on Binary Search Tree Operations on a Binary

The following operations are performed on a binary each tree...

- Search
- Insertion
- Deletion

Search Operation in BST

In a binary search tree, the search operation is performed with **O(log n)** time complexity. The search operation is performed as follows...

- **Step 1:** Read the search element from the user
- **Step 2:** Compare, the search element with the value of root node in the tree.
- **Step 3:** If both are matching, then display "Given node found!!!" and terminate the function
- **Step 4:** If both are not matching, then check whether search element is smaller or larger than that node value.
- **Step 5:** If search element is smaller, then continue the search process in left subtree.
- **Step 6:** If search element is larger, then continue the search process in right subtree.
- **Step 7:** Repeat the same until we found exact element or we completed with a leaf node
- **Step 8:** If we reach to the node with search value, then display "Element is found" and terminate the function.
- **Step 9:** If we reach to a leaf node and it is also not matching, then display "Element not found" and terminate the function.

Insertion Operation in BST

In a binary search tree, the insertion operation is performed with **O(log n)** time complexity. In binary search tree, new node is always inserted as a leaf node. The insertion operation is performed as follows...

- **Step 1:** Create a newNode with given value and set its **left** and **right** to **NULL.**
- **Step 2:** Check whether tree is Empty.
- **Step 3:** If the tree is **Empty**, then set set **root** to **newNode.**
- **Step 4:** If the tree is **Not Empty**, then check whether value of new Node is **smaller** or **larger** than the node (here it is root node).
- **Step 5:** If newNode is **smaller** than **or equal** to the node, then move to its **left** child. If newNode is **larger** than the node, then move to its **right** child.
- **Step 6:** Repeat the above step until we reach to a **leaf** node (e.i., reach to NULL).
- **Step 7:** After reaching a leaf node, then isert the newNode as **left child** if new Node is **smaller or equal** to that leaf else insert it as **right child.**

Deletion Operation in BST

In a binary search tree, the deletion operation is performed with **O(log n)** time complexity. Deleting a node from Binary search tree has follwing three cases...

- **Case 1**: Deleting a Leaf node (A node with no children)
- **Case 2:** Deleting a node with one child
- **Case 3:** Deleting a node with two children

Case 1: Deleting a leaf node

We use the following steps to delete a leaf node from BST...

- **Step 1: Find** the node to be deleted using **search operation**
- **Step 2:** Delete the node using **free** function (If it is a leaf) and terminate the function.

Case 2: Deleting a node with one child

We use the following steps to delete a node with one child from BST...

- **Step 1: Find** the node to be deleted using **search operation**
- **Step 2:** If it has only one child, then create a link between its parent and child nodes.

Case 3: Deleting a node with two children

We use the following steps to delete a node with two children from BST...

- **Step 1: Find** the node to be deleted using **search operation**
- **Step 2:** If it has two children, then find the **largest** node in its **left subtree** (OR) the **smallest** node in its **right subtree**.
- **Step 3: Swap** both **deleting node** and node which found in above step.
- **Step 4:** Then, check whether deleting node came to **case 1** or **case 2** else goto steps 2
- **Step 5:** If it comes to **case 1**, then delete using case 1 logic.
- **Step 6:** If it comes to **case 2**, then delete using case 2 logic.
- **Step 7:** Repeat the same process until node is deleted from the tree.

Example

Construct a Binary Search Tree by inserting the following sequence of numbers...

10,12,5,4,20,8,7,15 and 13

Above elements are inserted into a Binary Search Tree as follows...

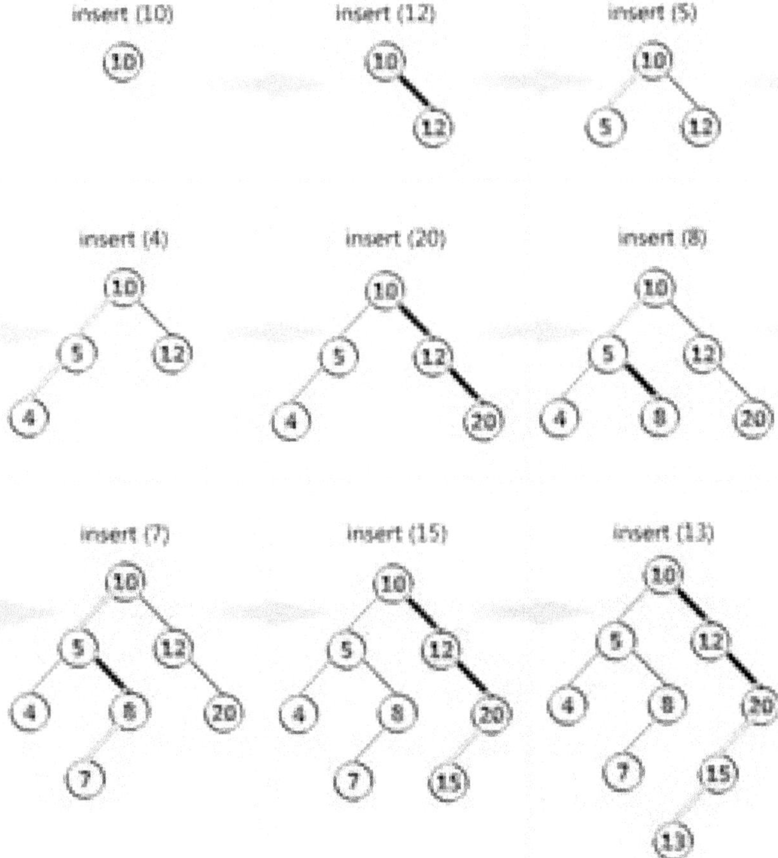

Program:

```
# include <stdio.h>
# include <conio.h>
# include <stdlib.h>
typedef struct BST
{
	int data;
	struct BST *lchild, *rchild;
} node;
```

```
void insert(node *, node *);
void inorder(node *);
void preorder(node
*); void
postorder(node *);
node *search(node *, int, node **);

int main()
{
        int choice;
        char ans =
        'N'; int key;
        node *new_node, *root, *tmp, *parent;
        node *get_node();
        root = NULL;
        printf("\nProgram For Binary Search Tree ");
        do
        {
                printf("\n1.Create");
                printf("\n2.Search");
                printf("\n3.Recursive
                Traversals"); printf("\n4.Exit");
                printf("\nEnter your choice :");
                scanf("%d", &choice);

                switch (choice)
                {
                case 1:
                        do
                        {
                                new_node = get_node();
                                printf("\nEnter The Element ");
                                scanf("%d", &new_node- >data);
                                if (root == NULL) /* Tree is not Created */
                                root = new_node;
                                 else
                                 insert(root, new_node);

                                 printf("\nWant To enter More Elements?(y/n)");
                                 ans = getch();
                        } while (ans == 'y');
                        break;

                case 2:
```

```
                        printf("\nEnter Element to be searched :");
                        scanf("%d", &key);
                        tmp = search(root, key, &parent);
                        printf("\nParent of node %d is %d", tmp->data, parent->data);
                        break;

                case 3:
                        if (root == NULL)
                                printf("Tree Is Not Created");
                        else
                        {
                                printf("\nThe Inorder display : ");
                                inorder(root);
                                printf("\nThe Preorder display : ");
                                preorder(root);
                                printf("\nThe Postorder display : ");
                                postorder(root);
                        }
                        break;
                }
        } while (choice != 4);
}
        /*
        Get new Node
        */
node *get_node()
{
        node
        *temp;
        temp        =        (node        *)
        malloc(sizeof(node));
        temp->lchild = NULL;
        temp->rchild = NULL;
        return temp;
}
        /*
        This function is for creating a binary search
        tree
        */

void insert(node *root, node *new_node)
```

```
{
        if (new_node->data < root->data)
        {
                if (root->lchild == NULL)
                        root->lchild = new_node;
                else
                        insert(root->lchild, new_node);
        }

        if (new_node->data > root->data)
        {
                if (root->rchild == NULL)
                        root->rchild = new_node;
                else
                        insert(root->rchild, new_node);
        }
}
        /*
        This function is for searching the node
        from binary Search Tree
        */
node *search(node *root, int key, node **parent)
{
        node *temp;
        temp = root;
        while (temp != NULL)
        {
                if (temp->data == key)
                {
                        printf("\nThe %d Element is Present", temp->data);
                        return temp;
                }

                *parent = temp;
                if (temp->data > key)
                        temp = temp->lchild;
                else
                        temp = temp->rchild;
        }
        return NULL;
}
/*
This function displays the tree in inorder fashion
*/
```

```
void inorder(node *temp)
{

        if (temp != NULL)
        {
                inorder(temp->lchild);
                printf("%d", temp-
                >data); inorder(temp-
                >rchild);
        }
}
        /*
        This function displays the tree in preorder fashion
        */
void preorder(node *temp)
{
        if (temp != NULL)
        {
                printf("%d", temp-
                >data); preorder(temp-
                >lchild);
                preorder(temp->rchild);
        }
}

        /*
        This function displays the tree in postorder fashion
        */
void postorder(node *temp)
{
        if (temp != NULL)
        {
                postorder(temp-
                >lchild);
                postorder(temp-
                >rchild);       printf("%d",
                temp->data);
        }
}
```

Output:

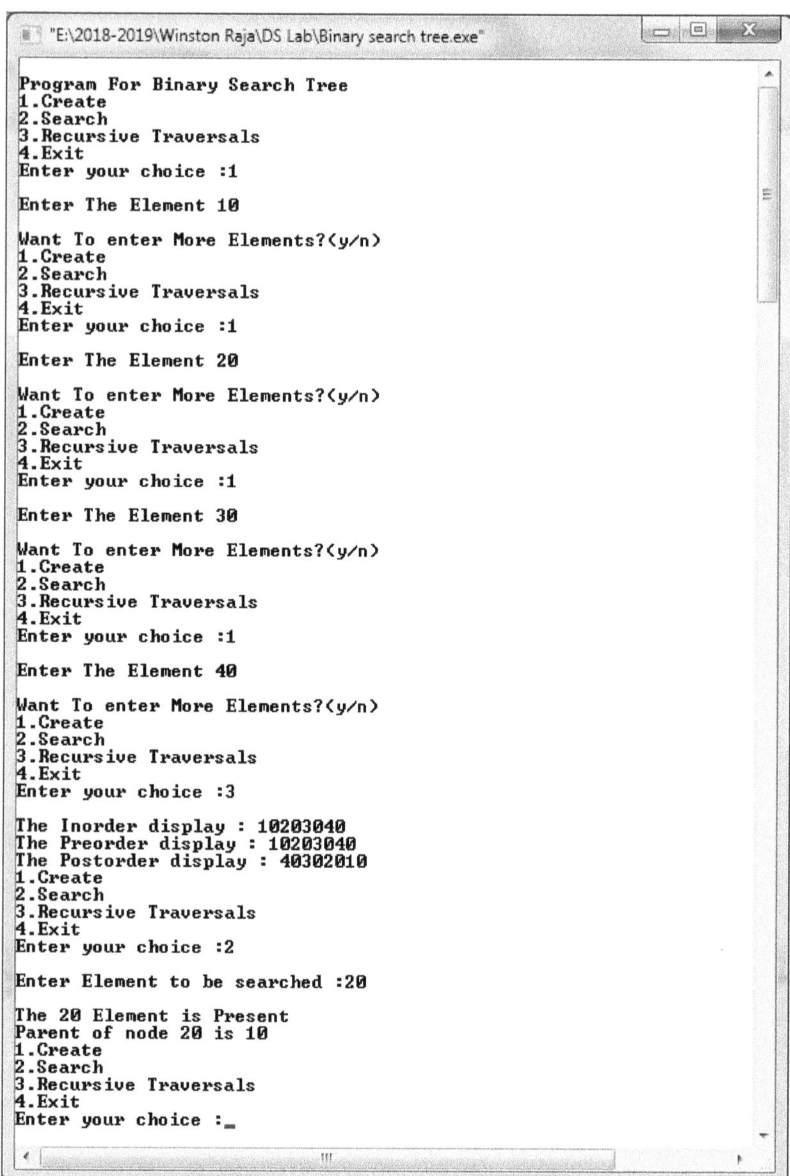

```
"E:\2018-2019\Winston Raja\DS Lab\Binary search tree.exe"

Program For Binary Search Tree
1.Create
2.Search
3.Recursive Traversals
4.Exit
Enter your choice :1

Enter The Element 10

Want To enter More Elements?(y/n)
1.Create
2.Search
3.Recursive Traversals
4.Exit
Enter your choice :1

Enter The Element 20

Want To enter More Elements?(y/n)
1.Create
2.Search
3.Recursive Traversals
4.Exit
Enter your choice :1

Enter The Element 30

Want To enter More Elements?(y/n)
1.Create
2.Search
3.Recursive Traversals
4.Exit
Enter your choice :1

Enter The Element 40

Want To enter More Elements?(y/n)
1.Create
2.Search
3.Recursive Traversals
4.Exit
Enter your choice :3

The Inorder display : 10203040
The Preorder display : 10203040
The Postorder display : 40302010
1.Create
2.Search
3.Recursive Traversals
4.Exit
Enter your choice :2

Enter Element to be searched :20

The 20 Element is Present
Parent of node 20 is 10
1.Create
2.Search
3.Recursive Traversals
4.Exit
Enter your choice :_
```

Result:

Thus the program is completed successfully and the Result is verified.

Exp.No:12 **Implementation of AVL Trees**

Date :

Search Operation in AVL Tree

In an AVL tree, the search operation is performed with **O(log n)** time complexity. The search operation is performed similar to Binary search tree search operation. We use the following steps to search an element in AVL tree...

- **Step 1:** Read the search element from the user
- **Step 2:** Compare, the search element with the value of root node in the tree.
- **Step 3:** If both are matching, then display "Given node found!!!" and terminate the function
- **Step 4:** If both are not matching, then check whether search element is smaller or larger than that node value.
- **Step 5:** If search element is smaller, then continue the search process in left subtree.
- **Step 6:** If search element is larger, then continue the search process in right subtree.
- **Step 7:** Repeat the same until we found exact element or we completed with a leaf node
- **Step 8:** If we reach to the node with search value, then display "Element is found" and terminate the function.
- **Step 9:** If we reach to a leaf node and it is also not matching, then display "Element not found" and terminate the function.

Insertion Operation in AVL Tree

In an AVL tree, the insertion operation is performed with **O(log n)** time complexity. In AVL Tree, new node is always inserted as a leaf node. The insertion operation is performed as follows...

- **Step 1:** Insert the new element into the tree using Binary Search Tree insertion logic.
- **Step 2:** After insertion, check the **Balance Factor** of every node.
- **Step 3:** If the **Balance Factor** of every node is **0 or 1 or -1** then go for next operation.
- **Step 4:** If the **Balance Factor** of any node is other than **0 or 1 or -1** then tree is said to be imbalanced. Then perform the suitable **Rotation** to make it balanced. And go for next operation.

Example: Construct an AVL Tree by inserting numbers from 1 to 8.

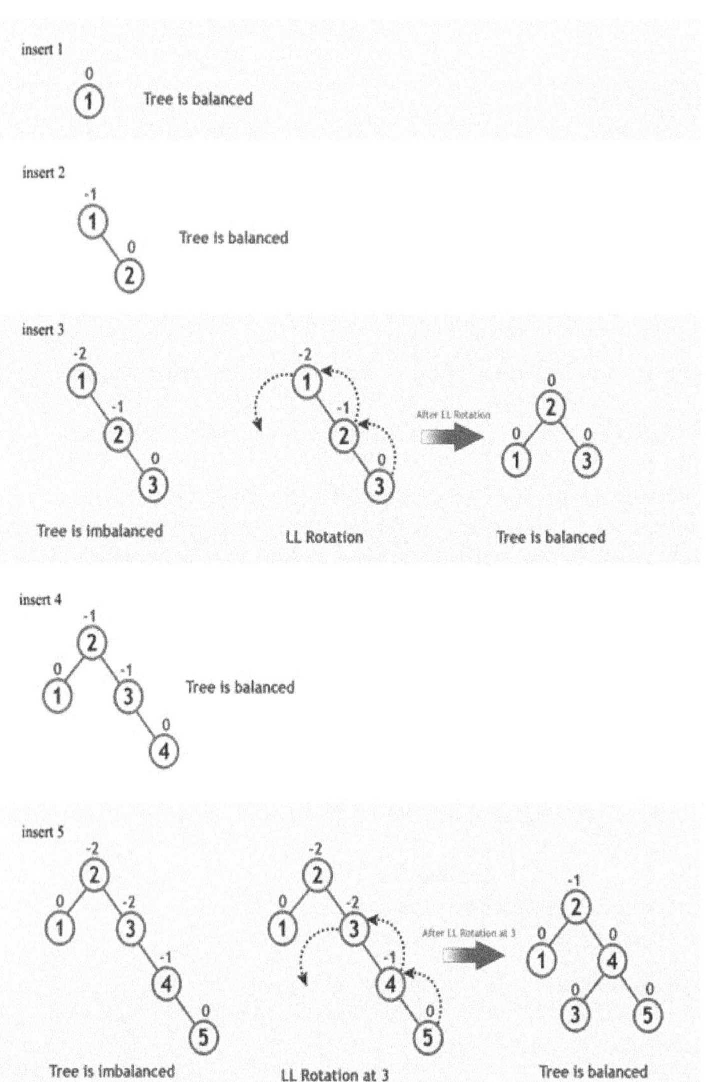

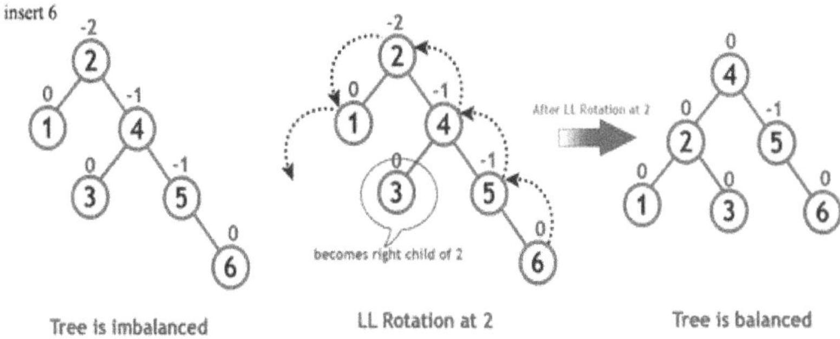

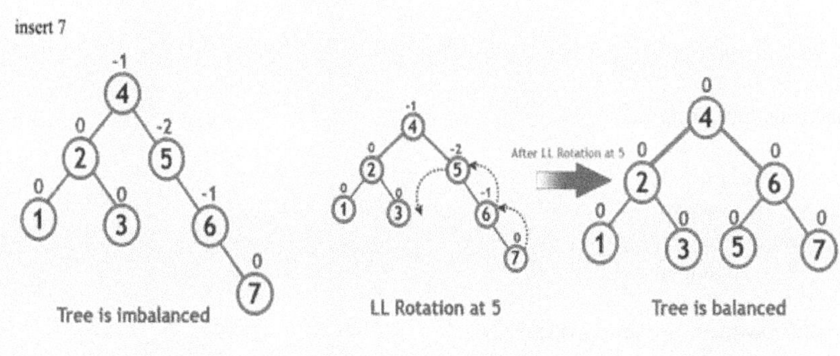

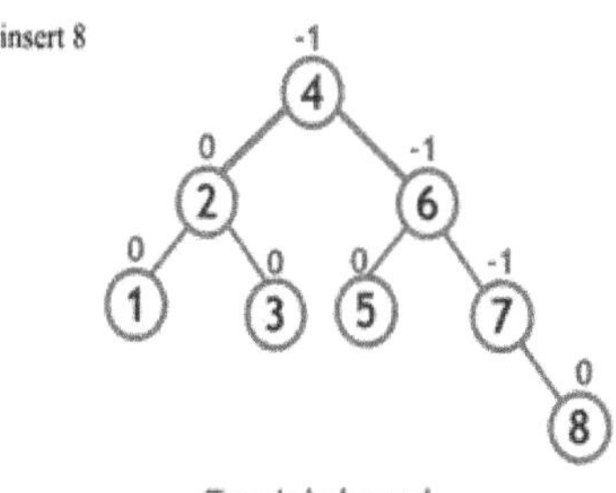

Deletion Operation in AVL Tree

In an AVL Tree, the deletion operation is similar to deletion operation in BST. But after every deletion operation we need to check with the Balance Factor condition. If the tree is balanced after deletion then go for next operation otherwise perform the suitable rotation to make the tree Balanced.

Program:

```
#include<stdio.h>
#include<stdlib.h>
struct avltree
{
	int data;
	struct avltree *left,*right;
	int height;
};
static int height(struct avltree*t)
{
	if(t==NULL)
		return -1;
	else
		return t->height;
}
int maxheight(int h1,int h2)
{
	if(h1>h2)
		return h1;
	else
		return h2;
}
static struct avltree*sleft(struct avltree*k2)
{
	struct avltree *k1;
	k1=k2->left;
	k2->left=k1->right;
	k1->right=k2;
	k2->height=maxheight(height(k2->left),height(k2->right))+1;
	k1->height=maxheight(height(k1->left),height(k1->right))+1;
	return k1;
}
static struct avltree*sright(struct avltree*k2)
{
	struct avltree *k1;
	k1=k2->right;
	k2->right=k1->left;
	k1->left=k2;
	k2->height=maxheight(height(k2->left),height(k2->right))+1;
	k1->height=maxheight(height(k1->left),height(k1->right))+1;
	return k1;
}
static struct avltree *dleft(struct avltree*k3)
{
```

```
k3->right=sleft(k3->right);
        return sleft(k3);
}
static struct avltree *dright(struct avltree*k3)
{
        k3->left=sright(k3->left);
        return sright(k3);
}
struct avltree *makeempty(struct avltree*t)
{
        if(t!=NULL)
        {
                makeempty(t->left);
                makeempty(t->right);
                free(t);
        }
}
struct avltree *insert(int num,struct avltree*t)
{
        if(t==NULL)
        {
                t=(struct avltree*)malloc(sizeof(struct avltree));
                if (t==NULL)
                {
                        printf("\n out of space");
                        return NULL;
                }
                else
                {
                        t->data=num;
                        t->height=0;
                        t->left=t->right=NULL;
                }
        }
        else if(num<t->data)
        {
                t->left=insert(num,t->left);
                if(height(t->left)-height(t->right)==2)
                        if(num<t->left->data)
                                t=sleft(t);
                else
                        t=dleft(t);
        }
```

```
if(height(t->right)-height(t->left)==2)

            else if(num>t->data)
            {
t->right=insert(num,t->right);
          if(num>t->right->data)
t=sright(t);

else
t=dright(t);

}
            t->height=maxheight(height(t->left),height(t->right))+1;
            return t;
 }
 void display(struct avltree *t,int space)
 {
            int i;
            if(t!=NULL)
            {
                        display(t->right,space+1);
                        printf("\n");
                        for(i=0;i<space;i++)
                                    printf("\t");
                        printf("%d",t->data);
                        display(t->left,space+1);
            }}
 int main()
 {
            int i,n,num;
            char ch,enter;
            struct avltree*t;
            t=NULL;
            printf("\nOPERATIONS ON AVL TREE");
            printf("\nEnter the number of elements on the tree:");
            scanf("%d",&n);
            printf("\nEnter the elements:\n");
            for(i=0;i<n;i++)
            {
                        scanf("%d",&num);
                        t=insert(num,t);
            }
```

```
printf("\n\n The New Tree is :\n");
display(t,2);
printf("\n\n Do you wish to enter more elements into the AVL tree?(y\n):");
 printf("\nThe Tree Is\n");
 display(t,1);
 do
 {
         printf("\n enter the element to be inserted:");
         scanf("%d",&num);
         t=insert(num,t);
         scanf("%c%c",&enter,&ch);
 }
 while(ch=='y'||ch=='y');
 t=makeempty(t);
 return 0;
}
```

Output:

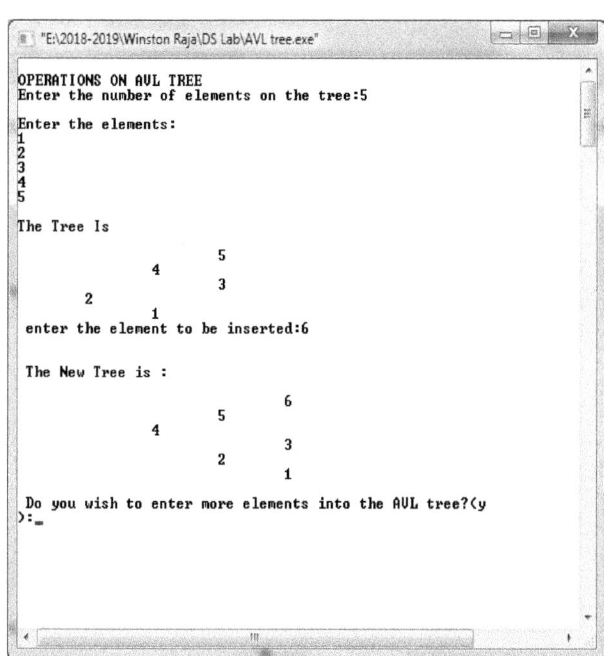

Result:

Thus the program is completed successfully and the Result is verified.

Exp.No:13 **Implementation of Heaps using Priority**

Queues. Date :

A priority queue is a data structure that allows at least the following two operations: Insert, and DeleteMin, which finds, returns, and removes the minimum element in the priority queue.

The basic model of Priority Queue is given below: DeleteMin(H)

Priority Queues are used for external sorting. They are also important in the implementation of Greedy Algorithms, which operate by repeatedly finding the minimum.

Priority Queues are implemented by binary heap. Heaps have two properties namely, a structure property and a heap order property.

Structure Property:

A heap is a binary heap that is completely filled, with the possible exception of the bottom level, which is filled from left to right. Such a tree is known as a Complete Binary Tree.

Heap Order Property:

The property that allows operations to be performed quickly is the heap order property. Since we want to be able to find the minimum quickly, it makes sense that the smallest element should be at the root. The heap order property is stated as below: In a heap, for every node X, the key in the parent of X is smaller than (or equal) the key in X. with the exception of the root.

AIM:

To implement Priority Queue using Binary Heap in C Language.

ALGORITHM:

STEP 1: Start.

STEP 2: Create a binary heap with a list of data which satisfies the condition, the minimum value is stored in the root. This condition should be satisfied in all the subtrees of the binary heap.

STEP 3: To insert a new value into the existing heap, create a node for the new value at the bottom of the heap.

STEP 3.1: Compare the value with root of the subtree. If the value is less than the value in the subtree, exchange the values.

STEP 3.2: Repeat the STEP 3.1 for all the subtrees, so that the root always contains the minimum value.

STEP 4: To delete a minimum element, delete the value in the root. Now the root becomes empty.

STEP 4.1: Check the values in the left and right nodes of the root. Place the minimum value in the root. Now root of the subtree becomes empty.

STEP 4.2: Repeat the above STEP so that the minimum value is removed from the root.

STEP 5: Stop

Program:

```
# include <stdio.h>
int arr[100],n;

void display()
{	int i;
	if(n==0)
	{
		printf("Heap is empty\n");
		return;
	}
	for(i=0;i<n;i++)
		printf("%d ",arr[i]);
	printf("\n");
}/*End of display()*/

void insert(int num,int loc)
{
	int par;
	while(loc>0)
	{
		par=(loc-1)/2;
		if(num<=arr[par])
		{
			arr[loc]=num;
			return;
		}
		arr[loc]=arr[par];
		loc=par;
	}/*End of while*/
	arr[0]=num; /*assign num to the root node */
}/*End of insert()*/

void del(int num)
{
	int left,right,i,temp,par;

	for(i=0;i<n;i++)
	{
		if(num==arr[i])
```

```
            break;
    }
    if( num!=arr[i] )
    {
            printf("%d not found in heap\n",num);
            return;
    }
    arr[i]=arr[n-1];
    n=n-1;
    par=(i-1)/2;   /*find parent of node i */
    if(arr[i] > arr[par])
    {
            insert( arr[i],i);
            return;
    }
    left=2*i+1;  /*left child of i*/
    right=2*i+2; /* right child of
    i*/ while(right < n)
    {
            if( arr[i]>=arr[left] && arr[i]>=arr[right] )
                    return;
            if( arr[right]<=arr[left] )
            {
                    temp=arr[i];
                    arr[i]=arr[left
                    ];
                    arr[left]=tem
            }       p; i=left;
            else
            {


                    temp=arr[i];
                    arr[i]=arr[right
                    ];
            }       arr[right]=tem
                    p; i=right;
```

```
            left=2*i+1;
            right=2*i+2;
    }/*End of while*/
    if( left==n-1 && arr[i]<arr[left] ) /* right==n */
    {       temp=arr[i];
                arr[i]=arr[left];
                arr[left]=temp;
        }
}/*End of del()*/

main(
)
{       int choice,num;
        n=0;/*Represents number of nodes in the heap*/
        while(1)
        {
                printf("1.Insert\n");
                printf("2.Delete\n");
                printf("3.Display\n");
                printf("4.Quit\n");
                printf("Enter your choice :
                "); scanf("%d",&choice);
                switch(choice)
                {
                 case 1:
                        printf("Enter the number to be inserted : ");
                        scanf("%d",&num)
                        ; insert(num,n);
                        n=n+1;
                        break;
                 case 2:
                        printf("Enter the number to be deleted : ");
                        scanf("%d",&num);
                        del(num);
                        break;
                 case 3:
                        display();
                        break;
                 case 4:
        break;
```

```
                default:
                        printf("Wrong choice\n");
                }/*End of switch */
        }/*End of while */
}/*End of main()*/
```

Output:

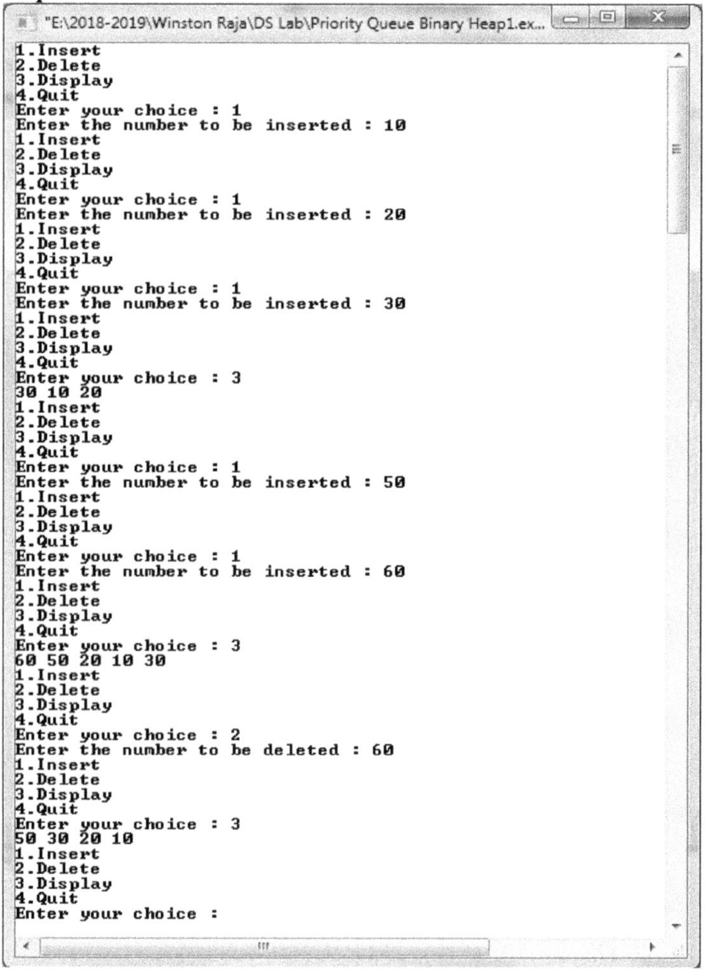

```
"E:\2018-2019\Winston Raja\DS Lab\Priority Queue Binary Heap1.ex...
1.Insert
2.Delete
3.Display
4.Quit
Enter your choice : 1
Enter the number to be inserted : 10
1.Insert
2.Delete
3.Display
4.Quit
Enter your choice : 1
Enter the number to be inserted : 20
1.Insert
2.Delete
3.Display
4.Quit
Enter your choice : 1
Enter the number to be inserted : 30
1.Insert
2.Delete
3.Display
4.Quit
Enter your choice : 3
30 10 20
1.Insert
2.Delete
3.Display
4.Quit
Enter your choice : 1
Enter the number to be inserted : 50
1.Insert
2.Delete
3.Display
4.Quit
Enter your choice : 1
Enter the number to be inserted : 60
1.Insert
2.Delete
3.Display
4.Quit
Enter your choice : 3
60 50 20 10 30
1.Insert
2.Delete
3.Display
4.Quit
Enter your choice : 2
Enter the number to be deleted : 60
1.Insert
2.Delete
3.Display
4.Quit
Enter your choice : 3
50 30 20 10
1.Insert
2.Delete
3.Display
4.Quit
Enter your choice :
```

Result:

Thus the program is completed successfully and the Result is verified.

Exp.No:14 Graph representation and Traversal algorithms

Date :

Graph data structure is represented using following representations...

1. **Adjacency Matrix**
2. **Incidence Matrix**
3. **Adjacency List**

Adjacency Matrix

In this representation, graph can be represented using a matrix of size total number of vertices by total number of vertices. That means if a graph with 4 vertices can be represented using a matrix of 4X4 class. In this matrix, rows and columns both represent vertices. This matrix is filled with either 1 or 0. Here, 1 represents there is an edge from row vertex to column vertex and 0 represents there is no edge from row vertex to column vertex.

For example, consider the following undirected graph representation...

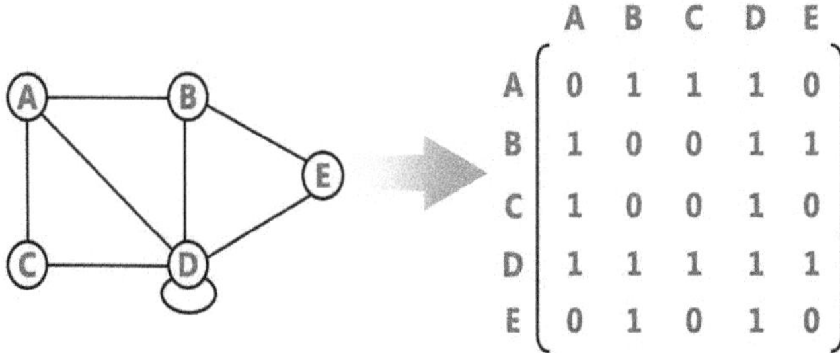

Directed graph representation...

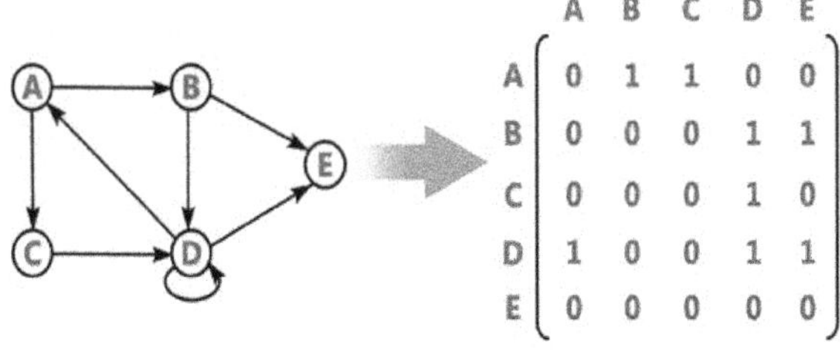

Incidence Matrix

In this representation, graph can be represented using a matrix of size total number of vertices by total number of edges. That means if a graph with 4 vertices and 6 edges can be represented using a matrix of 4X6 class. In this matrix, rows represents vertices and columns represents edges. This matrix is filled with either 0 or 1 or -1. Here, 0 represents row edge is not connected to column vertex, 1 represents row edge is connected as outgoing edge to column vertex and -1 represents row edge is connected as incoming edge to column vertex.

For example, consider the following directed graph representation...

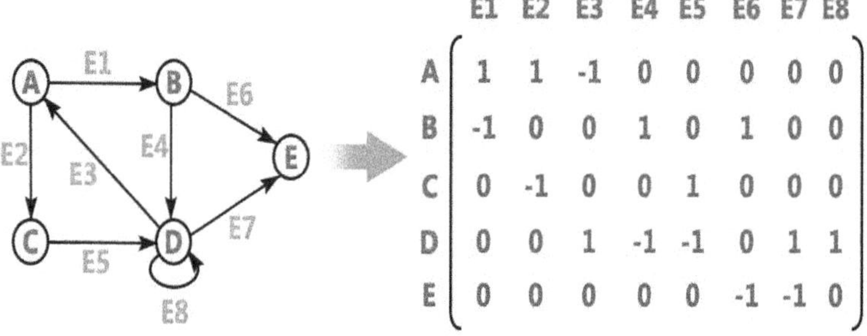

	E1	E2	E3	E4	E5	E6	E7	E8
A	1	1	-1	0	0	0	0	0
B	-1	0	0	1	0	1	0	0
C	0	-1	0	0	1	0	0	0
D	0	0	1	-1	-1	0	1	1
E	0	0	0	0	0	-1	-1	0

Adjacency List

In this representation, every vertex of graph contains list of its adjacent vertices. For example, consider the following directed graph representation implemented using linked list...

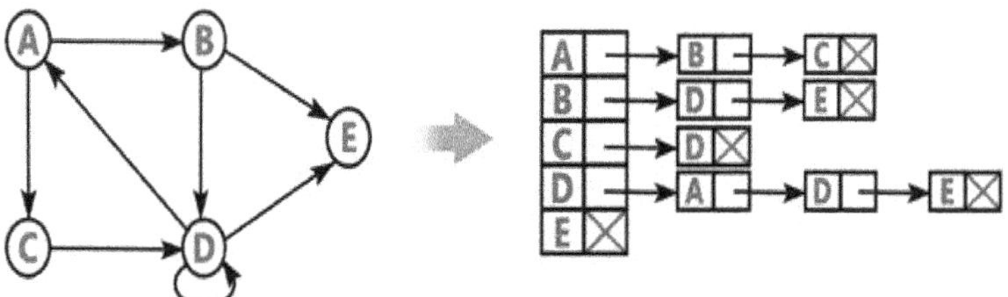

This representation can also be implemented using array as follows..

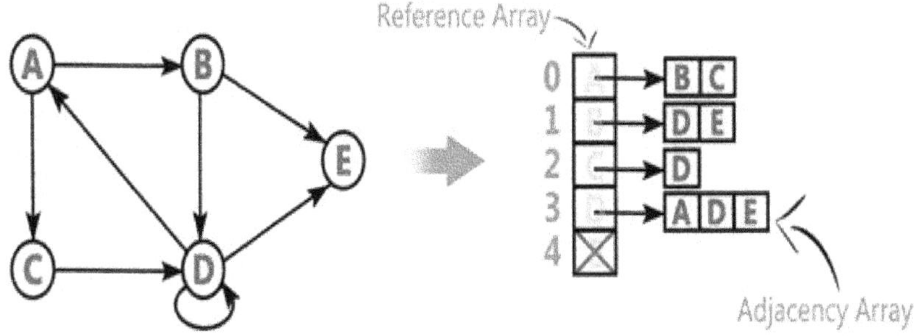

There are two graph traversal techniques and they are as follows...

1. **DFS (Depth First Search)**
2. **BFS (Breadth First Search)**

DFS (Depth First Search)

DFS traversal of a graph, produces a **spanning tree** as final result. **Spanning Tree** is a graph without any loops. We use **Stack data structure** with maximum size of total number of vertices in the graph to implement DFS traversal of a graph.

We use the following steps to implement DFS traversal...

- **Step 1:** Define a Stack of size total number of vertices in the graph.
- **Step 2:** Select any vertex as **starting point** for traversal. Visit that vertex and push it on to the Stack.
- **Step 3:** Visit any one of the **adjacent** vertex of the verex which is at top of the stack which is not visited and push it on to the stack.
- **Step 4:** Repeat step 3 until there are no new vertex to be visit from the vertex on top of the stack.
- **Step 5:** When there is no new vertex to be visit then use **back tracking** and pop one vertex from the stack.
- **Step 6:** Repeat steps 3, 4 and 5 until stack becomes Empty.
- **Step 7:** When stack becomes Empty, then produce final spanning tree by removing unused edges from the graph

Back tracking is coming back to the vertex from which we came to current vertex.

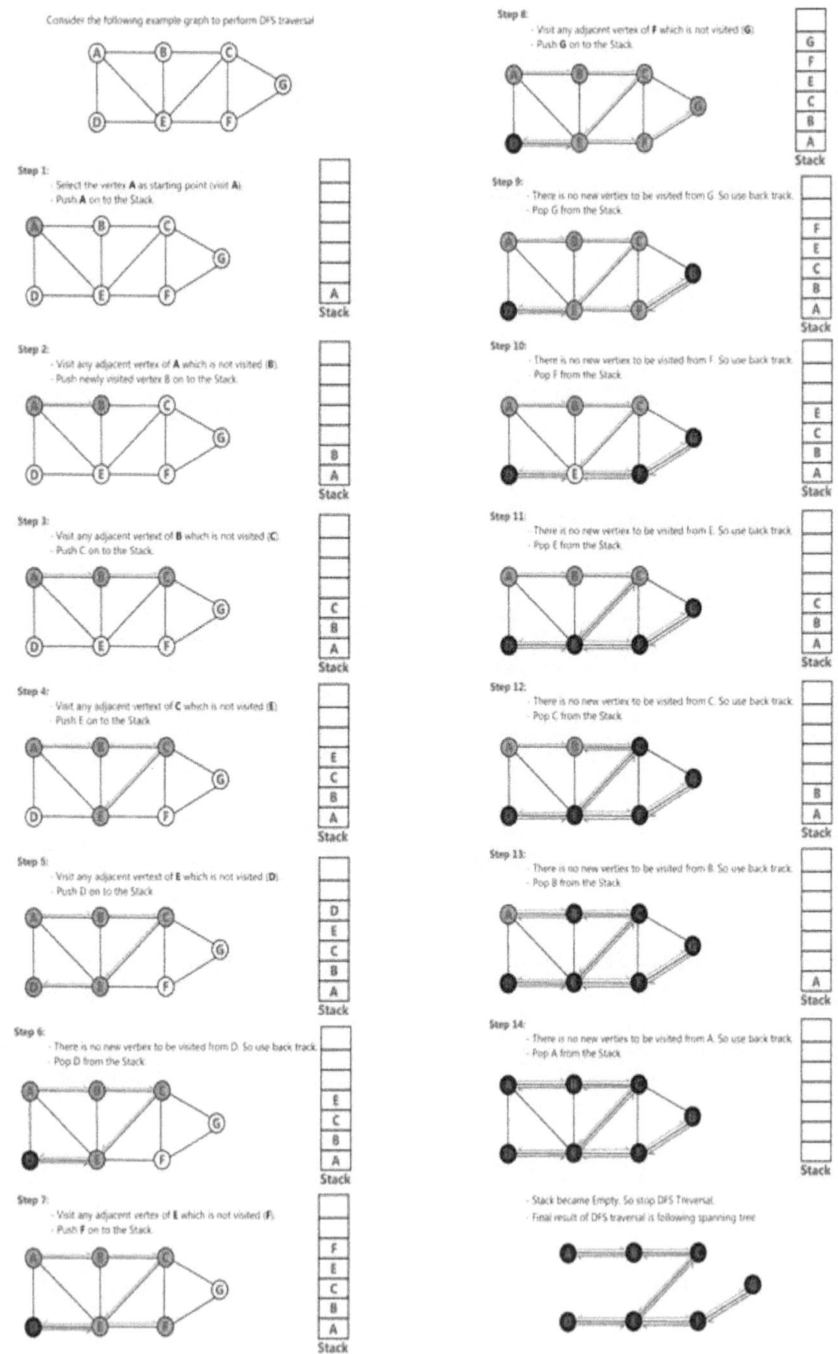

BFS (Breadth First Search)

BFS traversal of a graph, produces a **spanning tree** as final result. **Spanning Tree** is a graph without any loops. We use **Queue data structure** with maximum size of total number of vertices in the graph to implement BFS traversal of a graph.

We use the following steps to implement BFS traversal...

- **Step 1:** Define a Queue of size total number of vertices in the graph.
- **Step 2:** Select any vertex as **starting point** for traversal. Visit that vertex and insert it into the Queue.
- **Step 3:** Visit all the **adjacent** vertices of the verex which is at front of the Queue which is not visited and insert them into the Queue.
- **Step 4:** When there is no new vertex to be visit from the vertex at front of the Queue then delete that vertex from the Queue.
- **Step 5:** Repeat step 3 and 4 until queue becomes empty.
- **Step 6:** When queue becomes Empty, then produce final spanning tree by removing unused edges from the graph

Example

Consider the following example graph to perform BFS traversal

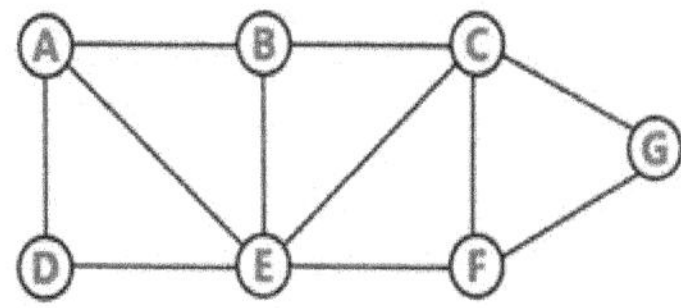

Step 1:

- Select the vertex **A** as starting point (visit **A**).
- Insert **A** into the Queue.

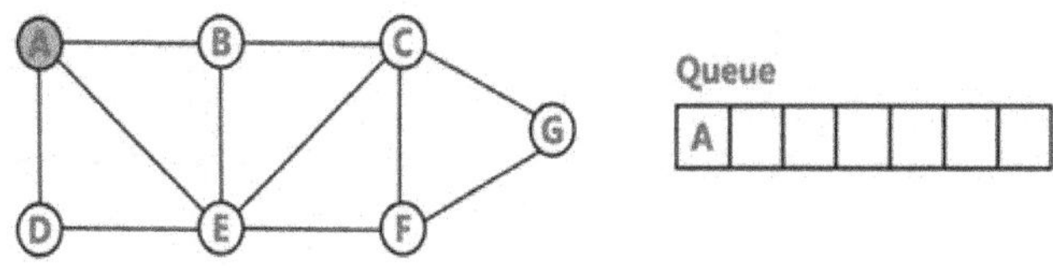

Step 2:

- Visit all adjacent vertices of **A** which are not visited (**D**, **E**, **B**).
- Insert newly visited vertices into the Queue and delete A from the Queue..

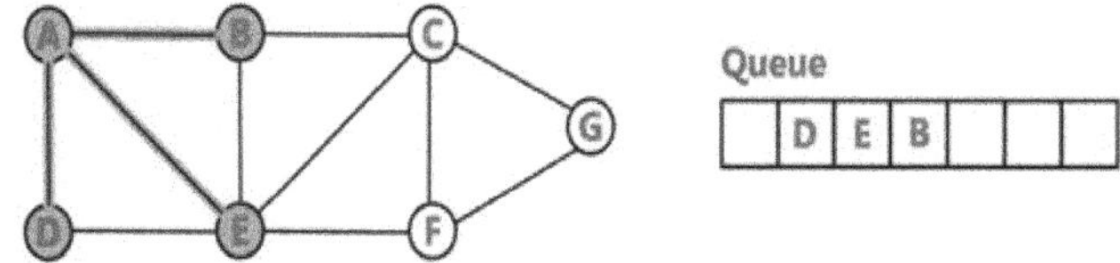

Step 3:

- Visit all adjacent vertices of **D** which are not visited (there is no vertex).
- Delete D from the Queue.

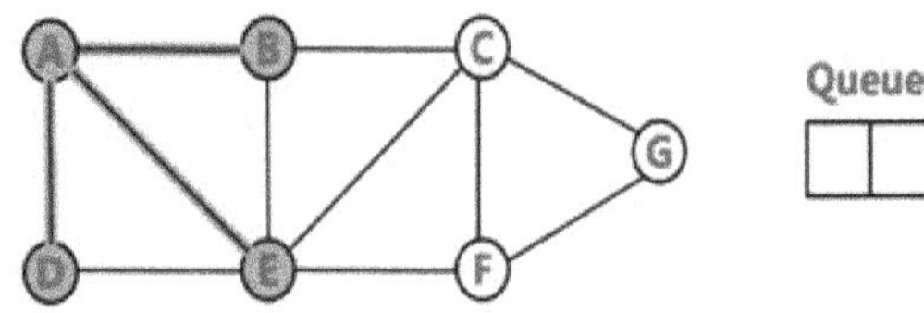

Step 4:

- Visit all adjacent vertices of **E** which are not visited (**C**, **F**).
- Insert newly visited vertices into the Queue and delete E from the Queue.

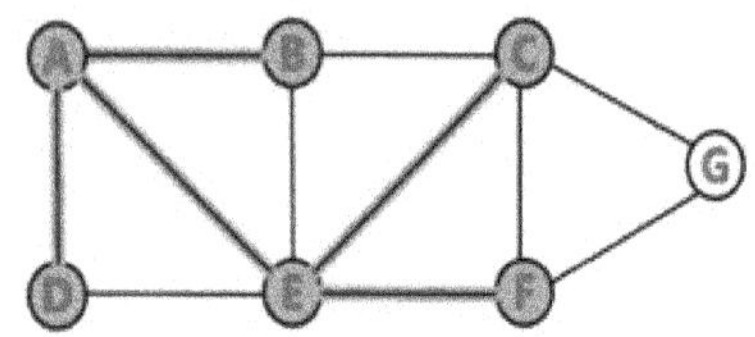

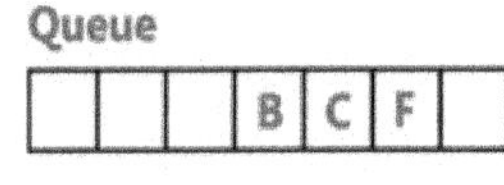

Step 5:

- Visit all adjacent vertices of **B** which are not visited (**there is no vertex**).
- Delete **B** from the Queue.

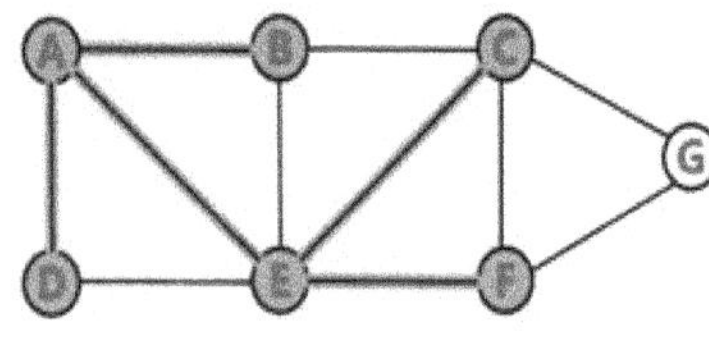

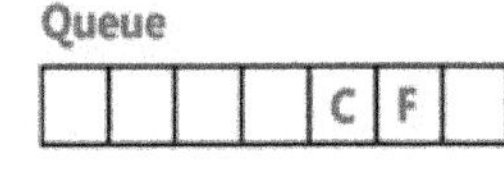

Step 6:

- Visit all adjacent vertices of **C** which are not visited (**G**).
- Insert newly visited vertex into the Queue and delete **C** from the Queue.

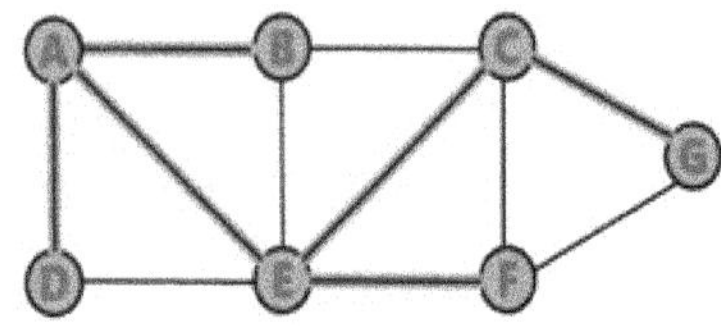

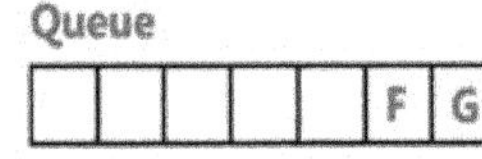

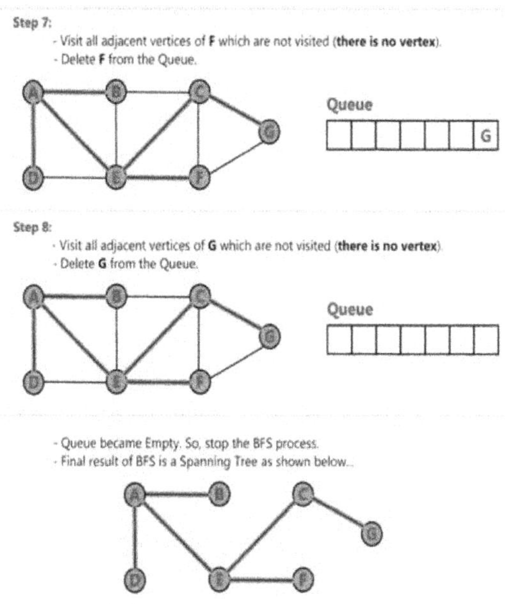

/* C program to implement BFS(breadth-first search) and DFS(depth-first search) algorithm */

```
#include<stdio.h>

int q[20],top=-1,front=-1,rear=-1,a[20][20],vis[20],stack[20];
int delete();
void add(int item);
void bfs(int s,int
n); void dfs(int
s,int n); void
push(int item); int
pop();

void main()
{
        int n,i,s,ch,j;
        char c,dummy;
```

```
        printf("ENTER THE NUMBER VERTICES ");
        scanf("%d",&n);
        for(i=1;i<=n;i++)
        {
                for(j=1;j<=n;j++)
                {
                        printf("ENTER 1 IF %d HAS A NODE WITH %d ELSE 0 ",i,j);
                        scanf("%d",&a[i][j]);
                }
        }
        printf("THE ADJACENCY MATRIX IS\n");
        for(i=1;i<=n;i++)
        {
                for(j=1;j<=n;j++)
                {
                        printf(" %d",a[i][j]);
                }
                printf("\n");
        }
        do
        {
        for(i=1;i<=n;i++)
                vis[i]=0;


       printf("\nMENU");
       printf("\n1.B.F.S");
        printf("\n2.D.F.S");
        printf("\nENTER YOUR CHOICE");
        scanf("%d",&ch);
        printf("ENTER THE SOURCE VERTEX :");
        scanf("%d",&s);
        switch(ch)
        {
        case 1:
bfs(s,n);
```

```
        break;
        case 2:
dfs(s,n);
        break;
        printf("DO U WANT TO CONTINUE(Y/N) ? ");
        scanf("%c",&dummy);
        scanf("%c",&c);
        }while((c=='y')||(c=='Y'));
}


//**************BFS(breadth-first search) code**************//
void bfs(int s,int n)
{
int p,i;
        add(s);
        vis[s]=1;
        p=delete()
        ; if(p!=0)
        printf(" %d",p);
        while(p!=0)
        {
                for(i=1;i<=n;i++)
                if((a[p][i]!=0)&&(vis[i]==0))
                {
                        add(i);
                        vis[i]=1;
                }
                p=delete();
                if(p!=0)
                printf(" %d ",p);
        }
        for(i=1;i<=n;i++
```

```
        } if(vis[i]==0)
        bfs(i,n);

}


void add(int item)
{
        if(rear==19)
        printf("QUEUE FULL");
        else

        {
                if(rear==-1)
                {
                        q[++rear]=item;
                        front++;

                }
                else
                        q[++rear]=item;

        }
}
int             {
delete()
int k;
if((front>rear)||(front==-1))
return(0);
else
{
k=q[front++];
return(k);
}
}
```

```
//**************DFS(depth-first search) code*****************//
void dfs(int s,int n)
{
        int i,k;
        push(s);
        vis[s]=1;
        k=pop();
        if(k!=0)
        printf("       %d
        ",k);
        while(k!=0
        )
        {
                for(i=1;i<=n;i++)
                        if((a[k][i]!=0)&&(vis[i]==0))
                        {
                                push(i);
                                vis[i]=1;
                        }
                k=pop()
                ;
                if(k!=0)
                        printf(" %d ",k);
        }
        for(i=1;i<=n;i++)
                if(vis[i]==0)
                        dfs(i,n);
}
void push(int item)
{
        if(top==19)
                printf("Stack overflow ");
        else
                stack[++top]=item;
}
int pop()
{
```

```
        int k;
        if(top==-1)
                return(0);
        else
        {
                k=stack[top--];
                return(k);
        }
}
```

Output:

```
"E:\2018-2019\Winston Raja\DS Lab\bfsdfs.exe"
ENTER THE NUMBER VERTICES 5
ENTER 1 IF 1 HAS A NODE WITH 1 ELSE 0 0
ENTER 1 IF 1 HAS A NODE WITH 2 ELSE 0 1
ENTER 1 IF 1 HAS A NODE WITH 3 ELSE 0 1
ENTER 1 IF 1 HAS A NODE WITH 4 ELSE 0 1
ENTER 1 IF 1 HAS A NODE WITH 5 ELSE 0 0
ENTER 1 IF 2 HAS A NODE WITH 1 ELSE 0 1
ENTER 1 IF 2 HAS A NODE WITH 2 ELSE 0 0
ENTER 1 IF 2 HAS A NODE WITH 3 ELSE 0 1
ENTER 1 IF 2 HAS A NODE WITH 4 ELSE 0 1
ENTER 1 IF 2 HAS A NODE WITH 5 ELSE 0 1
ENTER 1 IF 3 HAS A NODE WITH 1 ELSE 0 1
ENTER 1 IF 3 HAS A NODE WITH 2 ELSE 0 1
ENTER 1 IF 3 HAS A NODE WITH 3 ELSE 0 0
ENTER 1 IF 3 HAS A NODE WITH 4 ELSE 0 1
ENTER 1 IF 3 HAS A NODE WITH 5 ELSE 0 1
ENTER 1 IF 4 HAS A NODE WITH 1 ELSE 0 1
ENTER 1 IF 4 HAS A NODE WITH 2 ELSE 0 1
ENTER 1 IF 4 HAS A NODE WITH 3 ELSE 0 1
ENTER 1 IF 4 HAS A NODE WITH 4 ELSE 0 1
ENTER 1 IF 4 HAS A NODE WITH 5 ELSE 0 1
ENTER 1 IF 5 HAS A NODE WITH 1 ELSE 0 1
ENTER 1 IF 5 HAS A NODE WITH 2 ELSE 0 1
ENTER 1 IF 5 HAS A NODE WITH 3 ELSE 0 1
ENTER 1 IF 5 HAS A NODE WITH 4 ELSE 0 1
ENTER 1 IF 5 HAS A NODE WITH 5 ELSE 0 1
THE ADJACENCY MATRIX IS
 0 1 1 1 0
 1 0 1 1 1
 1 1 0 1 1
 1 1 1 1 1
 1 1 1 1 1

MENU
1.B.F.S
2.D.F.S
ENTER YOUR CHOICE1
ENTER THE SOURCE VERTEX :1
 1 2  3  4  5 DO U WANT TO CONTINUE(Y/N) ? y

MENU
1.B.F.S
2.D.F.S
ENTER YOUR CHOICE2
ENTER THE SOURCE VERTEX :1
 1  4  5  3  2 DO U WANT TO CONTINUE(Y/N) ? _
```

Result:

Thus the program is completed successfully and the Result is verified.

Exp.No:15 Applications of Graphs - Single-Source Shortest-Path

Date :

Dijkstra's Algorithm

DIJKSTRA(G,s)

Step 1 INITIALIZE-SINGLE-SOURCE(G, S)

Step 2 S ← Ø

Step 3 Q ← V[G]

Step 4 while Q ≠ Ø

Step 5 do u ← EXTRACT-MIN(Q)

Step 6 S ← S U {u}

Step 7 for each vertex v ∈ Adj[u]

Step 8 do if dist[v] > dist[u] + w(u,v)

Step 9 then d[v] ←d[u] + w(u,v) INITIALIZE-SINGLE-SOURCE(Graph g, Node s)

dist[s] = 0;

for each vertex v in Vertices V[G] - s dist[v] ← ∞

- s dist[v] ← ∞

Example

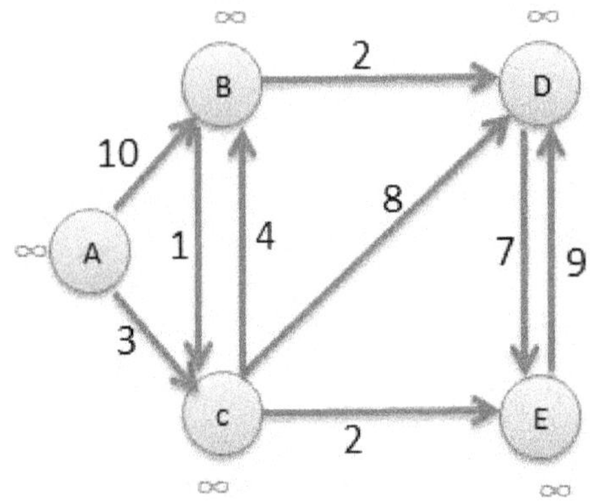

Procedure for Dijkstra's Algorithm

Step1

Consider A as source vertex

No. of Nodes	A	B	C	D	E
Distance	0	10	**3**	∞	∞
Distance From		A	A		

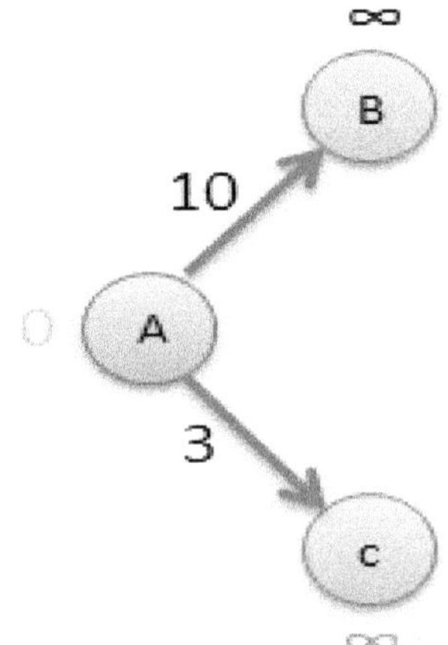

Step2

Now consider vertex C

No. of Nodes	A	B	C	D	E
Distance	0	7	3	11	**5**
Distance From		C	C	C	C

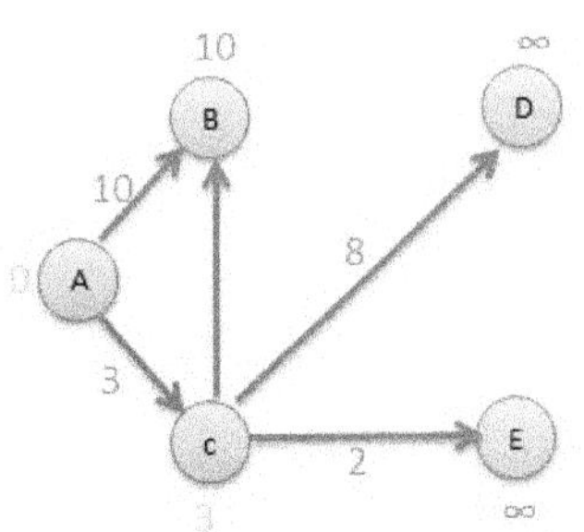

Step3

Now consider vertex E

No. of Nodes	A	B	C	D	E
Distance	0	7	3	11	0
Distance From		C	A	C	E

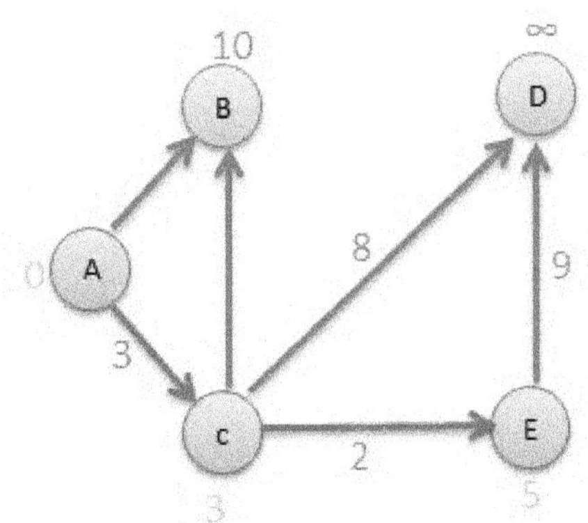

Step4

Now consider vertex B

No. of Nodes	A	B	C	D	E
Distance	0	**7**	3	9	5
Distance From		C	A	B	C

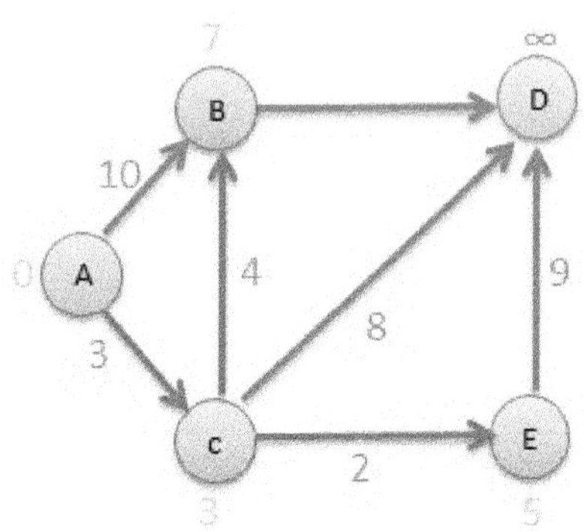

Step5

Now consider vertex D

No. of Nodes	A	B	C	D	E
Distance	0	7	3	**9**	11
Distance From	A	C	A	B	C

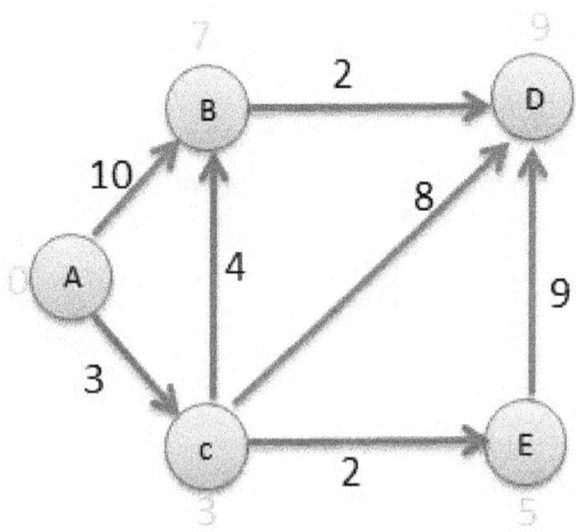

	A	B	C	D	E
	0	∞	∞	∞	∞
A	0	10	3	∞	∞
C		7	3	11	5
E				14	5
B				9	
D					16

Program:

```
#include<stdio.h>

#include<conio.h>

#define INFINITY 9999

#define MAX 10


void dijikstra(int G[MAX][MAX], int n, int startnode);


void main()

{

        int G[MAX][MAX], i, j, n, u;


        printf("\nEnter the no. of vertices:: ");

        scanf("%d", &n);

        printf("\nEnter the adjacency matrix::\n");
```

```
        for(i=0;i < n;i++)

                for(j=0;j < n;j++)

                        scanf("%d", &G[i][j]);
        printf("\nEnter the starting node::
        "); scanf("%d", &u);

        dijikstra(G,n,u);

        getch();

}


void dijikstra(int G[MAX][MAX], int n, int startnode)

{

        int cost[MAX][MAX], distance[MAX], pred[MAX];
        int visited[MAX], count, mindistance, nextnode, i,j;
        for(i=0;i < n;i++)

                for(j=0;j < n;j++)

                        if(G[i][j]==0)

                                cost[i][j]=INFINITY;

                        else

                                cost[i][j]=G[i][j];


        for(i=0;i< n;i++)

        {

                distance[i]=cost[startnode][
                i]; pred[i]=startnode;
                visited[i]=0;

        }

        distance[startnode]=
        0;
        visited[startnode]=1;
        count=1;
```

```
        while(count < n-1)
        {
                mindistance=INFINITY;
                for(i=0;i < n;i++)
                        if(distance[i] < mindistance&&!visited[i])
                        {
                                mindistance=distance[i];
                                nextnode=i;
                        }
                visited[nextnode]=1;
                for(i=0;i < n;i++)
                        if(!visited[i])
                                if(mindistance+cost[nextnode][i] < distance[i])
                                {
                                        distance[i]=mindistance+cost[nextnode][i];
                                        pred[i]=nextnode;
                                }
                        count++;
        }

        for(i=0;i < n;i++)
                if(i!=startnode)
                {
                        printf("\nDistance of %d = %d", i, distance[i]);
                        printf("\nPath = %d", i);
                        j=i;
                        do
                        {
                                j=pred[j];
                                printf(" <-%d", j);
                        }


}
while(j!
=startn
ode);
}
```

Output:

"E:\2018-2019\Winston Raja\DS Lab\Dijkstra.exe"

```
Enter the no. of vertices:: 4

Enter the adjacency matrix::
0 1 1 1
1 0 1 0
1 1 0 1
1 0 1 0

Enter the starting node:: 1

Distance of 0 = 1
Path = 0 <-1
Distance of 2 = 1
Path = 2 <-1
Distance of 3 = 2
Path = 3 <-0 <-1Press any key to continue . . .
```

Result:

Thus the program is completed successfully and the Result is verified.

Exp.No:16 Implementation of Binary Search Algorithm

Date :

Binary search algorithm finds given element in a list of elements with **O(log n)** time complexity where **n** is total number of elements in the list. The binary search algorithm can be used with only sorted list of element. That means, binary search can be used only with list of element which are already arranged in an order. The binary search cannot be used for list of element which are in random order. This search process starts comparing of the search element with the middle element in the list. If both are matched, then the result is "element found". Otherwise, we check whether the search element is smaller or larger than the middle element in the list. If the search element is smaller, then we repeat the same process for left sublist of the middle element. If the search element is larger, then we repeat the same process for right sublist of the middle element. We repeat this process until we find the search element in the list or until we left with a sublist of only one element. And if that element also doesn't match with the search element, then the result is "Element not found in the list".

Binary search is implemented using following steps...

- **Step 1:** Read the search element from the user
- **Step 2:** Find the middle element in the sorted list
- **Step 3:** Compare, the search element with the middle element in the sorted list.
- **Step 4:** If both are matching, then display "Given element found!!!" and terminate the function
- **Step 5:** If both are not matching, then check whether the search element is smaller or larger than middle element.
- **Step 6:** If the search element is smaller than middle element, then repeat steps 2, 3, 4 and
  5 for the left sublist of the middle lement.
- **Step 7:** If the search element is larger than middle element, then repeat steps 2, 3, 4 and 5
  for the right sublist of the middle element.
- **Step 8:** Repeat the same process until we find the search element in the list or until sublist contains only one element.
- **Step 9:** If that element also doesn't match with the search element, then display "Element
  not found in the list!!!" and terminate the function.

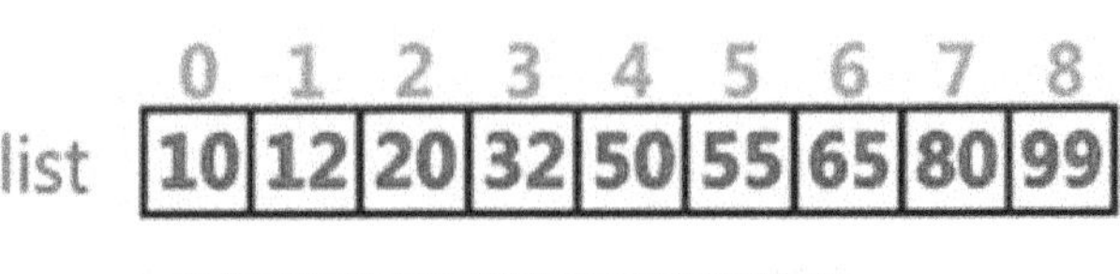

search element **12**

Step 1:

search element (12) is compared with middle element (50)

0 1 2 3 4 5 6 7 8

list 10 12 20 32 50 55 65 80 99

12

Both are not matching. And 12 is smaller than 50. So we search only in the left sublist (i.e. 10, 12, 20 & 32).

0 1 2 3 4 5 6 7 8

list 10 12 20 32 50 55 65 80 99

Step 2:

search element (12) is compared with middle element (12)

0 1 2 3 4 5 6 7 8

list 10 12 20 32 50 55 65 80 99

12

Both are matching. So the result is "Element found at index 1"

search element **80**

Step 1:

search element (80) is compared with middle element (50)

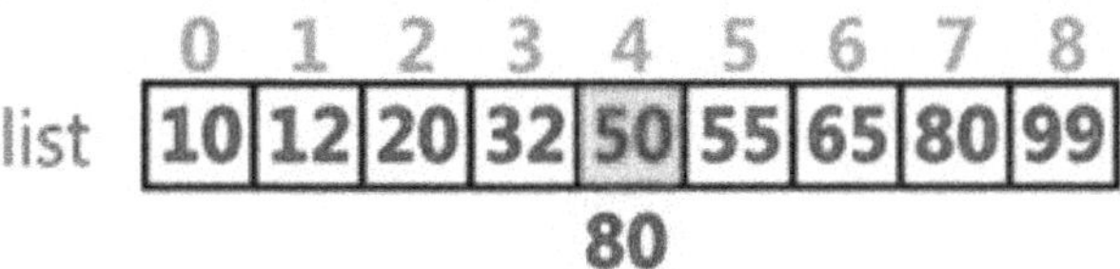

Both are not matching. And 80 is larger than 50. So we search only in the right sublist (i.e. 55, 65, 80 & 99).

Step 2:

search element (80) is compared with middle element (65)

Both are not matching. And 80 is larger than 65. So we search only in the right sublist (i.e. 80 & 99).

Step 3:

search element (80) is compared with middle element (80)

Both are not matching. So the result is "Element found at index 7"

Program:

```
#include<stdio.h>
#include<conio.h>

void main()
{
	int first, last, middle, size, i, sElement, list[100];

	printf("Enter the size of the list: ");
	scanf("%d",&size);

	printf("Enter %d integer values in Assending order\n", size);

	for (i = 0; i < size; i++)
		scanf("%d",&list[i]);

	printf("Enter value to be search: ");
	scanf("%d", &sElement);

	first = 0;
	last = size - 1;
	middle = (first+last)/2;

	while (first <= last)
	{
		if (list[middle] < sElement)
			first = middle + 1;
		else if (list[middle] == sElement) {
			printf("Element found at index %d.\n",middle);
			break;
	}
	else
		last = middle - 1;

	middle = (first + last)/2;
	}
	if (first > last)
		printf("Element Not found in the list.");
	getch();
}
```

Output:

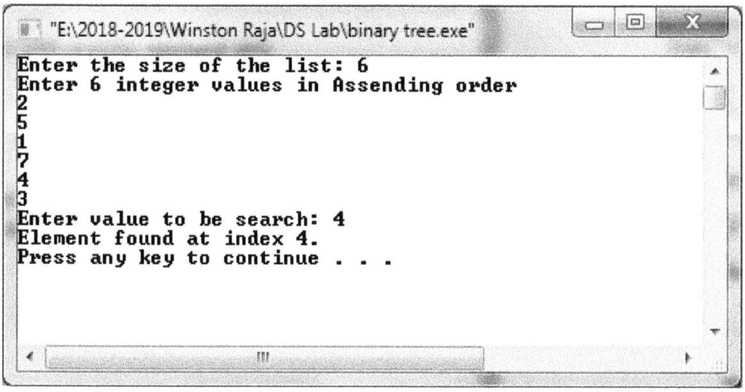

```
"E:\2018-2019\Winston Raja\DS Lab\binary tree.exe"
Enter the size of the list: 6
Enter 6 integer values in Assending order
2
5
1
7
4
3
Enter value to be search: 4
Element found at index 4.
Press any key to continue . . .
```

Result:

Thus the program is completed successfully and the Result is verified.

Exp.No:17 **Implementation of Linear Search Algorithm**

Date :

Linear search algorithm finds given element in a list of elements with **O(n)** time complexity where **n** is total number of elements in the list. This search process starts comparing of search element with the first element in the list. If both are matching then results with element found otherwise search element is compared with next element in the list. If both are matched, then the result is "element found". Otherwise, repeat the same with the next element in the list until search element is compared with last element in the list, if that last element also doesn't match, then the result is "Element not found in the list". That means, the search element is compared with element by element in the list.

Linear search is implemented using following steps...

- **Step 1:** Read the search element from the user
- **Step 2:** Compare, the search element with the first element in the list.
- **Step 3:** If both are matching, then display "Given element found!!!" and terminate the function
- **Step 4:** If both are not matching, then compare search element with the next element in the list.
- **Step 5:** Repeat steps 3 and 4 until the search element is compared with the last element in the list.
- **Step 6:** If the last element in the list is also doesn't match, then display "Element not found!!!" and terminate the function.

Example

Consider the following list of element and search element...

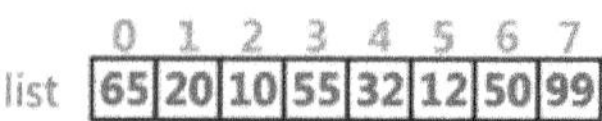

search element **12**

Step 1:

search element (12) is compared with first element (65)

	0	1	2	3	4	5	6	7
list	**65**	20	10	55	32	12	50	99
	12							

Both are not matching. So move to next element

Step 2:

search element (12) is compared with next element (20)

	0	1	2	3	4	5	6	7
list	65	**20**	10	55	32	12	50	99
		12						

Both are not matching. So move to next element

Step 3:

search element (12) is compared with next element (10)

	0	1	2	3	4	5	6	7
list	65	20	**10**	55	32	12	50	99
			12					

Both are not matching. So move to next element

Step 4:

search element (12) is compared with next element (55)

	0	1	2	3	4	5	6	7
list	65	20	10	**55**	32	12	50	99
				12				

Both are not matching. So move to next element

Step 5:

search element (12) is compared with next element (32)

	0	1	2	3	4	5	6	7
list	65	20	10	55	**32**	12	50	99
					12			

Both are not matching. So move to next element

Step 6:

search element (12) is compared with next element (12)

	0	1	2	3	4	5	6	7
list	65	20	10	55	32	**12**	50	99
						12		

Both are matching. So we stop comparing and display element found at index 5.

Program:

```
#include<stdio.h>
#include<conio.h>

void main()
{
	int list[20],size,i,sElement;

	printf("Enter size of the list: ");
	scanf("%d",&size);

	printf("Enter any %d integer values: ",size);

	for(i = 0; i < size; i++)
		scanf("%d",&list[i]);

	printf("Enter the element to be Search: ");
	scanf("%d",&sElement);

	// Linear Search
	Logic for(i = 0; i <
	size; i++)
	{
		if(sElement == list[i])
		{
			printf("Element is found at %d index", i);
			break;
		}
	}
	if(i == size)
		printf("Given element is not found in the list!!!");
	getch();
}
```

Output:

```
"E:\2018-2019\Winston Raja\DS Lab\Linear.exe"
Enter size of the list: 6
Enter any 6 integer values: 2
3
4
5
6
7
Enter the element to be Search: 5
Element is found at 3 indexPress any key to continue . . .
```

Result:

Thus the program is completed successfully and the Result is verified.

Exp.No:18 **Insertion Sort**

Date :

Sorting is the process of arranging a list of elements in a particular order (Ascending or Descending).

Insertion sort algorithm arranges a list of elements in a particular order. In insertion sort algorithm, every iteration moves an element from unsorted portion to sorted portion until all the elements are sorted in the list.

The insertion sort algorithm is performed using following steps...

- **Step 1:** Asume that first element in the list is in sorted portion of the list and remaining all elements are in unsorted portion.
- **Step 2:** Consider first element from the unsorted list and insert that element into the sorted list in order specified.
- **Step 3:** Repeat the above process until all the elements from the unsorted list are moved into the sorted list.

Following is the sample code for insertion sort...

```
//Insertion sort
logic for i = 1 to
size-1 {
  temp = list[i];
  j = i;
  while ((temp < list[j]) && (j > 0)) {
    list[j] = list[j-1];
    j = j - 1;
  }
  list[j] = temp;
}
```

Example

Consider the following unsorted list of elements...

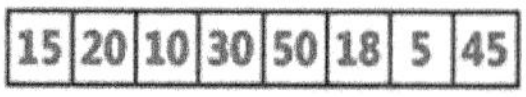

15	20	10	30	50	18	5	45

Asume that sorted portion of the list empty and all elements in the list are in unsorted portion of the list as shown in the figure below...

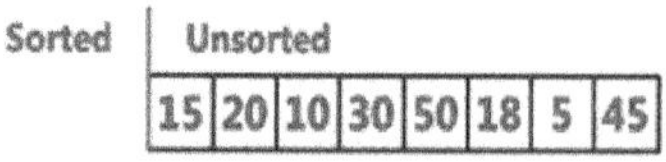

Sorted | Unsorted

15	20	10	30	50	18	5	45

Move the first element 15 from unsorted portion to sorted portion of the list.

Sorted | Unsorted

15	20	10	30	50	18	5	45

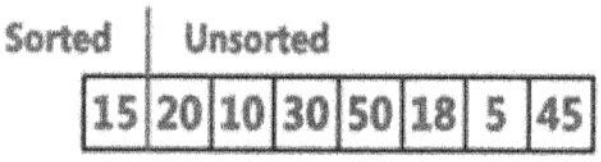

To move element 20 from unsorted to sorted portion, Compare 20 with 15 and insert it at correct position

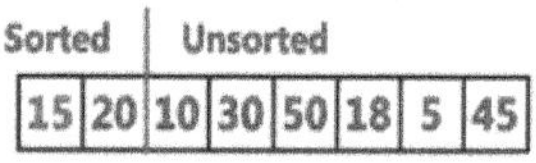

Sorted | Unsorted

15	20	10	30	50	18	5	45

To move element 10 from unsorted to sorted portion, Compare 10 with 20 and it is smaller so swap. Then compare 10 with 15 again smaller swap. And 10 is insert at its correct position in sorted portion of the list.

Sorted | Unsorted

10	15	20	30	50	18	5	45

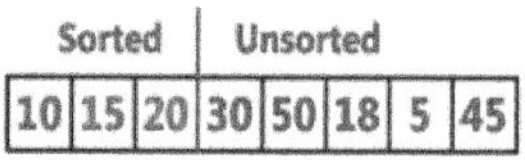

To move element 30 from unsorted to sorted portion, Compare 30 with 20, 15 and 10. And it is larger than all these so 30 is directly inserted at last position in sorted portion of the list.

Sorted | Unsorted

10	15	20	30	50	18	5	45

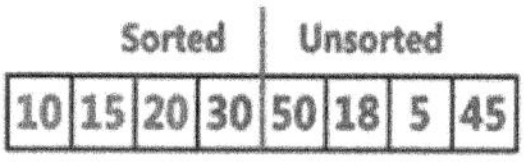

To move element 50 from unsorted to sorted portion, Compare 50 with 30, 20, 15 and 10. And it is larger than all these so 50 is directly inserted at last position in sorted portion of the list.

Sorted | Unsorted

10	15	20	30	50	18	5	45

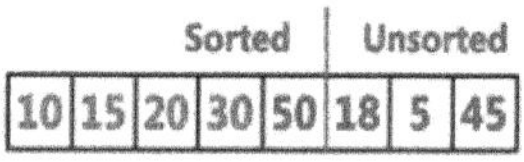

To move element 18 from unsorted to sorted portion, Compare 18 with 30, 20 and 15. Since 18 is larger than 15, move 20, 30 and 50 one position to the right in the list and insert 18 after 15 in the sorted portion.

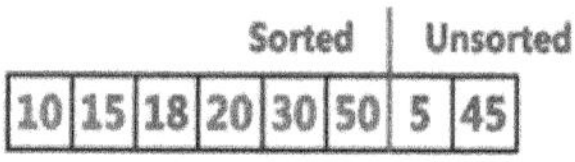

Sorted | Unsorted

10	15	18	20	30	50	5	45

To move element 5 from unsorted to sorted portion, Compare 5 with 50, 30, 20, 18, 15 and 10. Since 5 is smaller than all these element, move 10, 15, 18, 20, 30 and 50 one position to the right in the list and insert 5 at first position in the sorted list.

Sorted | Unsorted

5	10	15	18	20	30	50	45

To move element 45 from unsorted to sorted portion, Compare 45 with 50 and 30. Since 45 is larger than 30, move 50 one position to the right in the list and insert 45 after 30 in the sorted list.

Sorted | Unsorted

5	10	15	18	20	30	45	50

Unsorted portion of the list has became empty. So we stop the process. And the final sorted list of elements is as follows...

5	10	15	18	20	30	45	50

To sort a unsorted list with **'n'** number of elements we need to make **(1+2+3+......+n-1) = (n (n-1))/2** number of comparisions in the worst case. If the list already sorted, then it requires **'n'** number of comparisions.

Worst Case : $O(n^2)$
Best Case : $\Omega(n)$
Average Case : $\Theta(n^2)$

```
#include<stdio.h>
#include<conio.h>

void main()
{
        int size, i, j, temp, list[100];

        printf("Enter the size of the list: ");
        scanf("%d", &size);

        printf("Enter %d integer values: ", size);
        for (i = 0; i < size; i++)
        scanf("%d", &list[i]);

        //Insertion sort logic
        for (i = 1; i < size; i++)
        {
```

```
            temp = list[i];
            j = i - 1;
            while ((temp < list[j]) && (j >= 0))
            {
                  list[j + 1] = list[j];
                  j = j - 1;
            }
            list[j + 1] = temp;
      }

      printf("List after Sorting is: ");
      for (i = 0; i < size; i++)
            printf(" %d", list[i]);

      getch();
}
```

Output:

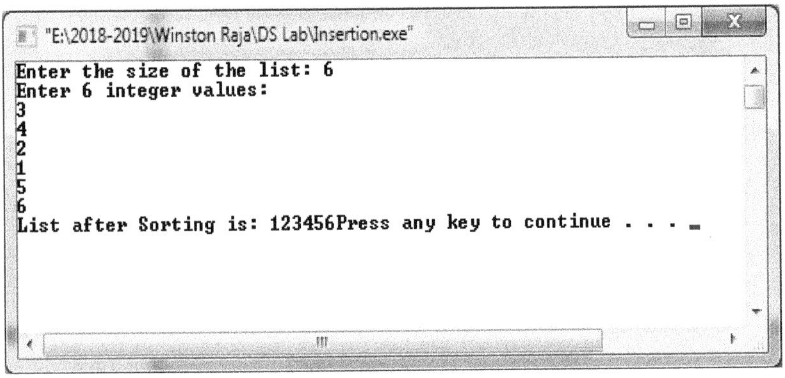

```
"E:\2018-2019\Winston Raja\DS Lab\Insertion.exe"
Enter the size of the list: 6
Enter 6 integer values:
3
4
2
1
5
6
List after Sorting is: 123456Press any key to continue . . .
```

Result:

Thus the program is completed successfully and the Result is verified.

Exp.No:19 **Selection Sort**

Date :

Selection Sort algorithm is used to arrange a list of elements in a particular order (Ascending or Descending). In selection sort, the first element in the list is selected and it is compared repeatedly with remaining all the elements in the list. If any element is smaller than the selected element (for Ascending order), then both are swapped. Then we select the element at second position in the list and it is compared with remaining all elements in the list. If any element is smaller than the selected element, then both are swapped. This procedure is repeated till the entire list is sorted.

The selection sort algorithm is performed using following steps...

- **Step 1:** Select the first element of the list (i.e., Element at first position in the list).
- **Step 2:** Compare the selected element with all other elements in the list.
- **Step 3:** For every comparison, if any element is smaller than selected element (for
  Ascending order), then these two are swapped.
- **Step 4:** Repeat the same procedure with next position in the list till the entire list is sorted.

Following is the sample code for selection sort...

```
//Selection sort

logic for(i=0; i<size;

i++){
   for(j=i+1; j<size; j++){
      if(list[i] > list[j])
         {
        temp=list[i];
        list[i]=list[j]
        ;
        list[j]=temp;
      }
   }
}
```

Example

Consider the following unsorted list of elements...

15	20	10	30	50	18	5	45

Iteration #1

Select the first position element in the list, compare it with all other elements in the list and whenever we found a smaller element than the element at first position then swap those two elements.

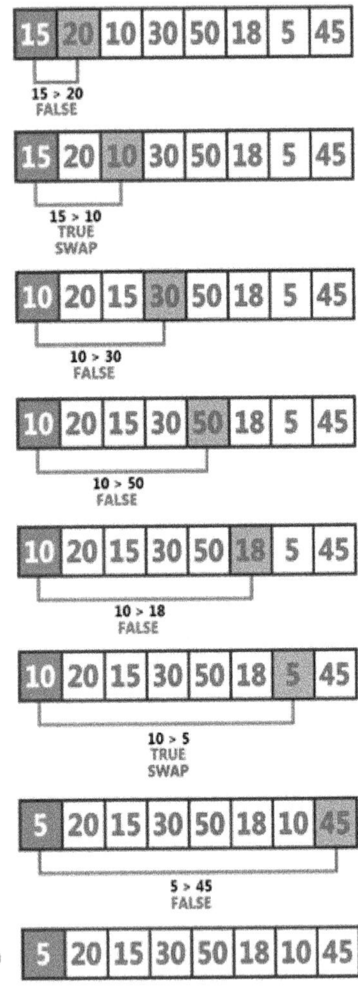

List after 1st iteration

Iteration #2

Select the second position element in the list, compare it with all other elements in the list and whenever we found a smaller element than the element at first position then swap those two elements.

List after 2nd iteration 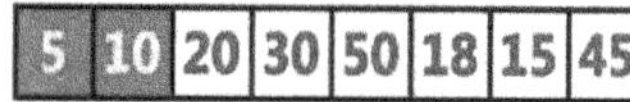

Iteration #3

Select the third position element in the list, compare it with all other elements in the list and whenever we found a smaller element than the element at first position then swap those two elements.

List after 3rd iteration

5	10	15	30	50	20	18	45

Iteration #4

Select the fourth position element in the list, compare it with all other elements in the list and whenever we found a smaller element than the element at first position then swap those two elements.

List after 4th iteration 

Iteration #5

Select the fifth position element in the list, compare it with all other elements in the list and whenever we found a smaller element than the element at first position then swap those two elements.

List after 5th iteration 

Iteration #6

Select the sixth position element in the list, compare it with all other elements in the list and whenever we found a smaller element than the element at first position then swap those two elements.

List after 6th iteration 

Iteration #7

Select the seventh position element in the list, compare it with all other elements in the list and whenever we found a smaller element than the element at first position then swap those two elements.

List after 7th iteration 

Final sorted list

To sort a unsorted list with **'n'** number of elements we need to make **((n-1)+(n-2)+(n-3)+......+1) = (n (n-1))/2** number of comparisions in the worst case. If the list already sorted, then it requires **'n'** number of comparisions.

Worst Case : $O(n^2)$
Best Case : $\Omega(n^2)$
Average Case :
$\Theta(n^2)$

Program:

```
#include<stdio.h>
#include<conio.h>

void main()
{

        int size,i,j,temp,list[100];
        clrscr();

        printf("Enter the size of the List: ");
        scanf("%d",&size);

        printf("Enter %d integer values:
        ",size); for(i=0; i<size; i++)
        scanf("%d",&list[i]);

        //Selection sort

        logic for(i=0;

        i<size; i++)
        {
                for(j=i+1; j<size; j++)
                {
                        if(list[i] > list[j])
                        {
                                temp=list[i];
                                list[i]=list[j]
                                ;
                                list[j]=temp;
                        }}}

        printf("List after sorting is: ");
        for(i=0; i<size; i++)
                printf(" %d",list[i]);
        getch();
}
```

Output:

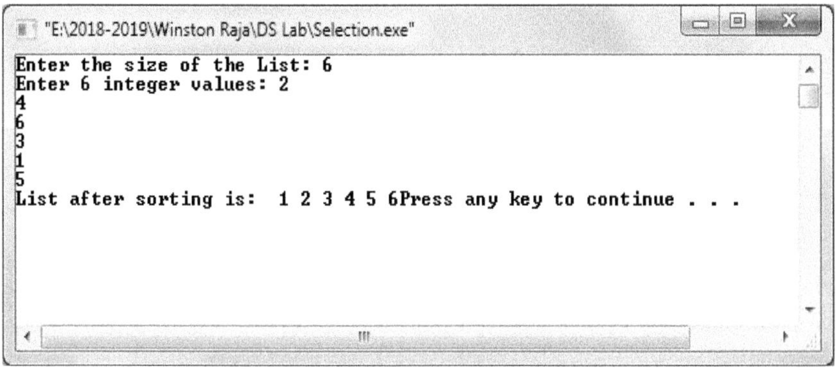

```
"E:\2018-2019\Winston Raja\DS Lab\Selection.exe"
Enter the size of the List: 6
Enter 6 integer values: 2
4
6
3
1
5
List after sorting is:  1 2 3 4 5 6Press any key to continue . . .
```

Result:

Thus the program is completed successfully and the Result is verified.

Exp.No:20 **Hashing With Open Addressing**

Date :

Hashing is a technique used for performing insertions, deletions, and finds in constant average time. The idea hash table data structure is merely an array of some fixed size, containing the keys. Typically, a key is a string with an associated value. Each key is mapped into some number in the range 0 to tablesize-1 and placed in the appropriate cell. The mapping is called a ***hash function***, which ideally should be simple to compute and should ensure that any two distinct keys get different cell. Since there are a finite number of cells and a virtually inexhaustible supply of keys, this is clearly impossible, and thus we seek a hash function that distributes the keys evenly among the cells.

In hashing there is a hash function that maps keys to some values. But this hashing function may lead to collision that is two or more keys are mapped to same value. Chain hashing avoids collision. The idea is to make each cell of hash table point to a linked list of records that have same hash function value.

Let"s create a hash function, such that our hash table has „N" number of buckets. To insert a node into the hash table, we need to find the hash index for the given key. And it could be calculated using the hash function.

Example: hashIndex = key % no of Buckets

Insert: Move to the bucket corresponds to the above calculated hash index and insert the new node at the end of the list.

Delete: To delete a node from hash table, calculate the hash index for the key, move to the bucket corresponds to the calculated hash index, search the list in the current bucket to find and remove the node with the given key (if found).

Let's say hash table with 7 buckets (0, 1, 2, 3, 4, 5, 6)

Keys arrive in the Order (15, 11 , 27 , 8)

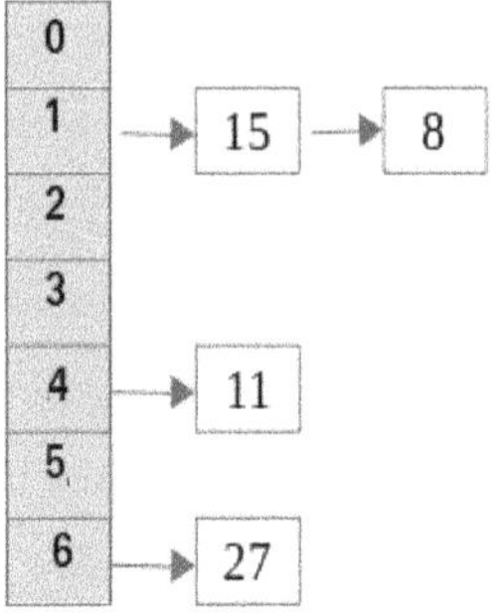

Open Addressing is a technique used to resolve collisions with linked lists. In an open addressing hashing system, if a collision occurs, alternative cells are tried until an empty cell is found.

AIM:

To implement Hashing with open addressing in C Language.

ALGORITHM:

STEP 1: Start.

STEP 2: Create a hash table.

STEP 3: Get the key values to be inserted.

STEP 4: Insert the key element into the hash table one by one.

STEP 5: If there is a collision while inserting a key element, resolve the collision by placing the key element in a free cell by following the function $F(i)=i^2$.

STEP 6: Perform STEP 5 till all the key elements are inserted in the hash table.

STEP 7: Stop.

Program:

```
#include <stdio.h>
#include <stdlib.h>
#include <string.h>
int tableSize = 0, totEle = 0;
struct node *hashTable =
NULL; struct node
{
        int age, key;
        char name[100];
        int marker;
};
void insertInHash(int key, char *name, int age)
{
        int hashIndex = key % tableSize;
        if (tableSize == totEle)
        {
                printf("Can't perform Insertion..Hash Table is full!!");
                return;
        }
while (hashTable[hashIndex].marker == 1)
{
        hashIndex = (hashIndex + 1)%tableSize;
}
hashTable[hashIndex].key = key;
hashTable[hashIndex].age = age;
strcpy(hashTable[hashIndex].name,
name); hashTable[hashIndex].marker =
1; totEle++;
return;
}
void deleteFromHash(int key)
{
```

```
        int hashIndex = key % tableSize, count = 0, flag = 0;
        if (totEle == 0)
        {
                printf("Hash Table is Empty!!\n");
                return;
        }


        while (hashTable[hashIndex].marker != 0 && count <= tableSize)

        {
                if (hashTable[hashIndex].key == key)
                {
                        hashTable[hashIndex].key = 0;
                        /* set marker to -1 during deletion
                        operation*/ hashTable[hashIndex].marker
                        = -1; hashTable[hashIndex].age = 0;
                        strcpy(hashTable[hashIndex].name, "\0");
                        totEle--;
                        flag = 1;
                        break;
        }
        hashIndex = (hashIndex + 1)%tableSize;
        count++;
}
if (flag)
        printf("Given data deleted from Hash Table\n");
else

        printf("Given data is not available in Hash Table\n");
return
;
}
```

```
void searchElement(int key)
{
        int hashIndex = key % tableSize, flag = 0, count = 0;
        if (totEle == 0)
        {
        printf("Hash Table is Empty!!");
        return;
        }
        while (hashTable[hashIndex].marker != 0 && count <= tableSize)
        {
                if (hashTable[hashIndex].key == key)
                {
                        printf("Voter ID : %d\n",
                        hashTable[hashIndex].key); printf("Name    :
                        %s\n", hashTable[hashIndex].name); printf("Age
                        : %d\n", hashTable[hashIndex].age); flag = 1;
                        break;
                }
                hashIndex = (hashIndex + 1)%tableSize;

        }

        if (!flag)
        printf("Given data is not present in hash table\n");
        return;
}
void display()
{
        int i;
        if (totEle == 0)
        {
```

```
            printf("Hash Table is Empty!!\n");
            return;
        }
        printf("Voter ID    Name        Age    Index \n");
        printf("----------------------------------------\n");
        for (i = 0; i < tableSize; i++)
        {
            if (hashTable[i].marker == 1)
            {
                printf("%-13d", hashTable[i].key);
                printf("%-15s",
                hashTable[i].name); printf("%-
                7d", hashTable[i].age);
                printf("%d\n", i);
            }
        }
        printf("\n");
        return;
}

int main()
{
        int key, age, ch;
        char name[100];
        printf("Enter the no of elements:");
        scanf("%d", &tableSize);
        hashTable = (struct node *)calloc(tableSize, sizeof(struct node));
        while (1)
        {
            printf("1. Insertion\t2. Deletion\n");
```

```
        printf("3. Searching\t4.
        Display\n"); printf("5.
        Exit\nEnter ur choice:");
        scanf("%d", &ch);
        switch (ch)
        {
                case 1:
                                printf("Enter the key value:");
                                scanf("%d", &key);
                                getchar();
                                printf("Name:");
                                fgets(name, 100,
                                stdin);
                                name[strlen(name) - 1] = '\0';
                                printf("Age:"); scanf("%d",
                                &age); insertInHash(key,
                                name, age); break;
                case 2:
                                printf("Enter the key
                                value:"); scanf("%d", &key);
                                deleteFromHash(key);
                                break;
                case 3:
                                printf("Enter the key
                                value:"); scanf("%d", &key);
                                searchElement(key);
                                break;
                case 4:
                                display();
                                break;
                case 5:
                                exit(0);

                default:
                                printf("U have entered wrong Option!!\n");
                                break;
        }
}
```

```
    return 0;
}
```

Output:

```
"E:\2018-2019\Winston Raja\DS Lab\Hashing.exe"
Enter the no of elements:6
1. Insertion     2. Deletion
3. Searching     4. Display
5. Exit
Enter ur choice:1
Enter the key value:4
Name:Raja
Age:20
1. Insertion     2. Deletion
3. Searching     4. Display
5. Exit
Enter ur choice:4
Voter ID      Name              Age     Index
---------------------------------------------
4             Raja              20      4

1. Insertion     2. Deletion
3. Searching     4. Display
5. Exit
Enter ur choice:1
Enter the key value:44
Name:sam
Age:23
1. Insertion     2. Deletion
3. Searching     4. Display
5. Exit
Enter ur choice:4
Voter ID      Name              Age     Index
---------------------------------------------
44            sam               23      2
4             Raja              20      4

1. Insertion     2. Deletion
3. Searching     4. Display
5. Exit
Enter ur choice:1
Enter the key value:2
Name:Jeeva
Age:24
1. Insertion     2. Deletion
3. Searching     4. Display
5. Exit
Enter ur choice:4
Voter ID      Name              Age     Index
---------------------------------------------
44            sam               23      2
2             Jeeva             24      3
4             Raja              20      4

1. Insertion     2. Deletion
3. Searching     4. Display
5. Exit
Enter ur choice:_
```

Result:

Thus the program is completed successfully and the Result is verified.

www.ingramcontent.com/pod-product-compliance
Ingram Content Group UK Ltd.
Pitfield, Milton Keynes, MK11 3LW, UK
UKHW021709190726
13853UKWH00001B/480